PRAIS... ...HE GRE...

"With introspection and good humor, Brown tells a lively and often appalling story…a vivid depiction of just how hard first-year teaching and its implicit lesson that urban schools urgently need to attract and retain more thoughtful and dedicated people such as Brown."

—The Washington Post Book World

"[Brown is] an appealing and sympathetic figure with a seemingly genuine talent for teaching… yet he finds himself in charge of a class that is always on the verge of chaos…"

—The New York Times

"I loved reading this book. Dan Brown has not only the teaching gene, but the writing gene. His account of a year in a tough classroom is one of the best that I have read."

—Diane Ravitch, author of *The Death and Life of the Great American School System*

"A lively and searchingly intelligent work on urban education which is also a vivid and compelling story of the highest possible political significance at this moment in our history. Parents and teachers alike will be grateful to Dan for his disarming honesty."

—Jonathan Kozol

"Brown's persistence… earned him a range of experiences that allowed him to become a clear-eyed and trustworthy guide to the inescapable everyday social problems with which so many public school children live. If we want to ameliorate some of these problems we need to know what we're dealing with and acknowledge the impact of poverty on students. We also need to try to keep bright young people like Brown teaching in our public schools."

—Chicago Tribune

"[*The Great Expectations School*] is not only a great read, it's a vivid portrait of the teacher retention challenge… Each student in Dan's class becomes someone the reader cares about—they all deserve the finest teachers and those teachers deserve a system that supports them…"

—Susan Fuhrman, President, Teachers College, Columbia University

"Among the many first-year teaching accounts, it's one of the best. [Brown's] students sparkle with life, and his tales from the classroom shimmer with real-life stress and inspiration."

—NEA Today

"In [Mr. Brown's] book, we see that good teachers are the linchpin to solid reform."

—Newsweek

"Brown chronicles his first year teaching with heart, humor, and disarming candor."

—Scholastic Instructor

"My favorite first-

ithor of *See Me After Class*

"Mr. Brown has w   he joys, sorrows, absurdities, terror:

reet College of Education

"Powerful and moving . . . Dan Brown has a story that we need to hear—and respond to."
—Deborah Meier, author of *The Power of Their Ideas* and *In Schools We Trust*

"Mr. Brown's a hell of writer in his own right, and he's just published a wallopingly good book -- his first, which is difficult to believe."
—*The Jewish Exponent*

"A compelling, scary, funny, touching look at urban education in the US."
—*Christian Science Monitor*

"Touchingly, Brown's dedication and imagination helped save those kids—and himself."
—*The Sacramento Bee*

"Dan Brown's heartfelt account of the thrills and frustrations of a first-year teacher grips like a novel. A must-read for anyone who has dreamed of a job that makes a difference."
—Anya Kamenetz, author of *DIY U* and *Generation Debt*

"A riveting human drama full of heroes and villains, humor and tragedy. Brown is an exciting new talent and his writing is so clear and suspenseful that the pages turn themselves. I couldn't put this book down."
—Clara Bingham, co-author of *Class Action: The Story of Lois Jenson and the Landmark Case That Changed Sexual Harassment Law*

"A compelling and illuminating journey through the American public education system… Brown's highlights the personal success-stories— the dedicated teachers, the kids overcoming massive odds—he encountered on the way. One finishes reading *The Great Expectations School* wishing those in charge of public education in this country spent less time administering overvalued standardized tests on students, and more on inspiring those students to truly learn. A good way to start would be listening to teachers like Dan Brown and some of his colleagues."
—Scott Anderson, author of *Moonlight Hotel* and *The Man Who Tried to Save the World*

"A powerful, heart-breaking story that challenges our image of inner city schools and the children who populate them. Important and moving, *The Great Expectations School* grabs your attention from the first page and refuses to let go."
—Gilbert M. Gaul, two-time Pulitzer Prize winning journalist

" *The Great Expectations School* splashes some ice-cold reality on usual policy pabulum that comes from inside-the-Beltway."
—Barnett Berry, co-author of *Teaching 2030* and President, Center for Teaching Quality

"A poignant portrait painted with skill . . . Read it and weep—and wonder no more about the human dimensions of the achievement gap."
—Gene I. Maeroff, author of *Building Blocks: Making Children Successful in the Early Years of School*

THE GREAT
EXPECTATIONS
SCHOOL

THE GREAT EXPECTATIONS SCHOOL

A Rookie Year in the New Blackboard Jungle

DAN BROWN

Foreword by **RANDI WEINGARTEN**
President of the American Federation of Teachers

Arcade Publishing
NEW YORK

Arcade Publishing books may be purchased in bulk at special discounts for
sales promotion, corporate gifts, fund-raising, or educational purposes. Special
editions can also be created to specifications. For details, contact the Special Sales
Department, Arcade Publishing, 307 West 36th Street, 11th Floor, New York, NY
10018 or info@skyhorsepublishing.com.

Arcade Publishing® is a registered trademark of Skyhorse Publishing, Inc.®,
a Delaware corporation.

Visit our website at www.arcadepub.com.

10 9 8 7 6 5 4 3 2 1

Library of Congress Cataloging-in-Publication Data is available on file.

ISBN: 978-1-61145-033-0

Printed in the United States of America

For my Mother, Sonandia, and Colleen
My rescuers, in the order that I met them

Contents

Author's Note

This book shares the journey of a teacher and the life of a classroom: an intersection of youth and experience, energy and discipline, empowerment and failure. As the drafts developed, and I circulated my work to teachers from a broad scope of backgrounds and school environments, I realized that the essence of my story did not stem purely from my own idiosyncratic misadventures in the classroom. Some inner-city teachers I know only vaguely have thanked me for articulating *their* stories. The insights and issues, whether systemic or personal, that spring from this narrative may pull back a curtain on a sector of our society that is largely invisible. One year with class 4-217 in the Bronx's P.S. 85 can illuminate the mushrooming crisis in lower-class America and the individual specks of hope that may propel us to act, or at least to care.

The contents of this book are based on my notes and recollections, though many names have been changed to protect privacy, and in a few circumstances real people have been merged into composite characters.

Cast of Characters

P.S. 85 Teachers
(★ rookie teacher)

Kindergarten: Allie Bowers★

1st grade: Trisha Pierson★
Aaron Rose

2nd grade: Corinne Abernathy★
Andrea Cobb

3rd grade: Elizabeth Camaraza★
Janet Claxton
Sarina Kuo
Stacy Shanline
Tim Shea★
Carol Slocumb

4th grade: Karen Adler, 4-110
Marnie Beck, special ed
Edith Boswell, gifted Performing Arts Class
Dan Brown★, 4-217
Pat Cartwright, 4-219
Catherine Fiore, 4-210
Melissa Mulvehill, 4-220
Cordelia Richardson
Wilson Tejera, bilingual

5th grade: Cheryl Berkowitz, gifted Performing Arts Class
Paul Bonn, 5-110
Evan Krieg, 5-205
Marc Simmons, 5-207

Jeanne Solloway, 5-213

Prep teachers: Fran Baker, literacy
Ethel May Brick, literacy
David de la O★, computers
Deborah Friedberg, gym
Adele Hafner, science
Wendell Jaspers★, floater
Wally Klein, librarian, union rep
Ava Kreps, art
Valerie Menzel, computers
Cat Samuels★, social studies
Jim Zweben, gym

P.S. 85 Administrators

Dom Beckles, Success for All coordinator
Kendra Boyd, principal
Barbara Chatton, new-teacher mentor
Al Conway, math coach
Rhonda Cooper, payroll secretary
Len Daly, Mr. Randazzo's assistant
Marge Foley, literacy coach
Sonia Guiterrez, assistant principal
Mr. Joe, security
Helen Kirkpatrick, special ed coordinator
Julianne Nemet, health clinic staff
Bob Randazzo, assistant principal
Diane Rawson, assistant principal
Marianna Renfro, special ed coordinator (summer)
Nurse Tina, nurse
Dilla Zane, regional superintendent

Class 4-217 Students

Sonandia Azcona
Deloris Barlow
Cwasey Bartrum
Asante Bell
Seresa Bosun (enter in January)
Joseph Castanon
Evley Castro
Gloria Diaz (enter in March)
Gladys Ferraro
Dennis Foster
Tayshaun Jackson
Reynaldo Luces (enter late September)
Maimouna Lugaru
Fausto Mason
Julissa Marrero
Bernard McCants
Verdad Navarez
Athena Page
Lakiya Ray
Destiny Rivera
Edgar "Eddie" Rollins
Eric Ruiz
Manolo "Lito" Ruiz
Tiffany Sanchez
Jennifer Taylor
Epiphany Torres (enter in January)
Hamisi Umar
Daniel Vasquez (enter in late September)
Clara Velez (enter in April)
Gladys Viña
Marvin Winslow (enter in late September)

Other P.S. 85 Students

Corrina Castro-Fernandez, Visual Arts Club
Lilibeth Garcia, Visual Arts Club
Jihard Gaston, Mr. Rose's class
Dequan Jones, Karen Adler's class
Mary, Kimberly, Asonai, and Sayquan, Pat Cartwright's students
Jimmarie Moreno-Bonilla, summer school
Thankgod Mutemi, Janet Claxton's class
Theo Payton, Mr. Rose's class
Jodi West, Visual Arts Club
Kelsie Williams, Success for All student

New York City Teaching Fellows Staff

Susan Atero, placement fair interviewer
Sarah Gerson, summer advisor
Charles Kendall, Mercy College adjunct teacher
Liesl Nolan, Mercy College supervisor

THE GREAT EXPECTATIONS SCHOOL

Prologue

Even if I had known what I was doing when I punched the chalk-board, I still wouldn't have expected my fist to crash through it. Lakiya Ray's face froze in a crazed openmouthed grin, but the rest of the class looked appropriately petrified. My eyes bulged, and I brushed sweat from my temple.

"Mr. Brown, you wiped a little blood on your face."

"Thank you, Destiny." I dabbed at the red wisps on my forehead and glared at the back wall's "Iroquois Longhouses" bulletin board, safeguarding my eyes from meeting those of any terrified children. *Especially Sonandia.*

I righted Tayshaun's upended desk and sat on it, my cheeks tingling. "None of you deserve to experience fourth grade like this. Class is dismissed."

June/July

From the Floor to the Moon

I THOUGHT I HAD UNUSUAL REASONS for becoming a public school teacher in the Bronx. Nine months before my left hook to the blackboard, while I was in my final semester studying film at the Tisch School of the Arts at NYU, professors started encouraging outgoing seniors to drive cabs, bus tables, or do anything possible to keep alive our passion for making art once discharged from our bohemian sanctum of university life. The undergrad movie degree might not wow decent-paying employers in the gritty real world.

Several of my film school pals planned to move to Los Angeles and become personal assistants to talent agents. Others decided not to work their first year out of school, intending to subsist on Netflix, ramen, and a word processor. I wanted to live on Manhattan's Lower East Side, which meant four figures in rent. I needed a job.

A weird month as a clerk for the U.S. Census Bureau in the summer of 2000 taught me that office work brought on either loopiness or depression. I couldn't see myself in sales. Apparently the economy was in the drink. What do you do when you're twenty-two?

Twenty-four hundred of New York City's teachers in 2003 were first-year New York City Teaching Fellows, members of a program initiated under ex-chancellor Harold Levy in 2000 to solve the chronic shortage of teachers in many of the city's toughest schools. Using the program model of Teach for America, the Board of Education agreed to hire college graduates with no academic background in education and quick-certify them with a three-year Transitional B Certificate. The city aimed its extensive subway ad campaign at altruistically minded career-changers. ("Take your next business trip on a yellow bus," was one slogan.) While teaching, Fellows would be enrolled in subsidized night and summer courses for a master's degree in education.

Encouraged by my career-teacher mom and buoyed by the idea of working with New York City children in schools where there was a desperate need for teachers, I applied. If accepted, I had no idea what, where, or how I was going to teach, but I saw a strange allure in requesting a job that no one else would take.

For my personal statement in the application, I wrote about my baseball fanatic dad. When I was six, he took me to my first ball game, a midsummer Phillies-Astros day game at Veterans Stadium in Philadelphia. The heat index hit triple digits and Nolan Ryan mowed down the home-team batters, making for an uneventful 2–1 loss for our guys. Crossing the Walt Whitman Bridge on the drive home to Cherry Hill, New Jersey, I decided aloud that I did not like baseball. My father, captain of the 1970 University of Pittsburgh squad, clutched for his breast and started to veer out of our lane. A moment later, he recovered and nodded. "No problem," he croaked. "That's okay." Several years later, I asked if I could join Little League and he became my coach.

The story was meant to illustrate my learned life lessons in patience, family solidarity, and unconditional support. Looking back, it's a reach. A few weeks later, though, I received a letter of acceptance.

My film school friends looked at me as though I'd just enlisted for the war. "Maybe this'll give you good material," my roommate said, eyeing me like a head trauma patient. Indeed, if nothing else, the coming year would at least be interesting.

However, after four years of studying storytelling in academia, I never counted on a neighborhood of concrete in the Bronx to reveal my world's gutsiest heroes and desperately flawed shortcomers, the craziest violence and strangest surprises, the darkest failures and the most unexpected second chances. What I got was a life-altering tilt-a-whirl ride, all of it more vivid and twisted than anything I could have concocted in fiction.

Along with over half of my fellow Fellows, I was assigned to teach in the Bronx. On the morning of Saturday, May 17, 2003, a placement fair for specific school assignments at a South Bronx high school began fifteen hours after I handed in my NYU dorm key.

Due at the fair at 8 a.m. and psyched up about the idea of leaving college and beginning a new era, I decided to catch a midnight movie and pull an all-nighter in the Odessa Diner by Tompkins Square with some cherry pie and my notebook. Over lukewarm black coffee, I scribbled in my journal about the crooked path that had led me to this new life chapter.

During winter break of my senior year, my reading specialist mom had enlisted me to help direct twenty second-graders in a child-friendly production of *Romeo and Juliet*. I spent two days with the kids, riling pint-sized Tybalt and Mercutio for their emotional sword-crossing, coaching Romeo (who gave up a good nine inches to his romantic costar) to act lovesick, and explaining ruefulness to sweatpants-clad Friar Lawrence.

Mrs. Haenick, the drama-novice classroom teacher, thanked me over and over for saving the show. "You've got this way of talking to them!" she told me backstage, beaming with surprised approbation, as if I had just sawed someone in half.

Something clicked in me during those two days: *I can work with kids . . . and love it.*

By 4:30 a.m., my writing had devolved into exhausted drivel and the diner staff was visibly perturbed at my lingering. Bleary-eyed, I stumbled to the street to seek a bunch of Red Bulls. The ghost-town city creeped me out, and I hailed a cab to Grand Central Terminal. I napped against a pillar near the 4-5-6-S exit until a police officer's boot nudged me awake. A subway platform bench became my home for the next three hours while I sang entire Beatles albums to myself to stay conscious.

When the fair opened, I wandered the jam-packed corridor for fifteen minutes, wading through several major traffic fluxes initiated by shouts like, "Eighty-six needs six common branches! They're over there! C.I.S. 170 is taking special ed now!" My mystification at this strange, serious game of "placement fair" manifested in a fear that I was behind in the race; these people were portfolio-carrying professionals and I was some kind of kid impostor, a summer-camp white boy from Cherry Hill, New Jersey.

Then a beacon of clarity appeared. I found a sign that read "District 10 Placements" with a nearly empty sign-in list. Soon I was summoned into an office by kind-faced Susan Atero, who scanned my résumé for fifteen silent seconds.

"*The Mummy Returns* . . . you worked on that? In Santa Monica, it says?"

"Not that film, the director, Stephen Sommers's, next film. It's called *Van Helsing.*"

"*The Mummy Returns* is my *favorite* movie of all time," Susan enthused. "I watch it with my sons almost every week. What is the director like?"

"Stephen's very energetic. He lives and breathes movies," I related, as if he and I were old bowling buddies. The truth was that I had driven out to L.A. for the summer with my cousin, only to find my previously secured internship on the Paramount Pictures studio lot handed over to someone with "a connection." I spent several demoralizing weeks bouncing between the Culver City public library Internet station and Kinko's, hunting for unpaid positions and faxing my résumé all over town. Eventually, an assistant to the coproducer of *Van Helsing* invited me to hang out several days a week in the production office screening room, photocopying scripts when necessary. Once, for my most auspicious assignment, I arranged a folder of creature concepts for a presentation and, as advised, did not commingle pictures of Dracula with the Winged Beast from Hell. It all came to a dubious end when I had to leave town prematurely after a traffic ticket busted my budget. I met Stephen Sommers once, and I spent most of our three shared minutes confusing him with details about how a robot snapped my picture going through a red light.

I nodded emphatically at Susan. "*Van Helsing* is going to be spectacular."

"Hmm." Promptly, her smiling mien sobered, and my hope that I could ride Hollywood name-dropping to a quick commitment form disappeared. I was suddenly certain that she knew all about the lame pseudo-employment prominently featured on my résumé.

"Daniel. What strengths will you bring to an inner-city school?"

I regretted not preparing seriously for this. I took a deep breath, aware that my pause had bloated into a hesitation. "I care about kids and I think one of my greatest strengths is my ability to communicate. [*Maybe not right this minute, but . . .*] I'm confident that I can find a common language of mutual respect with my students. I also think that being a younger man is an asset because of the lack of male teachers and male role models in the community. I'm a collaborator and a fast learner, and I can internalize criticism and feedback from anyone: student, colleague, or administrator." I stopped and another idea sprang to mind. "I'm very excited to become a teacher. I am dedicated to improving myself and doing anything possible to help my students. I'll go the distance." I winced inside at the final melodramatic declaration.

Ms. Atero gave a generic nod. "What are your weaknesses?"

This question is a trap. The key is to twist some kind of strength into sounding like a weakness, like "I overprepare" or "I'm a perfectionist, so I need to work on how I occasionally bend deadlines because I want anything with my name on it to be as well done as possible." At the time, my mind was clouded with fatigue and intimidation from Ms. Atero's transformation from congenial conversant to stone-faced interrogator. I swallowed my rank all-nighter saliva. "I don't know. I might be in over my head."

We stared at each other for a moment. Susan's smile returned like a sunburst. "You're going to see some stuff, but it'll be worth it!" The ominous statement was defused by its joyful dispensation. She said, "I'm going to represent you in District 10 to set up visits to schools that could be a good match for you. You're all set!"

A thrill surged within me as I headed to the school stage to get fingerprinted for my city employee file. Then in my fifth year in New York, I had lived in five different apartments, played pickup basketball at the neighborhood blacktop, knew the subway lines inside out, rocked out at CBGB, bought from street vendors, lingered for hours in the Central Park gazebo beyond Strawberry Fields, and watched the World Trade Center towers fall before my eyes. As I pressed my fingers hard to the inkpad, I felt a swell of pride in going to work for the city I loved.

On June 16, 2003, the incoming Fellows congregated in Avery Fisher Hall at Lincoln Center for opening ceremonies, where the keynote speaker declared the event the largest assemblage of talent at one time ever to fill this room. A middle school student spoke about how her teacher, a third-year Fellow, had changed her life. When the Fellow and her star student reunited onstage, a school band played "Amazing Grace," and many new teachers cried.

Three days later, I was randomly assigned to Mr. Aaron Rose's first-grade class at P.S. 85 for a "structured observation." The 2002–2003 school year was in its penultimate week, so Fellows were warned that we might see classes conducted more informally than usual. I was glad to be headed into a functioning inner-city classroom and away from the barrage of motivational lectures that had dominated the week up to that point. (A room-shaking applause line: "The young teachers have the fresh ideas! Does that veteran teacher really have thirty years of experience or just *one* year of experience *thirty times!*")

I took the D train to 182nd–183rd Street and exited onto the Grand Concourse, a broad throughway with three medians and aggressively honk-happy traffic. I passed the ancient brick Gospel Love Assembly where a morose queue of about twenty waited for a free meal. On a side street, some teens and a naked toddler pranced near a fire hydrant geyser. Small establishments selling carpet, divorce documents, and groceries lined the dogshit-smeared pavement. I was the only white face crossing the Concourse to 184th Street, where airbrushed murals paid homage to deceased neighbors.

I walked through the monolithic school's main entrance, under the stone threshold marked "Public School 85: The Great Expectations School."

I waited in the second-floor Teacher Center resource room with a dozen other new Fellows until Principal Kendra Boyd, a tall woman in her late fifties, enthusiastically greeted us. She spoke to the rookies about P.S. 85's mission for three specific aims: *clear expectations, academic rigor,* and *accountable talk.* I figured Mrs. Boyd had to be a brilliant and methodical woman (maybe even an unorthodox genius with that side-ponytail) to run a massive school like this.

Barbara Chatton, the in-house mentor for first-year teachers, also held the floor for a few minutes. Barbara informed us about P.S. 85's strong commitment to supporting new teachers, because they are the future of education and everyone knows how hard it is to be new. I desperately wanted Barbara to be my mentor and Mrs. Boyd to be my principal.

When the meeting broke, I was directed to the aluminum annex in the parking lot. Inside the "minischool," which houses kindergarten and first-grade classes, the environment was colorful and air-conditioned. Lively bulletin board displays lined the walls. Behind the windows of their classroom doors, teachers gestured exuberantly to rapt audiences of children. I couldn't restrain an excited grin.

I knocked on Mr. Rose's door in the middle of a lesson. "Hi, I'm Dan Brown from the Teaching Fellows."

Mr. Rose was a tall black man with a deep voice. With a genuine smile, he shook my hand firmly and said, "Terrific. Mr. Brown, welcome."

Mr. Brown. Get used to it, I thought.

During "independent work," a complete-the-sentence work-sheet on pronouns, I sat with two scowling boys, Theo and Jihard, who refused to write their names. "Jihard, if I were telling you about how much I like Theo's pen, I'd say I like *blank* pen. I like . . ." I waved at Theo and the pen.

Jihard frowned and mumbled, "His pen."

"Yes! Excellent! In that sentence 'his' and 'Theo's' would mean the same thing. 'His' is a pronoun for 'Theo.' Because it's 'his' pen and it's 'Theo's' pen! And Theo, if I were telling you about how much I like . . . what's that girl in the black T-shirt's name?"

"Yollymar."

Jihard interrupted, "That ain't Yollymar! Thas Daniella. She the line leader."

"If I asked you where Daniella bought that black T-shirt, but I didn't know her name, what would I ask?" Theo looked at me blankly and stood up. "Theo, sit down. Fill in the blank for me: Where did . . . get that shirt?"

"How I'm supposed to know?" Theo grumbled.

"Where did *she* get that shirt," Jihard stated.

"Yes! 'She' and 'Daniella' mean the same thing. 'She' is a pronoun for 'Daniella!' Jihard, you're a pronoun superstar. Theo, you get an assist." I gave them both five, and they got to work on their sheets. Jihard handed back a perfect paper, and Theo got two correct out of twelve, an improvement over his previously blank page.

When the time came for me to leave Mr. Rose's class, Mafatu and Yollymar presented me with crayon pictures and roly-poly Cory Jones gave me a pencil drawing of the two of us holding hands.

I walked away from P.S. 85 full of excitement and relief. I had witnessed no violence, sexual harassment, or ultra-jaded zombie teachers as I had anticipated from my preconceived image of an inner-city school. If confused Theo and moody Jihard were the "problem kids," the place didn't seem so bad. At least that's what I thought then.

★   ★   ★

Along with over seven hundred other Fellows, I was automatically enrolled in Mercy College, a graduate school contracted by the Department of Education to run the Fellows' coursework. Sarah Gerson, a third-grade teacher in Harlem, was my adjunct professor and "Fellow Advisor" for five hours each afternoon.

In the beginning, I kept a low profile at Fellow Advisor sessions, avoiding the group-hug atmosphere cultivated by Sarah and half of the group. I was also the youngest of the twenty-eight new teachers in the room. (The average age of a Teaching Fellow in 2003 was thirty-one.) We drew up unit plans, lesson plans, behavior plans, lists of rules, lists of routines, lists of ideal classroom materials, and lists of "higher-order thinking" questions. We wrote letters to ourselves, statements of our goals, statements of our strengths, and statements of our weaknesses. I distilled my goals into a sentence fragment: "Teach and model accountable character and citizenship while maintaining high expectations for helping students to become stronger problem solvers and self-motivated learners." (The high expectations bit was inspired by my P.S. 85 visit.) We walked on rhetorical eggshells for two hours once, talking about the n-word. There were many mentions of dedication, immersion, passion, and commitment.

We were packing up our satchels after another jargon-heavy discussion about poverty when Sarah offhandedly articulated my unease: "I hope these discussions give you something good to think about, but they're really nothing compared to being in the real situation. What we're doing right now is like reading a book about sailing. On September eighth, you'll be out there, probably in a defective vessel, alone in stormy waters."

After my structured observation at P.S. 85, I left letters for Mrs. Boyd and Ms. Chatton requesting an interview but received no response. Meanwhile, I had been assigned to spend my mornings as a seventh-grade apprentice teacher of summer school at M.S. 399, rumored to be the lowest-scoring middle school in New York City. The apathetic students terrorized their milquetoasty math teacher Mr. Akimo ("Fuck this nigger!") and shrugged at their imminent failure ("Seventh grade was out in the hall, man"). After a week, I submitted a grievance to the Fellows office, and over Independence Day weekend I received a miraculous e-mail informing me that I had been switched to familiar P.S. 85.

Heading up the P.S. 85 stairwell to the office to receive my classroom assignment on the morning of July 7, I came face-to-face with Mr. Rose. "Mr. Brown!" he called warmly, shaking my hand. He already had one Fellow in his room but said I should work with him too. In the office, he asked the secretary if I was needed anywhere specific. The baffled woman, apparently having no authority over Fellow room placements, shrugged.

Mr. Rose followed a tightly regimented program for the summer school half day. He did a half-hour read-aloud from *Help! I'm Trapped in the First Day of Summer Camp* by Todd Strasser, whose catalog includes *Help! I'm Trapped in the First Day of School, Help! I'm Trapped in the President's Body, Help! I'm Trapped in a Professional Wrestler's Body, Help! I'm Trapped in Santa's Body,* and *Help! I'm Trapped in a Vampire's Body.* Then the class moved on to Guided Reading, during which the teacher works intensively with one group while the other students do "focused activities," or busywork. Mr. Rose made three small groups, and the days glided by on cruise control.

One day during Guided Reading, I noticed that Jimmarie looked particularly sad. Jimmarie Moreno-Bonilla was a pretty Puerto Rican girl who carried herself with a quiet grace. She rarely raised her hand, but she watched intently during my *Help! I'm Trapped in . . .* performances. (Mr. Rose had happily relinquished the read-aloud responsibilities to me after my hyperanimated first recital.)

I asked Jimmarie if she wanted to talk about what was bothering her. We moved to the back of the room and she started sniffling. She told me that her father was a bad man and she wasn't supposed to see him, but he came over last night and started yelling and broke the phone. Now she couldn't talk to her grandma in Puerto Rico the way she did every other Sunday night. Also her grandma's planned Christmas visit to New York had been canceled because the ticket was too expensive.

Jimmarie used to live with her grandma in a house in Puerto Rico. She had her own white room that she could decorate however she wanted. Then her mother moved her to the Bronx, to Florida, back to the Bronx, back to Miami, then back to the Bronx. P.S. 85 had been her sixth school in three years. All she wanted was to return to Puerto Rico.

"My grandma is my heart," Jimmarie said quietly, mostly to herself, in her perpetually hoarse voice. "From the floor to the moon, that's how much I love her."

"Jimmarie, that's the most beautiful thing I've ever heard someone say about a grandma. You're a writer!"

"No, I'm no good at writing," Jimmarie said quickly, immediately associating *writing* with the overwhelming and mundane assignments from her struggles in school.

"Let's do it together. We'll make a book about your grandma. We can call it *From the Floor to the Moon*. Do you want to work with me to make a book for her?" Jimmarie's face warmed for the first time into a smile and I felt my insides turn over.

In the following weeks, Jimmarie and I made time each day to talk out ideas for pages and pictures. She had great difficulty writing down ideas that she could articulate orally. Usually, she would stop writing after the first few words. I brought in my mini-cassette recorder and recorded conversations with her, out of which we selected and transcribed the highlights. After we had compiled a list of notes for each page, I gave Jimmarie crayons to draw corresponding pictures. I also shot a roll of photos for the book. Jimmarie said she felt like a star.

I scanned her drawings into my computer and printed them out with her text on the page, leaving space on some pages for photographs. I bound three copies: one for Jimmarie, one for her grandmother, and one for me.

I think about my grandma so many times every day. I used to live with her in Puerto Rico, but now I live in New York City in the Bronx, so I miss her a lot. It's important for me to think about my grandma.

She always makes my favorite foods when we are together. She knows I love hot dogs and French fries and salad, but no salad dressing!

My grandma is a beautiful dancer. I love to watch her dance with my grandpa in her house. She will play a CD and they will dance, dance, dance.

She would dance with me too, but I really love it when she sings with me. She sings like a music star. We have the same voice.

My grandma always has the prettiest clothes and the prettiest shoes. My favorite is her red suit with black shoes. Her favorite color is red, so sometimes I think of red things when I think about her. And I think about her glasses and soft, black hair.

She also has the prettiest name. It is Migdalia Luz. I love my grandpa's name too. It is Juan Bonilla Rodriguez Nieve Cocsección Alberto Castro Martinez. I call him Poppy.

I have four imaginary cousins. Their names are Kimberly, Delma, Nachely, and Angelee. My grandma is their grandma too.

My grandma is my mom's mommy. My mom is the best mom in the world for me. You can tell my grandma was a good mommy to her.

My grandma was going to come visit my family and me in December, but the ticket costs a lot. I can still talk to her on some Sundays and write letters to her. When I talk to her, I get happy happy happy!

From the floor to the moon, I love you grandma!

I gave Jimmarie her two copies along with a hardcover of Sandra Cisneros's *The House on Mango Street,* thinking that she could identify with the author's inner-city Latina heritage, and we read the first two vignettes together. While we sat by her desk looking at her new books, Jimmarie gave me a tight hug, pressing her forehead into my shoulder, and whispered, "Thank you, Mr. Brown."

★　　★　　★

As summer training neared its finish (the Fellows' last day was August 1, preceding a two-week break), I was agonizing over having no placement for the fall. Would I be teaching kindergarten math enrichment or a fifth-grade homeroom next month? Would I end up as a roving substitute? Many other Fellows were in the same powerless boat.

In the summer of 2003, the public school system in New York City was in a state of change. Even the name of the Board of Education was altered to the Department of Education, with its headquarters moving from 111 Livingston Street to 65 Court Street in Brooklyn. Mayor Michael Bloomberg had made education reform his keystone municipal issue, and newly appointed chancellor Joel I. Klein was his man for the task.

In addition to implementing overhauls in curriculum and testing (largely inspired by the No Child Left Behind Act), Bloomberg and Klein revamped zoning lines. The old system of thirty-two districts was scrapped and consolidated into ten larger regions. District 9, which previously covered the South Bronx and was also the setting for Jonathan Kozol's required Fellow reading *Amazing Grace,* and District 10, which contained the Mid- to North Bronx, became Region One. To me, this meant that my *Mummy Returns* pal Susan Atero from the placement fair disappeared and my signed District 10 commitment form became worthless.

The sweeping administrative changes led to communication breakdowns. Teacher vacancies were out there, but no one knew where. The placement fairs had been such a shooting gallery that deep into summer training almost a third of the new Teaching Fellows still did not know where they would be teaching in September. Two Fellows in Sarah Gerson's advisory group got suddenly "excessed" by schools that had overhired during placement fairs. Fellow Advisors, who had virtually no contact with the Region One office, encouraged us to cold-call schools.

The Fellows also learned that the $4,750 Americorps education grants were suspended indefinitely, so despite the promise of total subsidization made during the application and orientation phases, ninety-five dollars would be deducted from each semimonthly paycheck to cover Mercy College classes. Sarah Gerson's room became a sea of bewildered head-shaking, like a bus tour group whose driver hasn't shown. That day was the first time I heard public education in New York described as "organized irresponsibility."

On Tuesday, July 29, Mr. Rose's class received an unannounced visit from Ms. Sonia Guiterrez, P.S. 85's no-nonsense assistant principal with wild, frizzy orange locks who *always* dressed in tight black suits. She stormed the corridors in a perpetual power walk, often shouting commands in open classroom doors in the half moment she passed by. I had just begun leading the daily math period when Guiterrez entered. She sat in the back and observed with an inscrutable expression, leaving immediately at the lesson's end.

Two days later, on my last day at summer school, the principal, Mrs. Boyd, entered the room like Ms. Guiterrez, just after I'd commenced the math lesson. She took notes for the entire forty minutes and left the room. Several minutes later, I was summoned to the principal's office, where Mrs. Boyd held my résumé.

"Mr. Brown, Mr. Brown, Mr. Brown. Tell me about yourself. You went to NYU film school, I see. Is that Tisch?"

"Yes."

"That's a very famous school. But now you want to be a teacher?"

"Yes," I said, and let a beat pass. My monosyllabic answers were not enough. "My long-long-term dreams are in writing and making movies, but my mother's a reading specialist and I spent some time working with kids at her school and that experience really made me believe that I have something to contribute as a teacher. I'm really excited about it. I've signed on with the Fellows for two years and I'm very committed to that. I want to help kids."

Mrs. Boyd nodded slightly. "Good, because I can tell you have the teaching gene. Ms. Guiterrez told me about the lesson she saw you do. She was actually supposed to observe Mr. Rose, but this worked out quite fortuitously. She said your communication skills with the children are exemplary. I went to see for myself and I must say I agree."

"Thank you."

"How do you feel about science, Mr. Brown?"

"Clueless," I wanted to respond. Despite science's indisputable importance to the world, I had generally avoided it as a student. I thought of handling wet dirt during my "Soil and Percolation" unit in elementary school.

My hesitation was noticeable. I was being offered a job as a science cluster teacher. A teacher on wheels. I didn't want that. I wanted my own classroom and my own students: Mr. Brown's class.

"Mr. Brown?"

"I'm interested to be part of the P.S. 85 community wherever I can help," I said.

"Good, because I think you have the teaching gene."

"Thank you." Here it comes.

"We need an upper-grade science cluster teacher. Do you want the job?"

"Yes . . . although I think I could really bring the most to the table as a classroom teacher. I think my ability to form relationships with students could create a very positive classroom culture across all subjects for the whole year, particularly with the school's older, more mature students."

"You make relationships as a cluster too," Mrs. Boyd countered.

"That's true, but an hour or less per week isn't the same as all day every day. Also, I think I could serve as a role model for a set group of kids, being a younger male teacher."

"Our roster is full right now for classrooms. All I have to offer you is this science position. This is it. Do you want to sign a commitment form?"

The terrified uncertainty of many of my placementless colleagues and Susan Atero's vanishing made the decision for me.

17

"Yes." I signed the form and we shook hands. Mrs. Boyd left the room to photocopy the form for my records. In the few seconds that she was gone, I realized that I had been holding my copy of *From the Floor to the Moon*. Jimmarie and I had been looking at it again when Mrs. Boyd called me into the office, and I had taken the book with me.

When my new principal returned, I asked if I could show her a project I had worked on with a student in Mr. Rose's class. Mrs. Boyd thumbed through the book.

"This is beautiful. This is fantastic work, Mr. Brown. Hmm. Jimmarie Moreno-Bonilla. Can I keep this and show it off?" She clutched the book eagerly.

It was my only copy. "Okay," I said.

"Thank you, Mr. Brown. This is terrific."

Later that day, I was congratulated by several teachers and administrators like a scout who had earned his stripes. Marianne Renfro, the veteran special ed coordinator and jack-of-all-trades administrator, gave me particularly warm wishes. I greatly appreciated the gesture from Ms. Renfro, since I knew her as a husky-voiced intimidator, feared and respected by students and faculty. "You're gonna make a helluva science teacher, Brown," she nodded, extracting a Winston from her metallic case.

I thanked her and mentioned that I was hoping for a classroom to open up.

"So you want to be the main man straightaway, huh? I respect that. Maybe I can say something to the Queen."

A week later, I got the call I had been hoping for. Mrs. Boyd offered me a position teaching a fourth-grade classroom.

Mr. Brown's class.

August

What Do You Want Us to Do?

ON MONDAY, AUGUST 18, the Fellows returned for the long haul, although the first day of school wasn't until September 8 (later than usual to compensate for the sweeping citywide administrative changes). I spent the two weeks off as a recluse, feverishly editing my NYU thesis film after an ill-planned Alaska-bound road trip fell through at the last minute.

Every summer since high school graduation, I had set a week aside with my buddies Greg and McKenzie to drive the byways of America. We had diamond-mined in Arkansas, danced on the Las Vegas Boulevard median at dawn, performed "Stand by Me" a capella in Virgin Records's Nashville office lobby, romped around Robot World in Wisconsin Dells, Wisconsin, and tramped across every state (except North Dakota) on the mainland. The cancellation of Road Trip V meant everything was changing.

Like many twenty-two-year-olds, I interpreted occurrences around me as cryptic signposts pointed toward my approaching moment of importance. All roads had led me to this strange adventure. I took the August 14, 2003, blackout as an omen, a silent message with a significant meaning that I couldn't grasp. Three months earlier, I was a college student directing and acting in my first 35mm film. Two months ago, a Los Angeles beach bum on a last-gasp vacation. Last month, a clueless young professional in the company of children named Phaedra and Cochise. Now I surveyed the dark city from my Lower East Side rooftop and sipped orange Vitamin Water, content for the moment to observe the crisis from above, with no idea of what was coming for me at eye level.

New Teacher Week opened with a near-melee inside Martin Luther King, Jr. High School. The auditorium probably held about a thousand people, but it looked to me like more than double that number wanted in for the morning session of "Identification and Reporting of Child Abuse and Maltreatment." People started pushing and one new teacher screamed, "I need to get into 'Abuse' *now!*" I caught the afternoon session.

The speaker, a bearded administrative veteran, launched into a speech about keeping our distance. "Our job, our responsibility as teachers, is to *refer.* As teachers, we *do not* treat the heartbreaking situations that can and will walk into our classrooms. We refer! There are trained professionals, contracted by the Department of Education, for counseling, physical therapy, and social work. We are not them. We are not their psychologists, social workers, nurses, parents, or friends. We are trained professionals in teaching and teaching only!"

Opened in 1931, formidable, brick Public School 85: The Great Expectations School rests on a steep concrete slope in the square between Marion and Webster avenues. One long, broad corridor built up six stories from the bottom of the hill, its length spans three blocks from 184th to 187th streets. The school stands in the center of the Fordham neighborhood in New York's 16th congressional district, which the 2000 Census reported to have a median household income of $19,311, ranking 436th out of 436 districts in the fifty states. And P.S. 85's district was deep in last place. Residents of the districts in 434th and 435th place respectively earn on average over $6,300 (32.6 percent more) and $2,600 (13.4 percent more) over the average 16th district resident. Also, those two districts are in West Virginia and Kentucky, where the cost of living is lower than in New

York City. The P.S. 85 community lives in the very bottom of the economic barrel in America.

The main entrance is on the first of four floors of classrooms, although the stairwell descends to a basement that houses special ed classes as well as the cafeteria. Below lies the subbasement that leads to the blacktop schoolyard, which serves primarily as the faculty parking lot. Exterior metal grates adorn all windows. The Great Expectations School looks like a prison.

At an opening faculty assembly, each of the eleven new teachers (all Fellows) stood when introduced. I saw Allie Bowers and Elizabeth Camaraza, my two lunch buddies from summer school. Allie, just a year out of Bard College, was kindergarten-bound, and I thought she would be a perfect fit with the little kiddies.

I admired raven-haired Elizabeth, who cursed and laughed and had made me feel legitimized in my summer exhaustion, confusion, and fear. She had gone from welfare lines to first class, raised two kids with her wonderfully nutty extended family in the Kearny, New Jersey, home where she grew up, and could sing both "London Calling" and "You Make Me Feel Brand New" at the top of her lungs. She was a natural-born leader.

Mrs. Boyd introduced Marnie Beck, the new fourth-grade special ed teacher. Marnie was a hard-nosed, forearm-tattooed Long Islander whom I had seen around at Mercy, usually puffing a Kool below her dark sunglasses. At first, I thought hiring gruff Marnie as the grade's sole special ed teacher was proof positive that New York City public schools were truly in the drink. I quickly learned that the woman had more love and expertise with tough kids than anyone else I would meet at P.S. 85. Marnie was a soldier, and she became one of my heroes.

I sat in a wooden auditorium seat amidst a clutch of young rookies, nervously eyeing the backs of incoming first-grade teacher Trisha Pierson and nebbishy computer guru David de la O. Next to me sat pretty, hipsterish Cat Samuels, the only new teacher who had not been at P.S. 85 for summer school. She would be a fourth- and fifth-grade literacy prep teacher, with my class slotted for Tuesday mornings. I asked what was playing in the headphones she was putting away. "Mission of Burma," she said. "I'm in a big Matador Records phase."

"Awesome. Pavement is one of my favorite bands," I offered, dropping the name of a Matador Records act with an accompanying thrill of credibility. I had an indie-rock ally!

After the schoolwide faculty meeting, Mr. Bob Randazzo held his own opening powwow for fourth- and fifth-grade teachers. A mustachioed, mousey man with an affable demeanor and singsong cadence in his speech, Mr. R. was the upper-grade assistant principal and my direct supervisor. Randazzo had been at P.S. 85 for over thirty years, most of them as an administrator. After calling the room to order, he said, "Welcome back everybody. First order of business: Marianne Renfro . . . is gone."

"YES!" A rousing sweep of applause broke out. I was stunned. Summer school had been an administrator love-in, with special ed coordinator Ms. Renfro at the center. "Thank God!"

Randazzo waved his hand to reclaim the floor. "And it's looking about ninety-five percent that I'll be retiring at the end of this year."

"Awwwww, Bobby . . ." The room now sounded like a sitcom audience track for a stray-puppy scene. "But I just want to remind everyone right off the bat that here in fourth and fifth grade, we take care of our own. If anyone at any point has any concerns, questions, tiffs, grievances, problems, successes, stock market tips (har har), you know you can always come to me. We don't have to go over each other's heads, because in fourth and fifth grade *we do our own laundry.*"

"That's right!" It was like a political rally. "Absolutely, Bob!"

My class was 4-217, pronounced "four-two-seventeen." The numbers felt like an awkward juxtaposition at first, but I got used to them quickly. The pale lime room looked giant and bare. It had air-conditioning, though, a blessing. I sat for a few silent minutes at my teacher's desk in the back, holding my classroom key. Ms. Vuong and Ms. Smith, two paraprofessionals assigned to help me organize my room, arrived. Ms. Vuong was in her third trimester and Ms. Smith had to be in her late sixties. They opened the coat closet's bulky sliding doors to reveal mountains of dusty textbooks resting on unsteady shelves.

"What do you want us to do?" Ms. Smith asked me.

I had no idea what anyone was supposed to do. In the opening meeting, Mrs. Boyd had announced her credo for teachers — "Your classroom is your résumé" — but I was blank on how to begin. Feeling like the greenest rookie in the world, I aimlessly rearranged stacks of textbooks until the magical arrival of Fran Baker, a kind and soft-spoken twenty-year teaching veteran. Mrs. Baker went to work expeditiously, bringing in her own magic markers and confidently assigning the helpers to make specific signs. I fashioned a Weekly Trivia Corner, my embellishment on the bare requirements. My first two questions were, "Who is the governor of New York State?" and "Who is the all-time NBA leader in assists?" Mrs. Baker half opened several hardcover picture books and placed them on the tall, protruding heater vent near the front of the classroom. She said, "The kids probably won't read these anyway. All they [the administrators] care about is that it looks pretty. In case Dilla Zane comes."

The mysterious name of Dilla Zane echoed in my head. It sounded like it belonged to a swamp beast. Who was that?

P.S. 85 received a special pass from the city to continue with Success for All (SFA), a scripted, "teacher-proof" literacy curriculum that the rest of the city had scrapped the previous June. The veteran teachers apparently hated SFA ("Slowly Fading Away" or "So Fucking Annoying," take your pick) but were stuck with it for ninety minutes every day, which, in the past year, had driven a deep wedge between the faculty and the administration.

Orientation meetings ran like doomsayer conventions, punctuated with gallows humor. During one particularly baleful meeting, the math and literacy coaches, Al Conway and Marge Foley, worried me when they both guffawed while slamming Region One; the "half-retired administrator," Mr. Randazzo; and "the Queen," Mrs. Boyd, for alienating teachers by insisting on sticking with poor curricula. Al and Marge also explained that the PA announcement "The red passes are in the office" means to close your door and allow no students to leave the room because of a security breach. However, when you hear "The green passes are in the office," you know the threat has been *neutralized*.

Apparently our *Math Trailblazers* was a confusing, "jumpy" text. *Everyday Math,* used by kindergarten through third grade, was more fluid and kid-friendly, but a bureaucratic tie-up prevented using it in grades four and five. There was no science textbook. For social studies, *New York* was supposedly a great text, but there were not enough copies to go around. I was lucky to find a class set in my closet. For science and social studies, we received pacing calendars with two or three lines dedicated to monthly focus concepts. Nobody got a full set of supplemental workbooks for any subject, and teachers had to bring in their own paper for photocopies.

My parents drove up from Cherry Hill to bring a boatload of supplies, including a blue stuffed dinosaur, Mr. Lizard, to encourage class spirit, and their old rocking chair, now rechristened as my Reading Chair. They also delivered boxes of magic markers, chalk, and construction paper, compliments of my roommate Greg's art teacher mom. As an extra touch, my mom brought several rolls of vibrantly colored, school-subject-themed border to enliven my bulletin board edges. The science border, speckled with microscopes and dino skeletons, was a particularly nice touch.

The following day, Ms. Guiterrez visited me. "Mr. Brown. That border is company made," she declared.

I nodded in cautious concurrence.

"It's distracting. Take it all down or turn it over. We're not a company. We're a school." And she stomped off. Guiterrez was technically the second- and third-grade interim assistant principal, but she took on supervisory responsibilities for fourth grade because Mr. Randazzo was often busy "crunching numbers."

I understood the push to avoid mass-produced inspirational posters in the classroom, although for whatever reason I still remember my fifth-grade teacher's Yoda poster: "The Force is with you when you *READ*." It never corrupted me as far as I could tell. Down the hall, Marc Simmons and Jeanne Solloway had all kinds of store-bought stuff on their walls. (Simmons had especially splurged on an American flag motif.)

This was a colorful border, displayed at the edges of the bulletin boards, not some prominently showcased company ad. I staple-removed my mom's border, flipped it over, and stapled it back with the blank, gray side facing out. It was the first time I was angry.

Who would be my kids? Everyone else had a set of blue index cards with evaluative paragraphs from the students' previous teachers.

On Tuesday, September 2, Mr. Randazzo told me that Adele Hafner had them and she would give the cards to me. Adele was a middle-aged enrichment teacher with a weathered face and grave demeanor. When I asked her if she had the guidance cards, she snapped in her authoritative Minnesotan twang, "Yeah. You'll get them."

I didn't. The next day, I passed Adele several times in the hall and she made no mention of the cards. I felt awkward about bringing it up since our brief discussion yesterday had been quite clear. When Adele still did not deliver them the day after, I sought her out again. I walked into a classroom where she was unpacking boxes. "Excuse me, Adele," I said tentatively, to no acknowledgment. "About the blue cards . . ."

"Mr. Brown, you don't know me well enough to call me a liar. I told you you'd get your blue cards and you'll get them. End of darn story!"

"Whoa, I didn't mean to sound like I was calling you a *liar* . . ."

"Except you did. I gave you my word you'd get them and that's that. Sound fair?"

"Okay, but I think there's been a miscommunication. I didn't intend for you —"

"No miscommunication. Alrighty? Good-bye."

Adele and I were supposed to be collaborators. She was scheduled to prep 4-217 (teach a fifty-minute science lesson during my out-of-class work period) every Thursday morning. Recalling Randazzo's speech about "taking care of our own," I went to his office.

Mr. R. nodded vigorously as I explained my conflict. "No problem, no problem. There are other issues there. I'll take care of it. Don't worry."

An hour later, the rubber-banded cards appeared in my mailbox.

I later learned that 4-217 had been Mrs. Hafner's room the previous year, and it was not her idea to relinquish it to a fresh-faced college boy while getting switched to a science cluster position in mid-August. Adele Hafner hated my guts for stealing her class. At least I got the cards. They read:

Lakiya Ray: Very, very slow. Very disrespectful to classmates and adults. Mother makes excuses for her behavior. She does not complete assignments. She gets an attitude 95% of the day. Very difficult child. She cannot get along with any of her classmates.

Fausto Mason: Fausto has deeply embedded good traits that have a hard time emerging. He is compulsive, impulsive, insultive [*sic*], and challenges authority at every turn. Although he is bright, he has a total lack of control that impedes his maturation (academically and socially). He is a real challenge! Good luck!

Eric Ruiz: Eric has made minimal improvement this year. He has difficulty focusing, needs help with organization skills. Referred with support of mother; referral went nowhere. Should be referred again. Eric is immature; he needs a great deal of direction.

Bernard McCants: Extremely temperamental child; has a tendency to be disrespectful to teachers; reading skills are good, but writing skills are poor. Math skills are also poor. Bernard has a knack for creative writing (poetry) and should be encouraged in this area.

Deloris Barlow: Deloris has potential to be an academically successful student. However, her propensity for using "inventive thinking" to explain her lack of classwork instead of applying herself is a major stumbling block. She is the embodiment of conflict as she challenges authority figures, as well as antagonizes & alienates her peers.

Asante Bell: Asante has great difficulty staying focused. Her interactions with classmates can be violent at times. She does not respect the property of others, including classroom materials. Writing skills are very weak. DO NOT place with Virginia Tyne.

Maimouna Lugaru: Maimouna is generally well-behaved, but is a follower. She finds a special friend and will go with the friend's every move. She loves to write, but gets lost by writing pages and pages. She needs responsibility to feel important in class.

Athena Page: Athena has excellent work habits and does quality work. At times she has shown a lack of self-control and has made careless and needless mistakes involving classmates. However on the whole, Athena is very sweet and studious.

Hamisi Umar: Hamisi is a hard worker; his behavior is generally ok. He tries to get away with fooling around, but he will respond to praise. Give him jobs/tutoring others and he is happy. Needs to develop writing skills. Loves to read, enjoys math.

Manolo "Lito" Ruiz: Has no grasp of basic mechanics despite numerous interventions. Can be a nice boy, but is extremely susceptible to negative influences in his environment. MANY problems at home.

Destiny Rivera: Destiny is a very quiet and sensitive student. Can be very emotional at times. Destiny needs to use the elevator. She is constantly misplacing work, becomes very distracted at times. Destiny would benefit from additional help in math.

<u>Sonandia Azcona</u>: Sonandia is an excellent student in both behavior and skill/ability. She is very courteous and participates regularly. Sonandia loves to write and has great creativity. Very beneficial to a student in need.

<u>Julissa Marrero</u>: Julissa is talkative and can be spiteful when provoked. She needs conflict resolution skills. She can be sullen when redirected. Her mother seems to be supportive and needs a Spanish speaking translator for communication.

<u>Cwasey Bartrum</u>: Cwasey often gets terrible headaches. Cwasey does all of his homework. Can be very disrespectful to teachers and classmates. Mother is supportive but her interventions seem to roll off his back. Needs help with writing mechanics.

<u>Tayshaun Jackson</u>: Highly talkative and demands constant attention. Can be combative with teachers. Tayshaun loves math and enjoys demonstrating this at the front of the class. Seems to have above average artistic potential.

<u>Verdad Navarez</u>: Verdad loves math — needs to improve writing/reading skills. Verdad is generally well-behaved, but can be stubborn. Verdad rarely volunteers to speak in class, he is sometimes lazy and needs to be pushed.

<u>Tiffany Sanchez</u>: Tiffany is a very promising student but lacks work ethics. She is very sloppy in her work and always has an excuse for missing homework. When reprimanded she becomes non-responsive. Tiffany also fidgets with anything within reach.

<u>Edgar Rollins</u>: Eddie is a very respectful child. Very shy. He needs help with math and science. No support from home. He does not like to be yelled at. He has been held back 3 times in the third grade. If he is absent for more than 3 days please follow up on him.

My roster listed twenty-five children, so seven kids' cards were missing, giving them a truly blank slate. I showed my class list to several flabbergasted P.S. 85 veterans.

"I have no idea why they always do that to first-year teachers."

"I can't believe they put Lakiya and Deloris together."

"Fausto alone will ruin your year. No one can control him."

"I'm so sorry."

On September 5, the final day of preparation before the first day of school, I paid the price for my cosmic collision with Adele Hafner. Mr. Len Daly visited my room. Daly was Bob Randazzo's best friend and henchman, a thirty-year teaching veteran who no longer taught classes but retained an administrative position with unclear responsibilities.

"You did the right thing talking to Bob about that situation you had," he said. "We're here if you need us. That's what it's all about. Don't hesitate to ask for help."

"Thanks, I appreciate it. I will."

"Seriously, we're down the hall. We're all nearby if you need us."

"Thank you."

Daly lowered his tone. "Don't need us too much. Especially in the beginning. Prove you can handle yourself." Now his hand gripped my shoulder with discomfiting firmness. "It's better for everyone."

September

The Disharmony

O**N SEPTEMBER** 8, I woke up at 5:05, methodically showered and dressed, purchased a bagel at the corner bodega, and boarded the F train. I strode through the Great Expectations School entrance with a quickened step, distributing good mornings to everyone I saw.

I had already prepared my chalkboard the previous Friday with the heading:

September 8, 2003

Mr. Brown

4-217

<u>TEAM</u>

I knew that establishing the "team" classroom culture had to happen right off the bat. I needed to be firmest when I was the least experienced, the paradoxical curse of new teachers. I hoped my "make our own class rules" activity was the right kind of opener.

At 7:58, I descended the stairs to the basement level where the students waited in the cafeteria. Each step down brought me closer to the nether din of high-pitched children sounds. I cracked an excited smile, stunned that my weeks of training and years of youthful experience had steered me to this unequivocally grown-up post. For twenty-two years I had been on one path and twenty-five Bronx children had been on another. Now we would meet. I needed no more convoluted symbols like the blackout to interpret. The real moment was upon me.

"Don't smile!" Ms. Slocumb, a second-year Fellow, whispered forcefully. "Seriously, no smiling!"

Holding a pen and clipboard purely as props, I entered the lunchroom to meet the students. I took in the Spongebob Squarepants bookbags, the girls' elaborate hair settings, jeans with winding embroidered flowers by the cuff, and the boys' Allen Iverson jerseys. Kids. They looked adorable, eager-eyed for the uncertainty-fueled first day of school. I circled the table, shaking each child's hand and introducing myself.

For the first of 183 times, we performed the morning lineup ritual: Mr. Randazzo raised his arm, the signal for silence. All responded by raising their arms in acknowledgment. Randazzo gave a perfunctory welcome speech, and the kids fell swiftly into two lines, separated by gender and ordered by height. He came around to give each class a rubric score of one to four depending on the degree of silence and neatness of the line. I marveled at the grand organization.

Line leaders Hamisi and Sonandia (two with encouraging blue cards), led the crew, halting every two doors in the corridor and every landing on the stairwell to look for the "go ahead" or "wait up" hand signal from me at the back. Meanwhile, I cased my problem-reputation kids. Imposing Lakiya Ray was the tallest in the class, a sour, tough-faced girl with tight braids. Eric Ruiz, whose previous teacher told me he was a "weird kid," was unreadable at first. Deloris Barlow, a skinny, pigtailed girl, was laughing a lot at the table before lineup but calmed down appropriately. Fausto Mason immediately tipped me off for trouble. Short and puffy-cheeked, he grinned and swaggered with a loose strut.

During summer training, I studied cases that made a convincing argument that students' achievement levels vary directly with their teacher's expectations of them, regardless of neighborhood or family background. I was determined from the first day to maintain high expectations for all my students, according everybody the blank slate I felt we all needed, even infamous Fausto Mason. After all, he had never had a male teacher and he had never had me.

I assigned the students to desks according to my carefully devised seating chart. Guided by the blue cards, I tried to arrange only one or two loose cannons per group. (City policy mandated that students sit in groups.) My class roster was also evenly divided between boys and girls and African Americans and Latin Americans, so I went for heterogeneous clusters.

After deflecting questions about my age, family size, and marital status, I launched into an even-tempered sermon about how 4-217 would succeed or fail as a group. "On the Yankees, either everyone wins or no one wins. If Derek Jeter has a great hitting game but doesn't back up his pitcher at shortstop, the team suffers. The Yankees are a strong team because they back each other up. They win because they work together. We need to help each other out for us all to do well. All I want to do is help you get smarter and have fun while it's happening. I'm very interested in trips, rewards, and games, but only if we work together. Does this sound fair?"

"Yes, Mr. Brown," the choral response resounded. The speech felt firm, and the kids sat silently with their eyes on me for every word.

"Excellent! Since we're a team, I thought it would be fair if we all made our class rules *together*. Who has an idea for a good rule for our team?"

Myriad hands shot up. I called on Cwasey, a shrimpy, bespectacled black boy with squinty eyes and a freshly shaved head.

"You should respect everyone. Like teachers and students and the principal."

"*Outstanding, Cwasey*! Brilliant! Respect for teachers and students and the principal. An outstanding first rule." I jotted it on the board. "What exactly is 'respect,' Cwasey?"

"Respect means you should treat everybody good, like you want to be treated."

I had a star. Cwasey Bartrum!

I called next on Sonandia, my line leader. "You should do all your work the best you can all the time."

Deloris said, "Nobody should steal nobody's stuff and treat everything like it's important."

Bernard piped up. "You should not fight in school cause there's better ways to . . . like . . . solve your problems."

"You should respect everyone," Dennis reiterated.

Lakiya prompted several giggles when she shouted in her bassy tone, "Do your homework!"

I ignored the chuckles because she had hit one of the key points. This wasn't going to be so lawless after all. These children were moral authorities! I consolidated their input into two broad rules regarding respect, effort, and honesty (rules I had of course planned from the beginning) and moved them to the "reading rug," a giant panther design I had bought on the Grand Concourse.

For the two weeks before the Success for All schedule began (when students would change rooms for their skill-level groups), teachers followed an introductory curriculum called *Getting Along Together*. For the first lesson, I had to read *Crow Boy*, an Eastern fairy tale about an outcast child who finds self-reliance. Introducing the story, I wrote the word "unique" on my chart paper, which Sonandia, my wordsmith, defined as "one of a kind." I told them we all have secret talents that we ourselves might not even know about yet. "Some of you on the carpet right now might be brilliant comic strip artists, creative writers, question-askers, room-organizers, or things we haven't even thought of. This year we will work together to discover those hidden gifts."

Two pages into my *Crow Boy* read-aloud, Fausto stood up and ambled leisurely toward the door, drawing the attention of the whole class. "Fausto. Fausto. *Fausto!*" I shouted. Fausto turned back toward the class.

"THAT STORY'S WACK, YO!"

I kept a straight face, but a majority of the class erupted in crazed laughter at Fausto's apparently genius comedic line. Fausto beamed while fifteen kids cracked up, Lakiya the loudest of all. She bellowed a forced, open-mouthed cackle, swaying violently in her seated position, knocking into classmates.

Ten seconds ago, we were all on the same page. Now it looked like a different class.

As the overwrought giggles receded, Fausto, now a superstar, still had not returned to his seat. I had to take this kid down. In deadpan, I said, "The story's not wack. Are you ready to stop acting like a kinder —"

"DAAAAAA! Mr. Brown talkin' gangsta, yo!"

"Mr. Brown said 'wack'!"

Destiny, Athena, Sonandia, and three others whose names I had not yet memorized sat patiently waiting for the story to continue. Everyone else was going bonkers.

"He say 'the story not wack'!"

Beads of sweat formed all over me. I looked at the clock: 8:43. Three hours and forty-seven minutes until lunch.

"Silence. Silence. Fausto! Sit!" I yelled at him as I would a wayward mutt.

Deloris piped up with a grin, "Mr. Brown, you turning red."

Bernard jumped in on my behalf. "Be quiet, yo! Let Mr. Brown read *Crow Boy!*"

Lakiya, still grinning, echoed Bernard's plea. "Shut up! Shut up y'all!" Suddenly, Fausto's face changed and he sat.

I had set myself against allowing "shut up" into the 4-217 vernacular, but my temperature was skyrocketing and at that moment I could handle the kids shutting each other up if it worked. And did Lakiya, a famous attitude-problem child, hold sway over other kids' behavior?

I battled through reading and discussing *Crow Boy,* often stopping mid-page because of rude laughter. One time, Fausto slapped

Destiny on the shoulder, a minuscule harbinger of the intergender aggression to come.

When I sent them back to their groups to write a story retell, or regurgitation of the plot, I felt like I had scaled a mountain in simply getting through the short book. Sonandia and several of her pals seemed to enjoy the story. In fifteen minutes, though, I was back to the beginning of another new lesson and new fight. I calculated that I would teach at least seven hundred lessons this year; they could not all be like this stop-and-start scrape job.

Our opening math lesson regarding bar graphs yielded slightly better results. I made a model graph, polling the kids and charting their favorite TV shows in a data table and spelling out my procedure on the board. They copied everything in their math notebooks or blank loose-leaf sheets I provided.

P.S. 85 draws its students from one of the poorest neighborhoods in the Bronx, but almost all of the kids had cable television to watch their favorite shows: *That's So Raven, Spongebob Squarepants, Kim Possible.* I soon learned that most of my students also owned state-of-the-art video-game systems. One teacher explained, "It's an investment in a twenty-four-hour babysitter."

Fausto got out of his seat eleven times during the twenty-minute math lesson. I tried to keep him at bay by calling on him when his hand was not raised. To my surprise, he had the correct answer every time.

After the kids answered the worksheet questions from the *Math Trailblazers* textbook and we had discussed them (although only ten of the twenty-one present completed the work), it was time for the Baseline Writing Sample. This would be a "before" example to compare with June work. The prompt was, "What would make a good teacher for me?"

Despite my coaxing, Lakiya, Deloris, and "weird" Eric again wrote nothing. Maimouna, my prolific student whose blue card warned about her tendency to "get lost by writing pages and pages," dutifully filled four pieces of loose-leaf with neon-purple ink.

One more lesson to go before the now direly needed lunch respite. Using a template devised during my summer training at Mercy College, I had created a "biography/autobiography" unit as an introductory meet-each-other literacy endeavor. For a model, I had a great kid-friendly biography of Martin Luther King, Jr. I decided on the spot that rather than read the whole book (an invitation for disruption), we would crawl one page at a time, charting the important elements of a biography.

PAGE 1: Birth date and place. Family background.

PAGE 2: Life before age 5.

PAGE 3: Life in elementary school. Friends, interests.

PAGE 4: An important experience or adventure as a young person. This may be a hint for something important the person does as an adult!

I stopped in the middle because after four and a half hours in the room together, we had made it to lunchtime. The kids jumped and pushed en route to the cafeteria. The mood was frantic and hungry and bore no resemblance to the beginning of the morning.

A phenomenon that lives only in our military, prisons, and elementary schools is the crucially serious transit *line.* I hated walking in line as a kid. I thought that if I could show I trusted my students to walk calmly and decently together, they would respect my trust and respect each other. Trust begets good teamwork.

When I reflected on the first hour of my first day, I realized everything I had done in that brief honeymoon period would come back to haunt me. My "team" spiel and my desire to offer everyone an evenhanded shake and social contract of respect were disasters of nuclear proportions. With my good-faith gesture, I had put myself in a position to be defied by one charismatic rebel, which of course happened immediately, opening the floodgates. Before I had won the respect and command of the class, I had allowed myself to be drawn into a graceless power struggle with the attention-seeking subverter. *From the Floor to the Moon* felt miles away.

Counter to my hopes, my lack of stern watchfulness during the first lineup enabled them to loudly screw off during future hall-walking time, since I had sent an initial impression that I was not fatally serious about our line. This resulted in a constant public fracas of shouting and shepherding the noncompliers during those formative first weeks. The disorder in the hall spilled wildly into the classroom, turning each morning, each return from lunch, gym, and computers, and each dismissal into an unwieldy and dangerous mess. I had been *too nice*.

The first day finished with forty minutes of doling out jobs — sweeper, dustpan holder, boys' line leader, girls' line leader, botanist, three librarians, two popularly demanded assistant librarians — and cleaning the floor, which had somehow become a cyclone scene of shredded papers, tissues, and pencil shavings. I handed out an exuberant welcome letter and supply list to parents that I had revised endlessly over the previous week.

I dismissed the kids out onto the subbasement-level blacktop as a gallery of legal guardians watched and waited behind the chain-link fence above. Seeing the adults waiting for us, my mood changed on a dime. I suddenly felt proud to be a leader in this procession of children, the first nip of excitement since my stairwell descent before the day even started.

The kids scattered immediately, and I headed back into school for the weekly eighty-minute Professional Development session. As soon as I hit the steps, I felt a shot of dull fatigue in my knees, as if they were about to give out. My heart throbbed and I felt a steely pounding in my wrists and forearms.

Barbara Chatton, my in-school mentor, advised me, "It's never as good as you think it is, and it's never as bad as you think it is. The day's over. Think of it as one door closing and another door opening."

That night I recounted the fiasco to everyone I knew. My roommate, Greg, and my neighbor Kadi wanted to rip Fausto apart. Their rage was contagious, and I started to feel worse. I called Jess.

I had only known Jess for nine days, but they were memorable ones. We had met while cavorting like fiends to Billy Idol's "Dancing with Myself" at a mutual friend's rooftop party in Brooklyn and had been more or less inseparable since. Meshing the stomach-tickling excitement of new romance with the annual end-of-summer dash for kicks, my feelings about Jess had quickly planted her very near to the center of my universe.

During the school day I thought I radiated failure, but Jess told me it's impossible to juggle so many flaming bowling pins of responsibility at once. I psyched myself up that this was a battle that I had asked for, and one that I was going to win. Now I knew their faces.

I decided two things. First, the kids would be disinclined to act out if there was a consistent reward system in place. This was something I had underestimated and thus had not implemented immediately on day one. Second, pleading with the collective for silence was exhausting and ineffective. I needed signals that could work efficiently and save my voice.

I made a "TEAM EFFORT" poster and divided it into halves for stars and strikes. If I counted to three, my newly hatched silent signal, and the room was still noisy, strike city! If they achieved quiet, star stickers all around. When the class accrued forty more stars than strikes (circa Halloween, I planned), we would have a 4-217 party.

I did not feel like smiling on my way downstairs for the second day.

Outside the 4-217 door, I sternly announced our new system to the line, translating their blank, tired looks as understanding. In the middle of my speech, a secretary tapped me on the shoulder and handed me three orange paper strips from the office, meaning I should expect three new students to arrive in my room in the next sixty seconds. Jennifer Taylor, Joseph Castanon, and Evley Castro dutifully appeared. Tall, mature-looking Jennifer shook my hand and said, "Nice to meet you, Mr. Brown." Evley had a sensitive face and shyly stared at his sneakers when I shook his limp hand. Joseph had a bowl haircut and an empty look in his eyes.

When chatter materialized during our bar graph lesson activity, I shook my head with slow intensity and boomed, "One . . . two . . . *I still hear talking* . . . *THREE*! That's a strike!" I felt like a jerk.

The kids reacted with spasms of disappointment, as if their final lotto number had failed to come up. They called out names of the offenders with twangy irritation. "Ber-NARD!" "Cwa-SEY!" "De-LOR-is!"

We had five strikes and one star when I realized I needed to doctor this whole operation. I started giving out spontaneous stars for strong individual efforts until we got the board even. Once the class received several stars, the kids started to like it.

Teachers are supposed to keep anecdotal records of misbehavior for documentation's sake. Mine quickly piled up.

SEPTEMBER 9

10:00 during *Simon Says,* Fausto punched Hamisi and Hamisi cried but did not fight back. Fausto did not apologize.

10:45 Lakiya will not stop talking no matter what! She makes mocking gibberish sounds when Deloris speaks.

11:30 Destiny says Joseph and Fausto told her they were going to beat her up at recess.

2:00 Unprovoked, Lakiya tells Tiffany, "I'm going to follow you home." Tiffany is terrified.

2:10 Randazzo tells the class "Mr. Brown is nice and you're taking advantage." I don't like that he says that.

SEPTEMBER 10

10:20 Destiny hyperventilating and can't stop. I send her to get water.

11:00 Had to scream at class. Lakiya completely rude and indignant. Laughing and yelling, "Preach!" Randazzo comes in, hearing the shouting, and lectures them. They're silent for him.

LUNCH (I'm not there) Fausto chokes Eric till Eric throws up. Gets in big trouble with Mr. Daly. Daly calls home and Fausto sobs. He says he will get beaten.

1:15 I have long conversation with crying Fausto about being a leader while I eat my lunch. Good man-to-man. He says he will step off confrontations. I believe him.

2:10 Fausto causes disruption in gym class immediately upon returning to group. Entire class game has to stop and wait.

2:35 Fausto pushes Destiny, she cries. *Lakiya* helps Destiny, very surprising.

2:45 Fausto picks up and drops Verdad in an awkward body slam. Verdad cries and becomes unresponsive.

I called all fifteen parent contact numbers I had. To the six I reached, I rambled praises and yammered about how I wanted us all to be working together. I encouraged the parents to read with their kids and to keep an eye on the nightly homework. I told Lakiya's mom about how Lakiya helped Destiny Rivera when Destiny was hurt and neglected to mention Lakiya's rampant disrespect during lessons. I wanted to win the parents onto my team now in the event that I would have to bring down the disciplinary hammer later.

Except for a few brief encounters in the parking lot at dismissal, this was my first contact with parents in the Bronx. As an outsider, my vague notion, fostered by Mercy College summer seminars, was that adults in the Bronx were either overworked, undereducated (hailing from P.S. 85 and the like), estranged from a spouse, tangled up with drugs, burnt out, or a combination of several. I did not know what to expect.

My initial impressions were that the parents wanted to hear what I had to say. Cwasey's mom volunteered to be a room parent on class trips. Lakiya's mother told me, "I appreciate your call." Tiffany's dad said, "I know Tiffany can get distracted, but she does good work when she's focused."

My two first-generation American kids from African families, Hamisi Umar and Maimouna Lugaru, had parents who spoke very little English. I knew Julissa and blue-cardless Gladys Ferraro's caretakers only spoke Spanish. I thought about ways to communicate with them. Then I passed out.

The following day was the anniversary of September 11, 2001. Some classes held discussion forums and responded to writing prompts about 9/11. Other teachers avoided the issue altogether because of the students' immaturity. Since many of my kids could not tell me their addresses, I opted against spending a chunk of class time on the tragedy. The self-censoring and expectation-lowering had begun.

At 8:30, Mrs. Boyd came on the loudspeaker and gave a speech about memorializing this day in history. Boyd got on the PA two or three times a day in September, taking her time on the microphone, incurring many frowns from momentum-losing teachers and spiteful comments from bored students. Instead of, "Mr. Randazzo, please call the office," we would hear, "I beg your pardon, teachers and students, and I apologize for this announcement in the midst of your literacy block, which I'm sure is making brilliant readers and writers out of you all [pause for guffaw], but Mr. Randazzo, would you please find a way to contact me, Mrs. Boyd, in the principal's office at your absolute soonest convenience. Once again, Mr. R., please contact the principal. Thank you and please return to your academic rigor and accountable talk."

Mrs. Boyd's 9/11 memorial message culminated with a prolonged moment of silence. I scanned the room, foreboding trouble in the pregnant quiet, but I was not ready for what happened next.

"SEPTEMBER 11TH IS WACK!"

Fausto leapt on top of the group three desks and jumped up and down, screaming incoherently. "FUCK SEPTEMBER 11TH!" he managed as I got my hands on him.

I grabbed him by the arms and yanked him down into a bear hug, blocking his path from any kind of crazed belly flop. Anything was possible. My face burned.

"I DON'T CARE, YO! GET THE FUCK OFF ME! SEPTEMBER 11TH IS BOOTLEG!"

I led him by the arm to Randazzo's office, telling Mr. R., "This one needs a time out." My physicality with Fausto surprised me, but the class cheered when I dragged him away.

With my biggest headache out of the room, I got reenergized to teach, as if I was on a hockey power play. My hopes got thrown in the gutter, though, when in the middle of our biography lesson, Eric suddenly lunged at Lakiya's face, awkwardly missing, and the two fell on the floor, wrestling viciously. I ripped them apart and angrily asked what it was about. Lakiya blurted, "He a faggot!"

At this exact moment I watched Lito Ruiz, the boy whose blue card identified him as "extremely susceptible to negative influences," heave a fistful of crayons at Verdad, my sullen, likable mathematician, who sat in the opposite corner of the classroom. "LIII-TO!" I shouted in what felt like comic slow motion. Verdad immediately retaliated by gunning his oversized eraser at Lito. He missed and hit Athena, who started crying. Several boys laughed maniacally, mocking Athena. Mr. Randazzo heard the noise and came in, shushing the class. The room went silent except for Bernard, who loudly sucked his teeth in an insolent snicker. Randazzo shook his head at me and blasted the class for being the most disrespectful group in the school. Sonandia covered her eyes.

Was this chaos my fault? I thought I had done everything I could to prepare to teach. My classroom was a print-rich environment. I modeled good character. I was organized and articulate in kid-friendly language.

I thought of a French movie that opens with a story about a man falling from the roof of a tall building. As he passes each floor he thinks to himself, "So far, so good, so far, so good." As his spirit looks down at his splattered corpse on the asphalt, he realizes it's not how you fall that matters. It's how you land. It's the mess that catches attention.

That night I decided two things: #1: Fausto was dead to me. His presence was cancerous. #2: I would aim high with content and ideas in class discussions (get back to those great expectations!), and if this amounted to blank stares all around, I would chalk it up. Jennifer and Sonandia would probably be able to follow me.

Decision #1 was rash and ridiculous. I could despise the kid, but I would still have to deal with his destructive actions. Also, he was a sad case. He said his mother beat the tar out of him. I felt sick for thinking so bitterly of an abused child. Decision #2 was built of virtuous intentions and horrendous logic. If I specifically geared activities toward the higher-achieving kids, I would alienate and lose the lower-achieving ones, who were already more likely to be discipline problems.

What was I supposed to teach to a room that held both Sonandia and Lakiya? Sonandia could read young adult books and analyze them critically with the right kind of guidance. She was capable of the higher-order skills in Bloom's taxonomy, a reference structure for teachers to analyze levels of abstraction in learning. Lakiya could not read a sentence fluently and refused even to write her name. The range of abilities in 4-217 was as wide as a Great Lake.

Upon arriving to P.S. 85 the next day, I got word that Fausto Mason had been permanently transferred out of my class. He was moving next door to Pat Cartwright, a tough black woman who had been in the army. This was Pat's second year as a teacher and first with a homeroom, and the administration felt she was better equipped to deal with Fausto than I was. I agreed. Pat explained, "He's just a rockhead. I'll whip him into shape."

With Fausto gone, I had my smoothest day yet. We began a

James and the Giant Peach read-aloud. We reviewed the Martin Luther King, Jr. biography and wrote outlines on graphic organizers for our autobiographies. We made bar graphs from data in the *Math Trailblazers* textbook. We paraphrased stories that I had modeled aloud and some that I had typed on a homemade worksheet. We made a chart of components for "Good Listening" in our *Getting Along Together* lesson. We reviewed the parts of the scientific method introduced in a previous lesson by Mrs. Hafner. We read "A Spaghetti Tale" in *Highlights* magazine and talked about fiction and nonfiction. We looked at a map of New York City and reviewed the names of the five boroughs until each kid (except Eric) could recite them. We cleaned the classroom and copied our homework.

I felt familiar pangs of exhaustion in my knees and throat as I shepherded the kids down the steps for the fifth time, but something unexpected happened when I released them into the parking lot. Jennifer turned around and walked back. "Thank you, Mr. Brown," she said, putting her arms awkwardly around my neck.

I hugged her back, feeling my stomach drop in surprise and joy. "You're welcome, Jennifer. Have a great weekend."

"You too. See you Monday!" Jennifer ran off to meet her friends. The quick handful of words we exchanged were among the most cursory and common in our language, but unknown to Jennifer, those ten seconds at the very end changed the first week of my new profession and my new life. The knocks and bruises of the screaming and conflict in 4-217 vanished and I smiled on the subway home, a first.

LIST OF INTERESTING DISCOVERIES AFTER WEEK ONE

1. Kids crave classroom responsibility. They compete for who gets to sweep and hold the dustpan. I need to use class jobs as rewards and withholding of jobs as punishment. However, sometimes the worst-behaved kids are the ones that benefit most from the tasks. I need to sort out a system with a publicly posted job board.

2. They love gym. Threatening "no gym" is a good threat to achieve temporary order. If I do cancel gym, though, I'm responsible for them, and I'll die if I don't get that afternoon prep after the 8:00–12:30 morning haul.

3. Many kids seem simply uninterested in academic achievement. For example, Eric, Deloris, and Lakiya do not do *any* work. They barely pick up their pencils. When I give an assignment, I need everyone working on it.

4. The kids are constantly touching each other and each other's belongings. At Mercy, this was mentioned as a by-product of poverty culture; they have no personal space and very few personal possessions, so there is no sense of respect for those ideas. Should I lock up my stuff?

5. The administration is stretched very thin and has been undermined by the city with the region's "no detention, no suspension" policies. No one seems to know why we can't have detention or suspension; we just can't. I might be on my own to discipline them, but I don't know what I can hold over them. Bluffing a punishment would be a fatal mistake; I have to follow through on every threat I make. I hope Mr. Randazzo can help me.

6. Other teachers have the same problems I do. I need to look closely at what the successful teachers are doing and emulate that.

As I ushered the children into the classroom for the first day of week two, the assault commenced. "Good morning, ladies and gentlemen. Go immediately to your groups. Take everything you need for the whole day out of your bags. First group to show me they're ready gets four points. Take your homework out so I can see it. Yes, Gladys, you can sharpen your pencil. Destiny, wait till Gladys finishes and goes back to her seat. Verdad, you're after Destiny. And 'mines' is not a word. No, Lito, you can't sharpen your pencil. Yes, it is fair, the line is too long. Bernard, separate your desk from Hamisi. Because I've already given you too many chances. No, *separate the desks!* Here, I'll do it. Yes, Hamisi, because you're going to talk to each other at inappropriate times. Take out your homework, everyone! Which group is going to be first to show me they're ready and get stars and get to use the closet? Joseph, get back in your seat! I have called no groups over to the closet yet! Sonandia, you're setting a wonderful example. Why is group two the only group following directions? Tiffany, why are you staring at the ceiling? Group two is about to earn a star, and it looks like group one is going to get a strike. One star for group two! Let's make it two stars, I'm feeling generous. Yes, Lito, now you can sharpen your pencil. Well, it's overheated again because Verdad sharpened ten pencils. You'll have to wait. Lakiya, take your hat off, take your homework out, sit down, and close your mouth. That is not the way to enter our classroom. It's 'May I drink water?' not 'I can drink water?' Gladys, raise your hand if you have something to say to me, and please speak in a nice voice and not like you're trying to destroy someone."

Some people say, "Even when sex is bad, it's good." I found that even when my days at P.S. 85 were good, they were bad.

On Monday I got through all of my lessons successfully, but that didn't stop Lito Ruiz from punching chatty Julissa hard in the face during math. Barely suppressing my rage at the violence, I told the class, "It is never ever okay for a boy to hit a girl or a man to hit a woman. Never. A good man would absolutely never hit a girl. No boys in this room will *ever* hit a girl."

"Why?" Cwasey piped up. He wasn't being rude this time. He really didn't understand why this issue got me so fired up.

"Because it's cowardly, and no man I respect would ever raise his hand to a woman. It hurts everyone involved and it's not right and it's not okay and on top of that this is my room and that's my rule," I steamed.

I could tell by Cwasey's face that he didn't get it. Neither did Bernard, Hamisi, or Lito, who had their heads down. Lakiya cackled, "Preach!" She got a kick from mocking my impromptu speeches about decency and community.

I left for my prep disgusted. Barbara Chatton had arranged for me to observe Paul Bonn's fifth-grade class for the period, and Paul told me he could show a range of systems and routines he had in place to keep the order.

At twenty-seven, Paul Bonn stood five foot eight with a dirty blond goatee and untucked golf shirt. The first time I saw him I hadn't taken him for a genius.

Paul was a second-year teacher and not part of the Fellows program. His interview at P.S. 85 was fifteen seconds long. An administrator asked, "Are you scared?" He said he wasn't and was immediately informed of his hired status. Bonn was brought on as a cluster teacher, but in October, class 5-110 got out of hand, despite rookie teacher Ms. Elmer's large and intimidating physical stature. Kids were freely treating the furniture like an obstacle course, dancing, and fighting at will. The administration removed Ms. Elmer and gave her a cluster schedule.

It was a suicide mission. Unassuming, mellow-voiced Paul Bonn went in there, though, and straightened them out.

His first day, Bonn told Mr. Daly to clear the area in the parking lot outside room 110's windows. When the class got noisy in the first hour, Paul pretended to lose his mind and *threw a desk out the window.* The kids were silent for the rest of the day.

The second day, a notorious discipline problem didn't want to do his work. Bonn called the kid's mom, who showed up immediately to hold the boy's hand for the next three hours. The mortified student did not say boo the rest of the year.

The third day, a few kids started laughing in line. Bonn made the whole class copy the dictionary for two hours and write two pages about the importance of lines.

The fourth day was perfect.

Now he was one of the most respected teachers in the school, coordinating the faculty football pool and engaged to Melissa Mulvehill, a redheaded fourth-grade teacher whom he impressed more than anyone with the monumental turnaround of 5-110.

Paul Bonn rarely raised his voice because his class was a finely tuned machine. Two paper passers swiftly completed their appointed rounds with rehearsed precision. Class security guards, positions assigned to kids with discipline problems in their background, tabulated disruptions to be submitted for later punishments. They policed their own!

Bonn took his kids to the rug to read *The Blind Men and the Elephant,* a second-grade-level book about a gang of sightless geezers who decipher that there's an elephant standing in front of them by using teamwork. The reading was brief, and at the last word the kids immediately returned to their groups, hustling to get out their notebooks. Bonn gave group points on the chalkboard to the first group with all members who had written their name and the date. When Tiquan spoke out of turn, he had to copy a page of the dictionary. The class ran seamlessly. I was wowed.

What could I cull from this observation to bring to 4-217? Bonn had several advantages that I didn't have. Fifth grade was graduation year, so Paul had the NGL (No Graduation List), the most feared P.S. 85 punishment, at his disposal. Also, dictionary-copying fell into the broad reach of *corporal punishment,* a territory where I was reluctant to tread.

Corporal punishment, as I understood it, encompassed touching a child, forcing one to stand, making a student face the corner, and dishing out punitive assignments of no academic value. I slowly learned that P.S. 85 turned a blind eye to all of these practices in the name of avoiding "incidents." However, Barbara Chatton strongly discouraged me from engaging in them, especially in my first few weeks. I agreed. I did not want to become a teacher who dealt out these kinds of penalties, although my current methods were not exactly clicking.

I thought Paul Bonn's group points were perfect. Since I already had my stars and strikes that applied to all of 4-217, bringing in Bonn's group points would encourage teamwork and discourage academic laggards. ("Deloris is not writing her name and that's costing group three points right now!") I planned to keep track of the points in a box on the blackboard and give out candy bars or wildly popular Yu-Gi-Oh fantasy game cards to the winning group on Friday afternoons.

I also borrowed *The Blind Men and the Elephant*.

At 10 a.m. on Friday, September 19, our principal, Mrs. Boyd, made a cryptic announcement on the PA. "Fellow eighty-fivers. There has been a . . . disharmony on Webster Avenue. Please stay in the building until you are further advised. Luckily, we are very safe right now. However, you should all know once again that there is a disharmony currently going on at the Webster Avenue intersection behind the school. Thank you and once again, we are safe."

A disharmony?

"Somebody been shot," Cwasey muttered.

A police chase had just ended at 187th Street and Webster Avenue with a massive shootout in the street. The suspect, who had a fake gun, was shot fourteen times by police and died in the crosswalk that I used every day to get to the One Way Deli to buy my lunchtime turkey sandwich. The intersection was sealed off with the coroner's wagon, and a massive bloodstain was visible from four stories above. Several bullets had tagged the doors and windows of the nearby apartment buildings.

The popping-gunshot scene was audible and visible to the classes on the opposite side of the hall from 4-217. The bullets went off adjacent to the minischool, the grades K–1 annex where I had first met Mr. Rose during his pronoun lesson in June. In Allie Bowers's kindergarten class, the kids instinctively knew to duck when the shots rang. Allie made them crawl into the hall, pretending to play a "waiting game" while they sat for thirty minutes.

Despite the bullet-ridden cadaver on the pavement outside the building, I had my best day yet. I ignored the disharmony and within two minutes the kids forgot about it too. We finished reading *The Hundred Dresses,* a beautiful book about a poor immigrant girl, Wanda

Petronski, who tells her cruel peers that she has a hundred dresses of all colors and materials, even though she wears the same ragged frock to school every day. Wanda has to move away suddenly, but through a poignant letter her regretful tormentors discover her elaborate and gorgeous drawings of a hundred dresses. I loved the book, and I think the kids did too. I did not respond when Lakiya said, "This story GAY!" It definitely went over better than *James and the Giant Peach,* which I had abandoned a few days earlier after sensing rampant confusion.

On the way down the steps for dismissal, Sonandia reached out and clasped my hand. When Athena saw this, she looped around to hold my other hand. Jennifer gave me a hug in the parking lot. She did it every day.

I collapsed on my bed at 6 p.m. on Friday, out cold for the next fifteen hours. I spent the weekend in my apartment catching up on back episodes of *Six Feet Under* and eating frozen pizza. I filled my plan book and brooded over the fatal shooting.

Cat Samuels actually saw the victim riddled with the cops' fourteen shots and fall dead to the rainy asphalt. She reacted with blank-faced horror. "If that's not enough to get me out of this hell, I don't know what is," she told me by the fifth-grade detention table where she served earsplitting lunch duty.

I got headaches in 4-217, but the cafeteria during upper-grade lunch was a migraine pressure chamber. Screams and squeals reverberated as children bounded over tables, wrestled on the refuse-strewn floor, and mashed up their fish patties for projectile fodder. It was a mammoth, virtually unchecked melee.

Cat and I had similar problems in silencing the whole class. As a prep teacher, though, she was at a disadvantage because she taught only one lesson per class per week. If it sputtered or got interrupted, she would leave feeling like a failure. When I had a lesson that tanked or a ridiculous student outburst, I could rebound or change gears immediately with a new activity with the same kids. I might lose the battle, but I had a shot at winning the war. Fighting isolated and out-manned battles, Cat felt overmatched. When she finished only one out of her first eighteen lessons in those initial two weeks, I couldn't blame her for considering leaving.

On Sunday night, I climbed into bed at 10:30 but never fell completely asleep. Sunday nights are dark times for teachers. Ugly moments from school rushed at me like a cinematic montage. I thought about the barrage of questions about pencil sharpening and the bathroom, the crying, the wild line on the steps, the clock-watching, and the yelling. So much yelling.

I tried to intellectualize my place in the universe, reaching only bleak conclusions. The dearly held idea that one person can change lives now felt like cheap, baseless dogma. It was an easy aphorism, like "love conquers all"; one that worked in movies and instantly disinte-grated in the giant, indifferent city. I thought, My kids are so needy, and I can never compensate for what they're missing in their lives. I can barely teach them math. I should do more, but I am failing at the basics.

No! Snap out of this void of negativity! I willed myself into a cold shower and slapped myself in the face. "It is always darkest be-fore the dawn," I said aloud, creeping myself out. Was this job mak-ing me a self-talker?

My morning route to school took me into the subway at Allen and Houston streets to board the uptown F or V trains. At Herald Square, I transferred across the platform where the D train, my uptown ex-press ride to the Bronx, originated. On lucky days, I would pull into the station on the F to find the open-door D waiting to leave. When the platform was empty, the wait was longer and the omen was ill.

On Monday, September 22, my F pulled into Herald Square but kept its doors shut long enough for the awaiting D train to close up and get moving while I haplessly watched. "The D train is an ass-hole," a woman in a business suit grumbled.

While I waited on the empty platform for the next D to show

up, I saw Karen Adler. Karen and I were introduced at the August Professional Development at P.S. 85, but we had never had a real conversation. She also taught fourth grade and was a second-year Fellow, although this was her first year as a classroom teacher. We struck up a tired-eyed chat, starting with how the D train is an asshole.

Karen graduated with an English degree from Vassar in 2002 and went straight into the Fellows. Her first year at P.S. 85 was as an in-school floating substitute (or "cover teacher") with an irregular schedule that was so terrible that she cried every morning before getting on the train. She commuted from Brooklyn, making a ninety-minute trek each way.

We were in the same boat as beleaguered fourth-grade teachers, but Karen's extra year of experience gave her a strong reference point to start the year. She was phenomenally organized and devoted to her students, but also she possessed an amazing, deeply ironic sense of humor about the job. I stopped eating lunch alone.

I visited my students' previous teachers for advice. Before the year started, some had offered quick tips like, "Eddie is very slow with math." Now that I had gotten familiar with my characters, I was hoping for more concrete ideas on how to help or simply control them.

Carol Slocumb looked the part of an old-guard Catholic schoolmarm, ruling her impeccably organized third-grade class with scowls and systems. I was surprised to learn that she was only a second-year Fellow, since she already had a reputation as an expert classroom manager. I soon respected Ms. Slocumb as one of the most kind-hearted people in the school, who put on that tough façade in the classroom because it was the only way to keep the students under control.

Carol had had Dennis Foster and Tayshaun Jackson last year. When I asked about them, she solemnly shook her head. "Tayshaun. He was pretty consistent until that mess with his brother. Then forget about it. It's a real shame because he's smart. And Dennis is such a sad story. Very, very slow. I stopped calling home because I knew the beating he would catch."

My understanding of the mess with Tayshaun's brother went as follows: The Jackson family has no father and six kids. The oldest is twenty. Tayshaun has a twin brother and they're the youngest. Last year, the twenty-year-old brother molested Tayshaun's twin, causing the twin to suffer a mental collapse that resulted in institutionalization. With his twin brother and best friend gone, Tayshaun decided he wanted to be expelled and started bringing matches to school. His intelligence made him even more of a negative force in the classroom, since his rebellious snickers were more conscientious objections than random grumblings. He drove Ms. Slocumb nuts.

Stacy Shanline looked like she belonged at Fashion Week rather than Public School 85. She had taught Sonandia, Destiny, and Lito Ruiz in third grade. "Sonandia is a doll. I love her. You can tell why she's so wonderful; her mom loves her. You know Olga, right?"

Of course I knew Olga Tavarez. She was a P.S. 85 paraprofessional who unobtrusively checked in on Sonandia several times a day. She made sure Sonandia was punctual and dressed neatly. She always smiled and said good morning to me. She held Sonandia's hand and said things like, "Have a great day, Sony. I love you."

Shanline continued, "Destiny is such a sad story. She's really a sweet girl, but her parents give her *nothing*. Her cousins are always beating on her and she has terrible asthma. She's really sensitive. Actually, she's more than sensitive. She's a wuss." I thought about how Destiny made a point to approach me every day with some statement that resembled, "My cousin zipped me up in a suitcase," or "This morning, my brother bit me in the knee."

"As for Lito," she went on, "he's the saddest story of them all. No father. In second grade his mother passed away." She lowered her voice. "We think it was AIDS. He stopped doing his work and got held back. The next year he didn't smile or do his work again but they had to move him up. When I had him, he barely did anything and he looked like the most cold-blooded kid you've ever seen. He lives with his grandmother, who doesn't speak English. He's not clean. He used to stink like shit. I mean actual feces."

Returning from Shanline's room, I picked up a memo in my office mailbox informing faculty that bulletin boards for math and literacy, compliant with rules outlined in our "Displaying Student Work" packets, were due up inside and outside the class by the end of the week. I had nothing that was close to presentation quality. I had hoped to start the week refreshed, but by 8:00 on Monday morning my mind was whirling.

When I met my class in the cafeteria, an unfamiliar girl in pinstripe pajamas was chatting and laughing with Lakiya and Deloris (mortal enemies the week before). I asked the girl who she was. "Asante Bell. I'm in your class." She was right, although I had listed her as a no-show for missing the first ten days.

"Where have you been, Asante? This is the third week of school!"

She shrugged. "I had things to do."

The nonchalant response caught me off guard, but I knew better than to begin my relationship with this truant girl by sermonizing on the importance of showing up for school. Instead, my mind scrambled for where to place Asante in the delicate 4-217 seating scheme. I decided to put her with Lakiya, risking a two-headed monster in group five in the hope that their company would abate Lakiya's apathy.

Monday, September 22, was also the kickoff day of our Success for All literacy program. I was very hazy on how this 8:45–10:15 daily segment was supposed to run, but fortunately Fran Baker came in to coteach with me, and she was an expert. Although SFA was brutally maligned by my colleagues, I had been secretly anticipating its kickoff because it sent my homeroom kids to other teachers for a precious hour and a half. The 270-minute blocks without SFA were killers.

In welcome contrast to the gigantic range in abilities in my

4-217 class, SFA students were grouped by skill level. Mrs. Baker and I had kids on a third-and-a-half-grade reading level. SFA periods were regimented to the minute. The first twenty minutes were "Listening Comprehension," in which the children gathered on the carpet for a read-aloud. This was the only part of the tightly codified literacy block that afforded any teacher input. The rest of the period involved a litany of reviewing charts and administering tests.

On the first day of SFA, I understood nothing. When the children appeared empty-handed in my room at 8:45, I learned I needed to provide pencils for every kid in the group. Marge Foley had given me a fistful of official, shiny yellow New York City Department of Education pencils for my homeroom last Friday, but I had not sharpened them. While Mrs. Baker did the read-aloud on the carpet in the back of the room, I frenetically jammed pencils into my electric Boston sharpener, one of the fruits of my summer spree at Staples.

Near the chalkboard, the machine emitted a cacophonous drill-buzz that was clearly audible in the hall. Within seconds, assistant principal Ms. Guiterrez was scowling in my doorway. "What are you *doing,* Mr. Brown?" She left before I answered.

A minute later Mrs. Boyd was in my room. "You're making a racket, Mr. Brown," she muttered with deep annoyance. "Why are you doing this?"

"I just found out I need to supply pencils to the SFA kids, so I was trying to sharpen them while Mrs. Baker did the read-aloud," I said. Boyd's face did not resemble the woman I'd interviewed with in the summer.

Her slow and staccato cadence transcended ordinary hierarchical condescension. "Mr. Brown, you are a *teacher,* not a *pencil sharpener.* Okay? It's your job to be leading the class with Mrs. Baker, not doing petty tasks while she does all the teaching."

"Right, although I wanted to save time by getting this done now . . ."

"Bulletin boards are due up Friday. You got the memo, yes?"

"Yes."

"Your classroom is your résumé, Mr. Brown. I personally hired you, so I have a special interest in making sure that fine work is displayed. You have the teaching gene, but it's not worth a thing if you can't maintain the professional responsibilities that go with the job. Pull it together."

My teeth clenched as Boyd stormed out. I took a seat beside Fran Baker and left the pencils alone.

One morning, I received two more new students: Daniel Vasquez and Reynaldo Luces. Diminutive Daniel was quiet, so he was fine by me. My attention was drawn to Reynaldo, whose hysterical cry-heaving made for an instant spectacle. Randazzo said, "Reynaldo is transferring out of Boswell's room. Why anyone would want out of PAC [Ms. Boswell's gifted Performing Arts Class] I have no idea."

I had an idea about it. The boy's flailing, full-body sobs made it impossible to gain order, let alone teach. Several kids tried to comfort him, but he only wailed harder when Athena blurted, "That new kid is CRY-ing!"

I took Reynaldo out in the hall several times with consoling words and offered him drawing paper. He wrote a letter in Spanish to his mother saying he wanted a new teacher and he wanted to change his class. Reynaldo's social worker, Ms. Schultz, his guidance counselor, Mr. Schwesig, speech therapist, Ms. Ruiz, and Mr. Randazzo all took him out for brief bits, but each time he was escorted back shrieking and decimating any momentum in the room. I had never seen such long-distance endurance crying. Finally, Randazzo took Reynaldo away and I never saw him again.

During free writing time, I was happy to see the kids get excited with the freedom of jotting anything they wanted in their notebooks. Hamisi, one of my stronger academic students, wrote in his shaky hand, "I gat blood on shos when I shot the poles and ran the street" [I got blood on my shoes when I shot the police and ran down the street].

Maimouna, who always filled her page, wrote, "I go to school every day on time and wear my uniform every day. Do you know why? Because I want to get a good education. Mr. Brown is a very nice teacher. I work hard in school and I am good. Sometimes I get wiped."

"Wiped?" I asked her.

"Whipped," she whispered.

Dismissal was a disaster. I let them see me upset, which was happening more and more frequently. I took deep breaths to check myself. Deloris Barlow became my worst enemy in the afternoons, always the last out the door. When I would yell that she was holding up the class, she smiled and screamed, "Sorry! Sorry! SORRY!" With a grin she tried to hug me. "Sorry, sorry, sorry, Mr. Brown!"

Meanwhile, Verdad lost his bookbag, and at the water fountain I saw little Cwasey Bartrum shove Julissa Marrero to the floor. He thought Julissa was drinking for too long. When I yelled at Cwasey, he turned his back to me and said he didn't do it. "Who did?" He pointed at Tayshaun Jackson.

"Thas bootleg!" Tayshaun cried.

"Relax, Tayshaun," I said. "I saw *you*, Cwasey! Don't lie to me. Lying makes it worse."

"It wasn't me," Cwasey muttered coldly, turning away again. I felt betrayed, still clinging to the moment on the first day when Cwasey had readily proffered his respectful suggestions for our class rules.

Three minutes later in the parking lot, I released the kids and commotion broke out. I saw Cwasey weeping, holding the remains of his stomped eyeglasses. "Lito broke his glasses!" Dennis shouted. A rubbernecking crowd of students rushed Cwasey to see the damage. Lito was unapologetic at first, then decided to say he didn't do it, even though a crowd of witnesses screamed he absolutely had.

"Shut the fuck up!" Lito screamed, sprinting away. Cwasey sobbed inconsolably.

Pat Cartwright, my army neighbor who now had custody of Fausto, spotted me reeling in the parking lot during the dismissal fiasco and approached me with some helpful ideas. "Sneak attack them. Call their parents during the prep period so the parents are waiting for the kids when they get home. The rockheads want to see you rattled. It's sick. They try to push your buttons. And they lie so much that they convince themselves they're telling the truth. I'm just teaching lessons. I didn't give birth to twenty-six children!"

"Neither did I," I said, and we chuckled darkly.

I went to the movies by myself for temporary escape. On the walk home, I fueled up with some kind of hyperbolic moral mania. Send me the whole borough! I will not be cowed or muscled out by the misbehavers or bureaucrats! These kids are not bad people; many have just been raised in loveless and confining environments. I can give them something good. I can show them the importance of school and good character. I will live through this and I will win!

Daniel was easily the smallest kid in the class. He had just moved to the Bronx, sent from Detroit by his mother who could not afford to keep him. Now he lived with his grandmother, or "abuelita," who spoke no English.

With Reynaldo's crying marathon and its resulting mayhem, I was barely able to pay any attention to Daniel on his first day, which made me feel lousy. Being the new kid is an extremely fragile thing. At first, the teacher is the closest thing you have to a friend. I had not been there for him; I had to make it up to Daniel.

I didn't have a free second until the middle part of the 10:30 math lesson, when everyone was filling in their line graphs. I came around to Daniel's desk to find the board notes he was supposed to copy were chicken scratches in his notebook. He did not answer for a long time when I asked if he had ever studied graphs in Detroit.

"G-g-graphs . . . I don't know . . . Maybe a l-l-little." The kid was terrified, and his stutter was severe.

My mind raced. My first thought was that I could not teach him graphing in this ninety-second mini-conference. Daniel was clearly not close to a fourth-grade academic level. At the grade-level meeting in the Teacher Center next period, I would ask what to do. Meanwhile, I could already spot trouble brewing between Deloris and Destiny in the far corner of the room. Deloris's hand was inside Destiny's desk, and Destiny looked upset. In another ten seconds unchecked, one or both would be crying. Bernard, who sat next to Daniel, understood graphs well.

"Bernard, help Daniel out. I'll be back."

I speed-walked to the front of the room and planted myself between the two would-be combatants, stifling their tiff. I glanced at their math papers. Deloris's was blank. Destiny's was filled in, but she had mislabeled her axes in the beginning and, now confused, drew random points and lines all over the paper.

"I don't know what to do," said Athena from across the room.

"Me either," chimed Lito.

"Mr. Brown, can you help me?" Destiny asked.

It didn't seem to make sense. The class had done quite well with bar graphs, with Athena leading the way. I had explained and modeled everything and answered questions about line graphs during the mini-lesson. Everyone had appeared to get it. Athena and Lito had answered oral questions correctly. Now an avalanche of confusion overran the room.

I felt a literal tug at my sleeve. I looked down and saw Daniel's expectant eyes. "Help me," he said.

"Get back in your seat!" I screamed, not recognizing myself. My immediate impulse was to penalize Daniel's group points as a deterrent for his walking across the room without permission. Wandering to the coat rack, sink, pencil sharpener, and bookshelf had recently ballooned into a major problem, and I had publicly declared war on it at lineup that morning. I didn't want to zap Daniel, but something told me I had to.

"Two points off group six! Absolutely no walking around the class without permission! And two points off groups two, five, three, one, and four for calling out! Now pay attention carefully and we will review together, step by step, how line graphs work . . ." By the period's end, Athena fully understood line graphs (her face at the moment of clicking realization was priceless), but I wasn't sure about the rest of them.

Cat Samuels came in to teach a social studies lesson, and I made a speech about how Ms. Samuels controls huge numbers of points and also holds supreme clout over the Rewards and Detention lists.

Every Tuesday from 11:30 to 12:20, all fourth-grade classroom teachers had a prep period. We were supposed to meet for support and cooperative lesson planning, but the meetings were often canceled or hijacked by the administration for paperwork tasks. Despite many pleas for organized coplanning time, it only happened two times all year.

The subject of that day's common prep meeting was something on the very front of my mind: special education referrals. I recalled the mandatory summer training seminar at Martin Luther King, Jr. High School when the thundering Department of Education official had explicitly told us of our critical duty *to refer* children with special needs.

Dr. Helen Kirkpatrick, a gentle-voiced white woman in her sixties, ran the seminar. Her tone was genial but rueful. "It's nice to see some new faces. Is it four new classroom teachers in the grade?"

"Five," special ed Fellow Marnie Beck piped up. She may have been relegated to a room in the basement, but Marnie was a fourth-grade teacher and hated when people forgot her. Karen Adler, Pat Cartwright, Melissa Mulvehill, and I were the ones Dr. Kirkpatrick asked about, but Karen, Pat, and Melissa each had a year of experience as P.S. 85 cluster teachers. I was the real newbie.

Dr. Kirkpatrick introduced herself as the school's special ed supervisor. I remembered this was the position previously held by Marianne Renfro, although Renfro also used to occupy a regular administrator's office and conduct formal teacher observations. Ms. Renfro's name had been on the school stationery that officially announced my hiring back in July. I had never seen or heard of Dr.

Kirkpatrick until now, and I thought I had been pretty thorough in getting out to meet or at least recognize most of P.S. 85's key players.

"I used to run the SBST [School Based Support Team], but that's now been dismantled because of budget cuts. Ms. Martinez and I are trying to do the work that the SBST used to do, but since there used to be four of us and now there are only two, and combined with my new paperwork responsibilities, it's very tough."

The School Based Support Team was responsible for following up on teacher-initiated special ed referrals. If you had a student who you thought could not make it in a regular class, they would check it out. They were trained professionals.

A pained grimace came over Edith Boswell, the fourth-grade gifted Performing Arts Class teacher and a three-decade veteran. With passive fury, she appeared to be finally receiving some long-expected disappointing news. Early in the August Professional Development sessions, I had made Ms. Boswell's facial expressions my secret barometer for the legitimacy and importance of school announcements and initiatives. I heard that years ago she had won some kind of New York State Teacher of the Year award.

Dr. Kirkpatrick bit her lip and continued, "I'll say it directly, and trust me, I don't like saying it. Don't shoot the messenger, you know what I mean? But the school is looking to suppress referrals for administrative reasons. If you think you have a kid that might be special ed material, experiment with all possible alternative teaching methods for six to eight weeks." She paused. "That's it."

A bomb had hit the room. Edith Boswell's lips were pursed tighter than I had ever seen them. "What are the administrative reasons?" I asked, my first time speaking in a faculty meeting.

"Well, it's complicated," Dr. Kirkpatrick began uncomfortably. "A couple years ago, Eighty-five was SURR [School Under Registration Review], and we don't want to go back to that."

"No, we don't," Ms. Boswell murmured.

"For the people who are new, when you're a SURR school,

you've got city people coming in all the time, sometimes every day, watching you like hawks. It's very intense oversight. That's why we're still an extended-hours school. The way the city is realigning its education initiatives, one of the criteria for judging schools is the referral percentage. The lower, the better."

"So, no referrals," Catherine Fiore, a perpetually grouchy fourth-grade veteran, translated with disgust. Her motto, as she explained to me in an aside during an August meeting, was "I don't play."

Dr. Kirkpatrick fumbled, "Well, we can't say *no referrals* exactly . . ."

"Good, because I have a kid that can't read his name," Fiore shot.

"Me too. I can't teach a kid like that, no matter what alternative strategies you suggest," added Mulvehill.

"I have one too," I said, thinking of Daniel. I also thought of Lakiya and Eric, who could read their names but had a poisonous combination of low skills, outbursts of violence, and general disrespect for the class. They would definitely function better in a modified environment.

"These are complete nonreaders, you're sure?" Dr. Kirkpatrick asked, evidently hoping we were exaggerating. We were all sure. Dr. Kirkpatrick took a list of the illiterate students' names and homerooms, promising to check out each one personally. I walked back to room 217, stunned that schools were punished for recognizing and attempting to seek help for at-risk kids.

Later, Karen Adler and I got lunch at the corner deli — the gunplay in the street caused only a one-day lapse in our new routine — and ate in 217 at group two. I sat at Sonandia's desk. Karen was the lucky final recipient of Reynaldo Luces. She said he had stopped crying and now constantly drew pictures of red hearts, always giving them to her at the day's end.

We griped about the bulletin board work that was due up by Friday. I became alarmed when she said her kids' work was done and it just needed mounting. I had work from my students, but virtually none of it was pretty or "error-free," as mounted work was mandated to be.

"Spend all your class time on it, seriously," Karen said. "Or they'll be all over you." Then, in a dead ringer for Mrs. Boyd, she bellowed, *"Mr. Brown, your bulletin boards do not reflect enough academic rigor, and we're going to have a nice long chat, you and I, in my inner office."*

Karen had a secret skill for impersonation. She did a perfect Randazzo and Barbara Chatton, and a frighteningly dead-on Guiterrez.

I took Karen's advice about the bulletin boards and scrapped my afternoon map skills lesson. I told the class that this new birthday data table and bar graph would be our most important yet. "Everyone's finished work will be on display and then placed in your *permanent portfolios!*"

The empty red portfolio folders sat in a crate on my desk next to the ancient iron cumulative records canister. Teachers were supposed to insert one meaningful, official New York State standards–bearing piece of math and literacy work in the folder each month. Thus the portfolio charted progress and could also be used in an appeal for promotion for a student with poor Test scores.

The class heard what I said about the tremendous importance of this next piece of work, but the words did not seem to register. Everyone wanted to go to the bathroom. "Forget about teaching after lunch," Ms. Fiore had advised with aggressively furrowed brows.

I pressed forward. Our Birthday Bar Graph was exactly what every other class was doing for their boards. I made a model data table on the board with my columns — important vocabulary word, kids: columns! — labeled "Month" and "Number of 4-217 Birthdays." My Bonn-inspired paper passers handed out blank data tables to everyone, and we were all supposed to fill it out together.

"Raise your hand if you were born in January!" I boomed. Asante's hand went up. "One. Happy unbirthday, Asante!"

"Thank you, Mr. Brown," Asante said, giggling. Asante was a

hard-nosed kid. The other kids took her amusement as a sign that the activity might not be wack after all. I could feel the group's focus tighten. It felt good.

"Okay, who was born in February? I was! February ninth," I said, raising my hand. "Does anyone else share February as a birthday month with me?" Three hands went up. "All right, four, counting me!" I charted it on the board. The kids marked their data tables.

"Mr. Brown, how old are you?" Sonandia asked. Several other kids instantly echoed the question.

"Don't worry about it," I said, setting off a yearlong guessing game that I would have preferred did not exist.

"Okay, we've listed how many 4-217 students have birthdays in each of the twelve months. Do I have any volunteers who would like to impress me and tell me how to make a graph out of this, what is it called, what are these numbers called? Tiffany?"

"Data?"

"Yes! Data! Outstanding. Excellent use of mathematical vocabulary, Tiffany! A point for group four."

The members of group four pumped their arms in silent exultation.

"Okay, so who wants to tell me what to do first to make a graph out of this data?"

Athena spearheaded the axes-labeling, and I was pleased that Destiny, who had struggled through most of the unit, correctly explained how to draw the first bars for January and February.

Before dismissal, I had a beautiful and accurate bar graph on the board. I collected everyone's work, distributed the homework, lined them up, shepherded the group down the steps, accepted Jennifer's hug, and turned back into the school building, renewed.

Upstairs, I leafed through the afternoon's work and my jaw dropped. Out of twenty-five students, only five papers matched what I had on the board. Eight kids had written nothing, not including Daniel's indecipherable scribbles.

I sought counsel from the faculty coaches in Al Conway and

Marge Foley's sliver-office. Throughout my distressed account, Al nodded as if he could have finished my sentences for me.

"I know exactly what you're going through. When I was a first-year teacher, I was your age and had thirty-eight kids in my class. I had no idea what I was doing. So many times I thought, 'I'm out of here. I quit.' Maybe I should have, the way my marriage is going right now . . ." Al trailed off, chuckling nervously. "The important thing is, don't get discouraged. For the bulletin board, you said you got five pieces of good work, right? That's all you need! Display them and you're set. Don't worry about everyone's portfolio all at once. You'll get work out of them, but some are just . . . uncooperative."

He leaned closer and turned on his secret-telling voice. "For bulletin boards in the future, it doesn't even have to be a whole-class activity. Just pick a few top kids and bring them up for lunch or set aside some time. Tell them you have a special task for them to do. They'll love it. Or to make it easier on yourself, just write out what you want and have them copy it over in their own handwriting. That's how a *lot* of teachers do it. The bulletin boards are just to show Dilla Zane that things are under control. You have to do them, but don't let them kill you. There are too many other things trying to kill you." Then he offered to teach my class a sample math lesson and build my math center.

On Thursday, I stayed late to mount the magnificent birthday bar graphs against fadeless teal paper. I typed our procedure in flashy fonts, and used magic markers on sentence strips to delineate the New York State standards employed in this lesson. (M4a: Collect and organize data to answer a question. M4c: Make statements and draw simple conclusions from data. M6g: Read, create, and represent data.) The Birthday Bar Graphs were the main attraction, but I also made a smaller literacy display with some "Writing About Me: Autobiography Introductions" from the previous week.

When I got home, I opened a personal e-mail from Liesl Nolan, the program manager of the Mercy College New Teacher Residency Program. She had paid a random visit to 4-217 the previous day, checking out the bulletin boards and asking me how everything was going. Liesl had typed, "Dear Daniel, I wanted to thank you for welcoming me into your classroom last Wednesday. Your room looks great! I can only assure you that it will get better. You have great support with Barbara and your Mercy instructor, Charles. Utilize them. I truly admire your passion for doing this work! Thank you!"

On Friday, September 26, I received a surprise. Ten minutes before lineup, Ms. Guiterrez rolled into my classroom. "Mr. Brown, I have to talk to you about your bulletin board. Immediately." She walked back into the hall. This was her first time in my classroom since her summer complaint about my mom's border paper, not counting the pencil-sharpening incident on the first day of SFA.

I flashed paranoid. But wait a minute, my bulletin board looked sharp. Maybe this was Guiterrez's way of telling me I had a damn good-looking first bulletin board and to congratulate me for surviving my first month in the inner city.

Guiterrez did not look at me when I followed her into the hall. "What is wrong with this, Mr. Brown?"

My bulletin board was a replica of everyone else's on the second floor. "I don't know," I said, my brief hope that this was some kind of weird compliment dashed.

"Are you sure everything is spelled right?" she asked in the same even, accusatory tone.

I was supremely positive that every word on my board was spelled correctly. A second-place finish in the township bee back in '93 ("tyrannous" did me in) was a major event in my youth, and ever after, spelling was one area in which I excelled.

"What do you think is misspelled?"

"*That* word." She pointed at the word "announced." I had written it in magic marker as part of the Activity Procedure. The line read, "Students raise their hand if their birthday falls in the month that the teacher has just announced. The data is then recorded in the data table."

"*That* word is spelled incorrectly," she deadpanned.

I squinted and stared at the word. A–N–N–O–U–N–C–E–D. Announced.

"Is it the word 'announced'?"

"Yes, Mr. Brown."

I moved my face close to the board. A tiny piece, less than a centimeter, of the end of the "o" did graze against its neighbor, "u." Did that make the "o" resemble an "a"? Annaunced? No. It still looked like "announced." I squinted at her in befuddlement. What kind of conversation was this?

"I see no writing on this bulletin board," Ms. Guiterrez said icily, changing gears.

I did not know how to respond without insulting her intelligence, although I felt certain that my own intelligence had just been insulted several times in quick succession. I gestured meekly at the page-long student pieces displayed under my "*WE WRITE AUTO-BIOGRAPHIES!*" banner, just below the bar graphs. "There is this writing."

"There is no math writing on the bulletin board!" she snapped. Math *writing*? I had data tables and corresponding bar graphs. "Take it all down," Ms. Guiterrez said. "You must check with me first before you put anything on this board from now on. I am very troubled that you thought this was . . . acceptable." She walked away.

I paced around room 217, my blood up. I had never heard of any math writing requirement. And what was all that about "announced"? I didn't want to take my whole bulletin board down.

When I arrived at lineup, beet-red Ms. Linda Devereaux was reading the riot act to Bernard and Hamisi. "I'll take them for the morning, Mr. Brown. WHAT GOES THROUGH YOUR BRAIN THAT MAKES YOU THINK IT'S OKAY TO HIT EACH OTHER IN SCHOOL? DO YOU HEAR ME?" The boys stared at their shoes, looking bored.

Ms. Devereaux was the real P.S. 85 enforcer. A member of the first cohort of Teaching Fellows in 2000, she had had her classroom-teacher position involuntarily revoked in exchange for a job as the school's full-time disciplinarian. She offered her supportive services to all teachers, provided she was not sent frivolous cases. When kids disappeared into her Alternative Education Strategies room, you didn't need to worry about them. I knew Ms. Devereaux would be a crucial ally, especially since detention and out-of-school suspension had recently been abolished by Region One.

However, fifteen minutes after the cafeteria scolding, Hamisi and Bernard reappeared at my door, both smirking. "Ms. Devereaux told us to come back," Hamisi said. A minute later, Mr. Randazzo showed up holding an orange paper strip. Another new student.

"This young gentleman is Marvin Winslow. He's going to be with you."

"Wonderful to meet you, Marvin!" I shook his and his mother's hands. My eyes went to the charm around Mrs. Winslow's neck, a $ the size of a cantaloupe. "Welcome to 4-217."

"SFA is about to begin. That's our literacy program," Mr. Randazzo explained. "See if you can get him tested for a group," he said to me, and promptly left.

Marvin had a lazy right eye, but there was nothing otherwise remarkable about him at first glance. He was average height for his age, with neatly trimmed short black fuzz on his head. His eyes were serious and terrified. I asked him if his family had just moved to this neighborhood and he shook his head, mumbling sullenly, "My old school is a bad place."

I called the Success for All headquarters downstairs to locate someone to test Marvin for a level placement. Daniel was still unplaced and alternated between drawing and spacing out in the back of the room during the ninety-minute block that Mrs. Baker and I now ran together. Dom Beckles, P.S. 85's SFA coach, answered the call and agreed to evaluate both Marvin and Daniel.

Thirty minutes later, Beckles returned them to my room and gestured for me to meet him in the doorway. "Those two are nonreaders. They can't read a thing!" he whispered.

"Why are they in my class?" I asked.

"It's a bunch of fools running this school," Mr. Beckles said with conspiratorial hush. "They pull the same thing every year, it's ridiculous. You've got the Queen up there and she has no idea."

Just get me to 11:30! Then I have a prep, lunch, our first assembly, and the weekend!

When my regulars returned from SFA at 10:15, I moved Marvin next to Sonandia. Now was her chance to prove herself "useful to a student in need," as her blue card assured. Marvin frowned and sat silently.

Instead of slogging on with well-covered bar graphs or starting a new unit on a Friday, I opted to play Math Bingo. I figured games are a necessary part of school, and this could also be a bit of preassessment for our future multiplication unit. I scolded Maimouna for poor sportsmanship when she gloated in Gladys Ferarro's face, but otherwise everything looked good, like a real classroom. Even Lakiya played.

Midway through the third game, Lito and Cwasey (mortal enemies earlier in the week when the former stomped the latter's glasses) teamed up to use the fake-penny game pieces as projectiles, targeting Eddie. Eddie immediately retaliated, tossing his board and pieces across the room.

My brain exploded. Fury, building from Guiterrez's early visit, suddenly frothed over. I felt a unique blast of air erupt from my lungs: *"DO NOT THROW!"* My face became boiling and screwed up, my words fraying into a guttural bellow. I wheeled, locking my demented-looking eyes with Cwasey's fearful ones, and in a moment I stood over him. Everyone froze.

Keeping my crazed gaze fixed on the small, sitting boy, I dealt commands in a low voice. "Jennifer, collect the game boards. Dennis, take the plastic bag from my desk and collect the pieces."

Cwasey piped up in protest, "But he was throwing them at *me —*"

"ZAAAAAAAAAAAAAAHHHHH!" I cut him off with another

dragon-cry. Cwasey shut his mouth. Lakiya grinned. I had outcrazied them all.

During my prep, I sat in the Teacher Center with my head down. I was sure that I was losing my mind. Through the wall, I could hear Melissa Mulvehill screaming at her class. I realized everyone on the floor had heard me raging like a banshee.

Thirty minutes into the period, Mulvehill appeared in the Teacher Center doorway, as if looking for some quick advice. "I just had a kid piss his pants on purpose," she said in a rush, her voice registering something between horror and twisted amusement.

At least I didn't have that going on, I thought. Besides coaching several baby-teeth extractions, I had had no encounters with fluids since the previous week when Tayshaun Jackson puked up a pack of sour apple Now-and-Later candies at lineup.

During lunch, I brought Sonandia, Jennifer, Destiny, Evley, and Tiffany upstairs. They were excited to be in the classroom at an unusual hour. I gave each kid a fun-size 100 Grand bar and a printout of the Birthday Bar Graph procedure. They copied happily.

On 4-217's direct cafeteria-to-auditorium route for our first assembly, Marvin Winslow tapped me on the arm. "Mr. Brown," he said, looking at the floor, "I'm not good. I'm a bad kid."

"No, no, come on, Marvin. I know that's not true."

"I'm bad. I do bad things. I ate lunch by myself."

"You did? I'll make sure that doesn't happen again. I saw you hanging out with Dennis when I picked up the class. I'm sure Dennis will want to eat with you," I said.

"Yeah!" Dennis enthused from the line. I didn't know he could hear us.

"But I'm bad," Marvin insisted.

"We're friends!" Dennis cheered. "Right, Marvin? We ate lunch."

Suddenly caught between his inferiority complex and his new buddy, Marvin hesitated. "Yeah," he mumbled.

"We're friends, Mr. Brown!" Dennis repeated. At that moment, I loved him.

"Marvin, I'm a good judge of character. I can tell you've got a good heart. We're going to work together. I know you had problems at your old school, but you're not there anymore. You're at P.S. 85 with Mr. Brown."

Marvin nodded and fell silent.

The assembly was a gargantuan letdown. Mr. Randazzo spent a huge chunk of time raising and lowering his arm, trying unsuccessfully to implement the Silent Signal. The teachers had to mimic Randazzo's arm movements, like monkeys. Eventually he achieved quiet and gave a banal speech about being one month through the new school year. Then he announced the September scores from his morning lineup rubric.

Four-two-seventeen was dead last, deep in the cellar. When Mr. R. called up each room's Student of the Month, Sonandia accepted her honor with nonchalance. With the calling of each name, the auditorium roared with wild shouting since, to many, the program solely equaled a license to make noise. Some award recipients could not hear their names. Randazzo had not prepared the winners' certificates, promising they would receive them next month.

I was alone in the corridor after school, appending my exterior bulletin board with five pieces of gloriously error-free math writing when literacy coach Marge Foley approached me. Most teachers are out the door as fast as possible on Fridays, but Marge always stayed late. She regarded the bulletin board. "Good, looks good," she said.

"Great. It was a bit of a mess . . ."

"I know, I know. You did a good job." A brief pause hung in the air. "I think you have the makings of a very good teacher. Your language when you're questioning the kids and your scaffolding on prior knowledge is excellent. And you care, which goes a long, long way. But I have to be frank about something. You absolutely have to find or concoct some kind of more effective approach to your discipline. You have to decide on something that works with your personality and commit yourself to it completely. Do you have a main plan and a contingency plan for every second of the day? Do you have a system for putting their coats in the closet, for getting drinks of water, for dismissal, for lineup? Your kids are out of control a lot. People can tell. The ship could sink, if you know what I mean. I've seen it before. And you have a *tough* class. I know. But once you get some traction on the management side, it'll get easier. If you don't, it's going to be a very long year."

I thanked Marge for her advice. I didn't want to sink. I didn't want Sonandia and Jennifer and Evley and Tiffany and Julissa to sink. I *really* didn't want Marvin Winslow to sink. Four-two-seventeen was at a crossroads.

October

Motivation into Submission

I WORE A SERIOUSLY PISSED-OFF expression when I tramped into the cafeteria for morning lineup. I intended to march the children up-stairs and deliver a quick, authoritative speech to the class outside the 4-217 door, announcing new systems for entering the classroom: Go straight to your desks with all of your belongings, unpack your bag *completely,* because the closet will be off-limits until dismissal, wait for your group to be called before anyone uses the closet (Violation will risk a severe consequence in group points!), place your homework on your desk so I can see it, and get straight to work on this math sheet that I'm about to hand you as you enter the room. Names go imme-diately on the Rewards List for following directions, the Detention List for failure to do so.

But something unexpected happened first.

The 4-217 line routinely passed Wilson Tejera's fourth-grade bilingual class on the way to our room. Mr. Tejera's group began each day by singing "The Star-Spangled Banner" as they entered their classroom and got organized. The bombs were bursting in air as we walked by that morning. I didn't see it, but apparently, Hamisi made some kind of mocking gesture at the singing students, and Tejera was out in the hall like a shot.

Wilson Tejera was a short, bolo-tie-wearing man with bushy eyebrows and a Rollie Fingers–style curlicue mustache. He had been at P.S. 85 for seven years and seemed genial in my brief encounters with him.

At this moment, his face was a deep crimson, cheeks vibrating with rage. He bent down, putting his nose an uncomfortable fraction of an inch from Hamisi's. "Don't you ever . . . *ever* . . . laugh at our national anthem."

Hamisi looked past him. He had been yelled at by teachers before and spacing out was his way to handle it. I had witnessed this when Ms. Devereaux shouted at him.

Tejera's right hand flew up and seized Hamisi by the mouth, digging hard into his cheeks. *"Do you have any idea how many people died so that we can sing this song?"* Wilson's eyes gleamed. Now he had Hamisi's full, terrified attention. *"You have no idea what people have sacrificed."* Tejera clenched tighter. *"Never do it again."* He released Hamisi's face and disappeared into his classroom.

My mouth hung open. I half expected rebellious bedlam to break out right there in the hall. It wouldn't have been unjustified. Instead, no one reacted. Hamisi stared ahead, expressionless. Forgetting the traumatic face-squeezing from a few moments earlier, 4-217 would have looked like a perfectly behaved class. At our doorway, I issued instructions for the new systems in low-voiced commands. The kids followed them.

I took Hamisi aside and asked if he was all right. He looked at me strangely, as if to suggest, "I'm fine. Are you sure it isn't *you* who's not all right?"

An hour later, Success for All period was in full swing. I answered a knock at the door and saw Mr. Tejera, making his first ever visit to my room. "Mr. Brown, how are you?"

"I'm fine."

"Good. I wanted to speak to you about what happened in the hall earlier with . . ."

"Hamisi."

"Right. With Hamisi." He pursed his lips, picking his words carefully. "You saw me talk very sternly to him, but you didn't see me put my hands on him because I never did." He paused, indicating my turn to speak.

I had no idea what to say and started stammering a non sequitur. "I think it's great that you have the kids sing in the morning. It's a really good routine . . ."

Tejera calmly repeated himself. "You never saw me put my hands on him because I never did. I take the national anthem very seriously. Okay?"

My mouth curled into a small, bizarre smile. I imagined us in a spicy drugstore potboiler:

> *The spitfire hombre gnashed his sharpened incisors, thirsty to visit further vengeance upon defamers of his sacred national oaths. Reflexively caressing his bolo, he peered deeply into the timid neophyte's shit-brown eyes, reading Brown's vulnerability. Suddenly, unexpectedly,* disastrously *for the intimidator, a Zen calm glazed over the younger man's countenance, signaling a clean and abrupt end to his moral earthquake. With renewed confidence and sense of self, Brown stared back at Hamisi's assailant and knew what he must do . . .*

Mr. Tejera filled the void. "You're uncomfortable with that, aren't you?"

"Yes."

"Go with the flow." He knocked his fist against the doorpost for a punctuating dramatic effect and ambled away.

I reeled back to my Success for All group. If I went to the administration, I would be a rookie, a few weeks in, blowing the whistle on a veteran teacher. Tejera seemed to be on buddy terms with the higher-ups. Was this a battle worth fighting? Hamisi's mood had not even noticeably changed after the confrontation. I decided not to initiate anything about the incident, but if asked by anyone, I would tell everything.

The residual stress from the incident shortened my fuse. When Jennifer walked to the closet without permission, I blew up on her, deducted four group points, and zapped her with lunch detention. My introductory lesson for our place value unit lost some steam with my rule-enforcement digression, but I decided it was worth it. I had to build the ship before we could sail it. I felt lousy nailing Jennifer, one of the only kids who showed any appreciation toward me, but she had broken the rule, and I needed to be consistent. Disappointingly, the next offender out of her seat was Destiny, who started bawling when her name appeared in the detention box.

Lunch detainees sat at a separate cafeteria table from their homeroom friends. They queued up last in the lunch line, and the daily special would inevitably be gone by the time the detention kids got their turn, leaving only reviled peanut butter and jelly.

When I delivered them to the detention table, Jennifer sniffled in shame, but Destiny had a full-body sob attack. "Please, Mr. Brown. Please, please don't make me sit at the detention table!"

"Sorry, Destiny. Now you know the punishment for getting out of your seat without permission." I wheeled and left the room. Neither Jennifer nor Destiny broke the rules for the rest of the year.

I received a memo from Ms. Guiterrez to inform me that she would be formally observing me on Monday, with a pre-observation meeting slated for Thursday during my prep. At literacy coach Marge Foley's recommendation, I planned another graphing lesson for the big show. "Avoid confusion during observations," Marge said. "Teach them something they already know." I thanked Marge and sketched out my observation lesson plan that night. It was two typed pages, complete with aim, objective, task, prior knowledge tapped, Bloom's taxonomy implementations, key questions, quotes I planned to say during the lesson, several paragraphs of procedural description, and some other bells and whistles. Some parts were bold, italicized, underlined, or a few at once. I included a copy of the post-activity questions they would answer — in complete sentences, of course — and a completed model bar graph and data table of my own.

Ms. Guiterrez opened our pre-observation meeting with some casual questions. "How is my dear, sweet Evley?" He was the silent boy who arrived on the second day of school with Jennifer and moody Joseph.

"Evley's my best-behaved boy. He's very shy, but he's starting to come out of his shell more and more. His effort is good. He shows good imagination in his writing, although sometimes he gets lost in the middle of a sentence and stops making sense. I'm trying to have as many writing conferences with him as possible to get him to verbalize his ideas orally, to make sure they make sense, before he writes them down. He's a really smart kid," I answered, hoping a thorough response would not only answer her question, but demonstrate that I was working closely with and understanding my students, something I was not sure Ms. Guiterrez acknowledged.

"My heart breaks for him. We held him over one too many times. Do you have Deloris or Lakiya?"

"Both," I said.

"Ugh. They are terrible. And the parents are no help."

I immediately thought of Deloris's father's outgoing voice-mail message:

Wassup girl, this is MC Onyx. Uh, if it's really that imp-o-tant, hit me with a message at the beep.

Ms. Guiterrez scanned my lesson plan. She asked questions about what would happen first, next, and after that. She pressed me to tell her what exact words I would use with the children. Many answers to her questions were in black and white on my prepared sheet, but I answered straightforwardly, and she appeared satisfied. Then we hit a stumbling block. In order to maximize the use of space on my sample graph paper, I had scaled out two blocks on the y-axis for every one kid who liked a specific fruit. "Why did you make it big like that?" Guiterrez asked, like a cross-examiner cornering a witness into incriminating himself. She pointed to the two blocks between zero and one.

"I scaled it out. Otherwise the graph would have been small . . ."

"One is one, Mr. Brown. Have you actually been teaching it *like this*?"

Silence. I was stuck for words again. Does New York City not teach scales? Maybe scales had been outmoded by some super-progressive curriculum that I hadn't heard about because I was new.

"I have been teaching it like this, using scales. Two spaces for one, four spaces for two, six spaces for three, just as long as it's consistent," I said, each word coming out more tentatively than the last.

Guiterrez shook her head in bemusement at my evident stupidity. "One is one, Mr. Brown. It is very, *very* simple. One is one. Okay? Fix it and we will meet again tomorrow."

That night, Jess came over. "I think your hair is falling out," she said. "You're ridiculously stressed out." She was right on both counts. If I was writing in my notebook, before long many loose hairs would lie on the page. I didn't want to go bald at twenty-two.

I cringed at the idea of having to meet with Ms. Guiterrez. When my alarm buzzed on Friday morning, I pulled the comforter over my head, and for the first time, called in sick.

On Sunday, I took Jess to the Bronx. We got wings at Mom's Fried Chicken and walked around the perimeter of P.S. 85. "It's so . . . depressing," she observed, snapping a telephoto-lens shot of some kids sitting on a stoop. "It really is a modern ghetto. A racial ghetto."

"Yeah," I said, hoping the stoop kids didn't see the white girl in the J. Crew jacket taking their picture.

"Is there even one white kid at P.S. 85?"

"No."

"Unbelievable how society turns their backs. It's a cycle of disempowerment."

I nodded, but had no desire to tease out socioeconomics with her. I wanted to show her my new life, where I came every day, maybe to impress her. Now that we were here, I regretted the whole trip.

"Do you want to go to the movies?" I asked.

"Is there a theater close by?"

"No, downtown."

"Oh," she said, shrugging. "I'm down for whatever. This place is so *hopeless-looking.*" She inflected her last sentence to indicate an inclination to stick around and check out the impoverished spectacle.

"MR. BROWN! OH SNAP, IT'S MR. BROWN!" Lito Ruiz, Tayshaun Jackson, and several of their cronies emerged around the corner.

"What's up, Lito, Tayshaun?" I said, giving out three-part handshakes.

"Mr. Brown is da man," Tayshaun told his pals.

"Why you come around here on the weekend?" Lito asked.

"Just hanging out," I said. "I'll see you in class on Monday."

"All right!" Lito nodded, his smile eating his face. "Have a good weekend!"

The kids went their way and Jess and I headed toward the D train. "You're a celebrity," Jess said.

"Those kids antagonize me nonstop during the week. Lito just broke a kid's glasses and lied about it," I uttered. "It's a novelty for them to see me on the street. They don't even *like* me."

"You're wrong," she said. "You're their hero."

On Monday morning, I held a special class meeting. "The word is out that the behavior in 4-217 is not good. Ms. Guiterrez is coming in at 10:15 to watch *you,* each and every one of you, to see who's doing a good job, and who needs to be sent back to third grade. [Marge Foley assured me of the efficacy, if not truth, of this threat.] Ms. Guiterrez will be taking notes about *everything,* so if I were you, my behavior would be absolutely perfect, the way it should be. And I'll bet you if everyone behaves, the class will be a lot more fun."

After my speech, Evley raised his hand and asked to speak to me in the hall. He was exceptionally shy, and this request for a private conference was the first of its kind. I stepped outside with Evley, who looked at me with worried doe eyes. His voice was quiet and high-pitched. "Mr. Brown, you know my private part?"

I nodded, terrified of what was coming next. "Yes."

"It stings."

This was out of my job description. My face blushed. "Go to the nurse, now," I said, pointing in the vague direction of her office. "Just go to the nurse."

Evley shook his head in panicked refusal.

"Then go to the bathroom. Go, go, go!" I urged. Evley went, returning to the class soon after. He made straight for his desk without a word.

At 8:45, as I directed kids out the door to their SFA rooms, Evley approached me again.

"Everything okay, Evley?" I asked.

"When I'm sitting down it's okay, but when I stand up and walk, it *stings*." His voice cracked sharply on the last word. He did not wait for a response, joining the sea of students in the corridor.

At 10:15, Ms. Guiterrez did not show up for the observation, and I had to stall. Twelve interminable minutes later, she appeared. I began the lesson precisely as my plans dictated, and often-raucous 4-217 behaved like obedient students. I forgot about Guiterrez in a few minutes because it was a pleasure to teach such attentive kids. I opened the lesson by simply asking what are graphs, how graphs are useful, and to identify and explain each part of a graph. Hands shot up. I usually got zero to three raised hands, and almost always the same bunch of kids. Now everybody wanted to participate, and what's more, they had good answers! Eddie, Lito, and Lakiya wowed me with articulate mathematical definitions of axes, variables, vertical, horizontal, columns, and rows. I thought they had been out to lunch the entire unit. The class made beautiful, if small, bar graphs, adhering to Guiterrez's "one is one" school of scales.

The lesson fired me up to teach. Something had been getting through after all, despite the chronic chatting, fighting, and block-throwing. Ms. Guiterrez left at the lesson's end, giving me a nod that I translated as a pedagogical thumbs-up.

The rest of the day passed smoothly, except for an episode on the steps where Asante yelled at Deloris, "Shut the fuck up! My father's going to come and cut you like he cut that other guy!" When I took Asante out of the room to investigate the problem and tell her she couldn't say things like that, she started bawling.

"Deloris makes me crazy. She's always bothering me and making fun of me 'cause of my clothes and cause I live in a shelter in Queens. She never stops so I want to get my father on her. Then she'll stop."

Shelter in Queens? This explained the chronic lateness and absences. And no phone number. I put my hand on her shoulder. "Don't worry about getting your father. I'll make Deloris stop." I sent Asante inside the classroom and pulled Deloris out, unsure what magic words or threats I could pull out to mediate this cruel conflict.

"Deloris, why —"

"She always bothering me and hitting me!"

"Do not interrupt me. Listen. If you were friends with Asante yesterday, which I know you were, why —"

"I ain't friends with her! She bad and dirty!" Deloris burst out.

"Deloris Barlow!"

"Do not use my last name please."

"*Deloris Barlow.* No one says those kinds of mean things in my room. You don't have to be friends with Asante, that's fine. But you two will stay away from each other and you'll both be better off!"

Deloris laughed coldly. "What do you know, you just a first-year teacher! You don't know nothing!" She doubled over with a belly laugh. "You a *scrub*! You don't know nothing!"

"Go sit in Mr. Randazzo's office. *Get out of my sight.*"

She skipped down the hall with a smile. The class cheered when I came back into the room without Deloris, a scene reminiscent of Fausto's 9/11 ejection.

When school was dismissed, I told the secretary that I had a student who commuted to school alone from a shelter in Queens. She shook her head sadly. "What a shame. These kids move from place to place so much that they don't change schools till they settle down. Poor girl. When Mom gets her feet on the ground, she'll change schools."

I asked if there was anyone I could notify or anything I could do to expedite Asante's transfer to a Queens school. The secretary again shook her head. "Nothing we can do from our end."

I told Barbara Chatton about how the kids rose to the occasion for the big observation. She seemed pleased and repeated her credo: "It's never as good as you think it is and it's never as bad as you think it is." She sprang it on me that 4-217 had been a popular topic of discussion among administrators. The word was that my teaching was good, but my management needed work. This wasn't news until Barbara told me that the next day, class 4-217 would be broken up, so that I could spend the day shadowing Janet Claxton, a veteran third-grade teacher with stellar classroom management. "Then you can motivate them into submission," Barbara said, patting me on the shoulder.

At lineup the next morning, Mr. Randazzo leaned into my ear. "Janet Claxton's a great teacher. Probably one of the strongest in the school."

"I know, I'm looking forward to being in there with her," I replied.

"Good," Randazzo said in a low voice. "Really try to get all you can out of this. I don't want to give up on you." He slapped me on the back and walked away.

I was suddenly furious. Did I just receive encouragement or a threat? *Give up on me?* Since when was anyone considering giving up on me?

I had a waking nightmare image of Randazzo, Daly, Guiterrez, and Boyd lounging around the principal's office with cigars and cognac. "What about Brown?" Daly asks. "We did give him the shit class of the fourth grade."

Guiterrez blows a smoke ring and waves her hand dismissively. "His management is poor and his bulletin board is a disgrace."

Boyd shakes her head ruefully. "It's a shame because he had the teaching gene."

Randazzo snuffs out his stogie on my Department of Ed file and claps his hands together. "So we give up on him?"

Ms. Claxton was a tall, dark-skinned Jamaican lady in her mid-thirties. Her six-foot stature and authoritative voice scared children. She addressed the class as "ladies and gentlemen," and when a student misbehaved, she immediately yell-asked if that was the way a lady or gentleman should act. When the group got noisy, Ms. Claxton clapped her hands, twice slow and three times fast. One-two, *one-two-three*! The class repeated the rhythmic claps, and after the last one, you could hear a pin drop. I held my clipboard and marveled.

Ms. Claxton's kids followed directions and did their work, with Thankgod Mutemi the only exception. He was a frowning, angry boy who occasionally pounded his fist on his desk and wandered around the classroom. Janet told me later, "Thankgod is dangerous. Anytime I'm not with him, he instigates a fight. They tell me I'm the only one who can control him, but what good is that?" (Thankgod was expelled a month later.)

Ms. Claxton seemed like the perfect teacher for these kids: intimidating, tough, smart, consistent, and maternal. She gave me hope (and a hand-clapping silence system), although I was not sure how I could ever intimidate the students of 4-217. Scariness appeared to be a crucial ingredient in the recipe for classroom harmony.

The brutal façade took a toll on Ms. Claxton. Two years earlier, she had suffered a stress-related heart attack. She also commuted two hours each way to get to Marion Avenue, something that did not seem to make sense. Any school would be lucky to have a Ms. Claxton. Why did she schlep all the way to hellish P.S. 85?

Ms. Claxton extended a magical offer to me. "Deloris Barlow is incorrigible. I know. If I've had them, they're always my children. Anytime you want her out, just give me a call, and you can send her right up." I thanked her profusely for everything.

The next morning I received cheers when I arrived in the cafeteria for lineup. "Mr. Brown's here! All right!"

"Yay, Mr. Brown!"

"You're not gonna let them split us up again, right?"

"It was terrible!"

"Please don't let them split up the class. We want to stay with you!"

Thanks, Tayshaun, I thought. I didn't know you cared.

Despite the flare of class spirit in the lunch room, we instantly reverted to the deluge of mini-problems upon entering room 217. Hamisi was munching on Doritos and tried to hide them in his shirt when I noticed, so I trashed the whole bag. Six kids did not have pencils. Gladys Ferraro and Verdad suddenly could not bear sitting next to each other. Sonandia's group earned a star toward the much-rumored Halloween party, but Eddie cost everyone a strike and landed himself in lunch detention by roaming over to Lito's group without permission. Deloris called Destiny a fat lesbian again and Destiny cried. The little nothings were snowballing into a monster. I could feel the room tilting out of control.

Clap-clap. CLAP-CLAP-CLAP!

The kids stared blankly. Clap-clap. CLAP-CLAP-CLAP!

I was clapping hard with a crazed, welded-on smile. Clap-clap. CLAP-CLAP-CLAP! "Now you do it!" I shouted insanely. The kids could not discern whether I was serious or had just morphed into some psychopathic drill sergeant.

Finally, Sonandia clapped. I clapped back. Then they all followed. Then I clapped. They clapped again in response.

"Everybody get up!" I called.

The kids obeyed and I performed the rhythmic clap, striking a ready-to-pounce pose à la Michael Jackson's "Thriller" video. Everyone followed suit, cautiously smiling.

I kept the lively stop-start dancing going for a while, cavorting into consistently weirder freeze-poses. In moments, Destiny forgot all about Deloris's meanness. Eddie followed directions. Gladys F. and

Verdad were laughing together. In mid-gyration, I glanced at the door to see Ms. Guiterrez peering in with a "what the hell is this?" expression on her face. I didn't care. Thank you, Janet Claxton!

P.S. 85 had a computer lab on the third floor with thirty Dell laptops in a metal case on wheels. The kids had Computers fifty minutes per week for one-third of the school year. Grades four and five were assigned to the first cycle, from September to December.

The head computer teacher, Valerie Menzel, was young but proved herself a decidedly unfriendly colleague. Ms. Menzel randomly paired kids together for each computer, stridently demanding total silence as she demonstrated the multistep processes of changing font sizes and colors in Microsoft Word. If the kids talked or touched anything during her harangue, Menzel would stop and slam the kid's laptop shut like some sort of Joycean schoolmaster.

Since sustained total silence is hard for kids anywhere and was supremely impossible for 4-217, Menzel would usually end by either threatening never to have us back and reminding us how incalculably far beyond us the other classes were, or she would grumpily capitulate and say, "Type whatever you want." I would have been more inclined to respect Ms. Menzel's austerity if she had cogent lessons to deliver, but all my students did under her was copy sentences from the overhead projector.

I was disgusted that this was the extent of my kids' in-school exposure to computer technology. (My classroom had no computer, although I was promised one several times throughout the year. It never showed up.) Changing font colors for three weeks? Type whatever you want? I remembered, as a fourth-grader in 1990, getting excited about geography and history by playing the interactive Oregon Trail or Carmen Sandiego social studies games during specially designated class time. I learned keyboarding in school with Mavis Beacon Teaches Typing software, which was a blast.

Now in the new millennium, baffled students were told to type whatever they wanted on a blank screen with a blinking cursor. They had enough trouble writing anything with a pencil and paper when given very specific instructions. To me, this computer class exemplified the gap between schools in more affluent neighborhoods and P.S. 85.

This chilly mid-October morning was an indiscriminate-typing period. Gladys Ferraro and Bernard, unwilling partners, had been at each other's throats since entering the lab. When Ms. Menzel called open season on Microsoft Word, Bernard snatched the laptop. Gladys F. made a clumsy lunge to swipe it away and fell out of her seat. Lakiya saw this and laughed, causing Verdad, Eddie, and Asante to start laughing too. "Shut up!" Gladys F. cried. Ms. Menzel sped over and slammed Gladys F. and Bernard's laptop shut, confiscating it. Bernard clenched his fists in a slow burn. Minutes after returning to 217, Bernard upended Hamisi's desk, prompting Hamisi to swing his right fist into Bernard's temple. I tore them apart and sent them to Mr. Randazzo's office. Lakiya shouted that Hamisi "punched like a bitch," and five kids cackled in concurrence. I scrambled to regain control, but the sudden, vicious fight threw the class energy way off-kilter. The rest of the day was a mess that no amount of rhythmic clapping could salvage.

I had a recurring daymare of being shadowed by a small fleet of robotic Ms. Guiterrez clones. I imagined coming home to find one in my kitchen, dressed in floral pajamas, dancing to her iPod and cooking something that involved three frying pans. On the futon, a Guiterrez antagonized two others by insisting on watching reruns of *Growing Pains,* and the latter Guiterrezes lunged for the remote control. Another Googled herself on my computer, while a towel-turbaned Guiterrez sat on the edge of my bed, reading a printout of my journal. She snapped Bubble Yum and shook her head indignantly, mystified and offended by every word.

I have not met a teacher who has not occasionally wished for a specific kid or two to be absent. Every day I strode into lineup hoping not to see Lakiya Ray. She was always there. Eric Ruiz played with my hopes by coming in late four times a week.

But on Friday, I wanted them all there. It was Picture Day.

Lito Ruiz wore his Lamar Odom jersey. Cwasey sported a yellow collared shirt, something never again repeated by the resident Kid in Sweatpants. Sonandia's hair was up in Princess Leia side-buns. Even Asante was on time. We had everybody.

I could feel a landmark moment materializing as we arranged ourselves on the auditorium stage. The photographer, apparently free of any obligation to adhere to Department of Ed guidelines for how not to interact with children, snapped at my uncooperative characters. "Hey fool! Stop being stupid and stand up straight, or I'll *make* you fall down!" I stood beside Deloris Barlow, and we all smiled like a big family on vacation.

After the picture, Asante handed me a note from her mother. At dismissal the day before, I had scribbled a letter to Mrs. Bell asking if she had a contactable phone number or if we could arrange a conference in person. I opened Mrs. Bell's sealed envelope and found two splotched pages covered front and back in Asante's curvy handwriting with "I will be good in school." I sent home another note, this time fully explaining what I wanted.

Gladys F., always on time and usually cheerful, was not in the class line Monday morning. At 8:30, Ms. Guiterrez delivered her to 217. Gladys looked at the floor, and I noticed a nasty, swollen purple shiner on her left eye. "It's okay. She's fine. She fell," Ms. Guiterrez said. "Come to my office on your prep to talk about the observation."

She left before I could mention that I already had a meeting scheduled with Tayshaun Jackson's social worker during my prep, so I sent Sonandia up to her office with a note. She responded that we would meet after school. Every time I dealt with Ms. Guiterrez, I felt a watery sickness in my gut.

My prep was slated for 11:30, but 11:30 came and went and the scheduled teacher, Randy Croom, did not show up. At 11:37, a man on crutches entered 217, claiming he would cover my prep. My mouth opened in astonishment at who I was about to hand over 4-217 to: Wendell Jaspers!

Wendell, a sixty-year-old, snowy-haired first-year Fellow, had been my think-pair-share partner for a week of Region One training in August. In our introductory activity, he had turned to me and explained, in a geriatric Jimmy Stewart voice, "I always believed that this Teaching Fellows program was intended for people who have gone out and made their mark on the world to come into a classroom and share their experience and expertise with young people. That's why I'm surprised to see so many young people. Like you, for example. Someone like you has made no mark on the world whatsoever. It's not your fault; it's just your youth. So, I really don't know what you could bring into a classroom." Then, under his breath, "No mark whatsoever." Most of our week passed in frosty silence after that.

"I'm an ATR now," Wendell said as I handed him the 4-217 chalk. ATRs were subs. "Bounced around a bit trying to find a firm placement, but now it looks like I'm staying at Eighty-five, mostly with Cathy [Catherine Fiore]. She's a piece of work."

I told the class that Mr. J.'s word was law, and that he had consummate reign over the Rewards and Detention lists. Jaspers made a sour face and proclaimed, "Thank you, Mr. Brown, but I have no need for your lists. These children are about to learn that I'm playing a much more severe game than that."

I had no idea what that meant. Out of curiosity concerning the severe game, I decided to risk two extra minutes of lateness with Tayshaun's social worker. Jaspers withdrew a coin from his pocket and dramatically held it out, like Moses with his staff. I held my breath as he temporarily released one of his crutches.

"This . . . is a penny! Every student will receive one penny and one piece of paper. You will observe the penny. Whoever writes the most observations, wins."

"What do we win?" several kids shouted.

"For the winner, I will replace that penny with these" — Jaspers took cash out of his pocket — "two one-dollar bills."

"OH MA GOD!"

The class erupted with wild energy. Lito, Cwasey, and Joseph jumped up and down. Lakiya started hooting. Eddie paced frantically, and a desk in group five was suddenly on the floor. "Who will volunteer to give out the papers?" Jaspers yelled over the din.

Me! Me! ME! ME! ME!

I slipped out of the room and closed the door, the fracas clearly audible in the hall. The social worker, Ms. Rincón, politely deflected my apologies for being late and asked me what I thought of Tayshaun, so I launched into a state-of-the-union speech. I offered the idea of making comic books as an avenue for getting him engaged in narratives. I mentioned his exceptional computational math skills and his (occasionally excessive) sociability with his peers. I talked about how he shuts down so entirely when upset that it takes him a half hour just to speak again. Lastly, I mentioned his tendency to deal out homophobic epithets.

The social worker nodded. She told me Tayshaun's family is very tragic, touching lightly on his institutionalized twin brother and drug-afflicted single mom, her words corroborating Ms. Slocumb's account. After we finished our lengthy speeches, Ms. Rincón gave a nod of closure. "So what happens now?" I asked.

"I'll put it all in my report. Talk to Mom, see about the comic books. That's a really good idea, but it's tough to get progress. I have a lot of other cases."

"How many?"

"Seventy-seven."

I headed back to 217 to find a lawless rumpus. Baskets of classroom materials were dumped across the floor in the back of the room, with Lakiya and Verdad lifting fistfuls of linker-cubes and slamming them down against the tile. Joseph and Dennis were taking turns pummeling each other in the bicep. Destiny, Tiffany, and Athena (a newly formed vocal trio, inspired and named after the teenie-pop "Cheetah Girls") were singing in hyper-soprano. Marvin and Daniel, my two illiterate kids, had covered their desks in dark scribbling. Wendell Jaspers yelled for order, slamming a meter stick against terrified Sonandia's desk. The noise was ear-crushing.

"Mr. Brown is here! Mr. Brown is here!" Jaspers boomed in futility.

I shut off the lights. Clap-clap CLAP-CLAP-CLAP! Several kids looked up. Clap-clap CLAP-CLAP-CLAP! Half of the class returned the claps. I did it again. And again. By the seventh set of claps, we had silence.

Jaspers spoke loudly. "Mr. Brown, because of *extremely* unfortunate unruliness, we haven't gotten to review our observations and find out who our two-dollar winner is. Do you think we could spend a few minutes now to finish it off?"

I glared. Maybe if you had been on time, Wendell, we could have found our two-dollar winner easily within the allotted period. Maybe some of the extremely unfortunate unruliness is your fault. And not maybe, but definitely, the clock says it's lunchtime, and the last thing I want to do is allow your bungled lesson to impinge on my eating minutes.

"Sure," I said, receiving big cheers. "Silence! Or you'll get a *strike*."

Mr. Jaspers called on Maimouna, the quietest kid in the class, to read her list. She speed-mumbled for a minute, her face three inches from the paper. The resultant lag stoked the room's wildness. Jaspers didn't know what to do. When Maimouna finished, he called on several other kids, but kept no master list of observations. Confused and hounded, Mr. J. gave one dollar to Maimouna and one to Asante. Kids cried in protest as Jaspers left, and we got to lunch sixteen minutes late. The rest of the day was a loose mess.

Immediately after dismissal, Wendell approached me on the blacktop. "Mr. Brown, I really respect how you handle that class. They are a *tough* group. I don't know how you do it." I appreciated Wendell's compliment, but he immediately undermined himself. "I have my doubts about some of the young women here," he said, in confidential tones. "This really is a man's job."

I had a mental image of Janet Claxton breaking his crutches and bludgeoning him with them. "I have to go, Wendell."

I jogged upstairs, entered Ms. Guiterrez's office, and sat down.

"Mr. Brown, what can I say? Your lessons are very good. Your management and classroom environment are terrible."

My teeth clenched. It had been a hell of a day already. I was first to acknowledge that I didn't have complete order like Paul Bonn or beautiful student work bedecking the walls like Catherine Fiore. But I was not terrible.

"Your kids behaved fine for the observation, but observations are not shows. What is important is how they behave every day for you, and I know it's not like that. How do you feel in your classroom? How does the room around you make you *feel*?"

"All right."

Ms. Guiterrez shook her head. "If you would just walk in now and sit down at your desk, how would you feel? Would you feel good?"

I suspected a trick question. "Yes," I said tentatively.

"I don't think so. Your room is . . . not lively. It has no energy. On the walls, I mean." The August memory shot to mind of Guiterrez forcing me to turn my mom's colorful borders backside-up. "And worst of all, it is a mess."

She had a point that I had barely any student work on display. My teacher's desk was a chaos of papers. I had not made those things priorities.

"Ms. Barrow is going to help you get these things on track. When your classroom looks good, everything works better. Nobody likes to be in a terrible classroom. I also highly recommend that you walk around and look carefully at the rooms of some of the experienced teachers. It can be very helpful to you."

Ms. Guiterrez shared her office with Abigail Barrow, a well-dressed older lady who helped with lower-grade teacher resource support. With the mention of her name, Ms. Barrow roused herself from reading some memo and joined the conversation. I was not thrilled about this new mentorship proceeding under Guiterrez's scornful eye, but I needed help and here it was. Ms. Barrow asked what I was teaching right now.

"In math, we're doing place value. In writing, we're doing memoirs. In social studies, we're finishing map skills. We're going to start Native Americans next week."

Ms. Barrow's and Ms. Guiterrez's eyes lit up at the mention of Native Americans. Guiterrez inquired, "What are the focus points of that new social studies unit?"

"I think mainly the Iroquois and Algonquians from the *New York* textbook."

The women exchanged a knowing glance. Ms. Guiterrez asked, "You need to have all of this planned out before you begin. What are the *enduring understandings*?"

I hesitated. There was definitely a preconceived correct response to this. "I guess they will have an enduring understanding of the Native Americans' lifestyle and culture," I offered.

Wrong answer. Guiterrez asked in a deeply patronizing voice, "Mr. Brown, does it really matter if the students understand the lifestyle and culture of the Iroquois people?"

I thought it did. Wasn't that what elementary school social studies was about? I remembered making a diorama of ancient Egypt, and bringing in a kimono for my fourth-grade report on kabuki theater. We took mental field trips to the battle of Gettysburg, and stared at photographs from different vantages of the Taj Mahal. I recalled social studies at Johnson Elementary as a mishmash survey across time and continents, and I loved it.

Ms. Guiterrez threw off my concentration with her pronunciation of "Iroquois." She said it exactly like "Iraqi." I also was not sure if her pointed question was rhetorical, but she answered it aloud. "It doesn't matter. What matters is literacy. How is your social studies unit going to be a vehicle for improving literacy skills? Do you think it will make a difference on the Test if your students know a lot about Iroquois lives?"

Now I picked my phrases straight out of the New York State standards book. "Well, one assignment could be writing a journal entry from the point of view of a Native American child. It would be good for creating a narrative procedure and responding to literature."

Guiterrez laughed. "Okay! See? It's not so hard!"

I wanted out of that room. I did not like at all how every conversation with Ms. Guiterrez bore a discomfiting overtone of her exerting authority over me.

"The students should not write cold," she added. "They must do a prewriting activity on a graphic organizer."

I knew this already. Graphic organizers, or various kinds of thought outlines, went without saying. I wanted to add that I never intended to teach my students lists of meaningless facts; of course literacy skills would be central to our social studies activities. The moment had passed.

"Okay, I have some business to take care of," she said, grabbing some papers and striding purposefully out of the office, handing me a typed two-page evaluation for the formal observation. I got a satisfactory rating with the criticism, "There is no evidence of developmental lessons. . . . Their [sic] should be evidence of a print-rich classroom." As for missing the developmental lessons, I can only assume that Guiterrez figured that the kids were bar graph experts on observation day by blind luck or osmosis. And I couldn't help imagining inviting her to sit in on my upcoming "their-there-they're" lesson with the fourth-graders.

So began my short-lived but fruitful collaboration with Ms.

Abigail Barrow. She talked to me as if I did not know thing one about anything regarding school, children, or human interaction, but she supplied some useful materials, including a thick batch of supplemental readings, questions, and activities about Native Americans.

She also ran 4-217's closing map skills lesson by writing questions on big chart-paper sheets and posting them at five stations around the room. The kids got excited to work in teams and rotate to the stations. I kept Ms. Barrow's questions on the walls for months, scoring compliments from Mrs. Boyd for fostering a more print-rich classroom.

The Ms. Barrow meetings petered out because we both recognized that while the help with lessons was useful, it was really in behavior management where 4-217 had trouble. As a soft-spoken older lady who had been out of the classroom for years, she could not help me there. It looked bad for her when my kids acted up while she conducted the class.

Ms. Barrow left me an invaluable set of desk-size laminated maps with the United States on one side and the world on the other. The kids loved them, especially since each student got his own, and they provided endless material for geography lessons, games, and fast-fix time-fillers. Cat Samuels borrowed them often.

"They are lost in the woods," my new self-talking self explained to the bathroom mirror. "You have a map. You can teach them. You are Mr. Brown." I frowned at the lopsided Windsor knot of my tie and pulled it loose to redo it.

In reality, my confidence in my lessons was improving, but my attempts to control Lakiya, Deloris, Eric, Lito, Tayshaun, Cwasey, and Eddie went nowhere. I could not get all seven of them to be quiet at the same time. If they somehow were, Bernard would be squabbling with Verdad, or Destiny would be upset about something her best friend Tiffany had said to her. Occasionally, Athena or Gladys Ferraro called out disruptive things, which killed me, because I counted on them to be my stars. My sentences in class alternated:

one about the lesson, one about discipline, one to answer a question, one to mediate a conflict. Getting into a rhythm was impossible.

Meanwhile, Daniel and Marvin stagnated in the back of the room. One time, Dr. Kirkpatrick picked Daniel up and returned him a half hour later. She told me that back in Detroit, Daniel was in intensive one-on-one special ed, and he should never have been placed in a regular class. She also asked me if I had noticed his stuttering problem and the long gaps of time he took before responding to a question. I told her of course I had. She explained that his speech problems were a blessing in disguise, because they could be the tipping point to push through a recommendation to transfer him to a specialized school. I filled out several forms with my analysis and anecdotal records about him.

Two months later, Daniel Vasquez left P.S. 85 to begin to get the help he needed.

Marvin Winslow was proving himself to be a dangerous boy. He stole Tiffany Sanchez's purple pencil sharpener, and when she asked for it back, he cold-cocked her in the cheek. I was reading with Dennis and Joseph and didn't see it. Sonandia tapped me on the shoulder and plainly said, "Tiffany is crying 'cause Marvin hit her."

I spun to see Marvin darkly scowling at the sobbing girl. I flew into a rage.

"How dare you ever hit a girl! That is the weakest, most cowardly thing anyone could do! How dare you bring that into our classroom!"

I told Sonandia to take Tiffany to the nurse for ice. When they left, I continued my verbal lambasting, telling Marvin he was on lunch detention for a week, and if the class earned that Halloween party, he had certainly just thrown his invitation in the gutter.

"I don't care. I don't care," Marvin muttered. "I don't care."

He did care, because when the class lined up for lunch he remained in his seat, catatonic. The line got restless, and Tayshaun and Bernard started pushing each other. With the whole class's impatient urging, Marvin finally joined the line. Upon entering the cafeteria, he separated from the group and pressed his face into the wall, crying, "I'm bad, I'm bad, I'm bad, I'm bad, I'm bad."

"What you did to Tiffany was very bad, but you are not a bad person. Look at me. Marvin, look at me! If you accept your punishment for breaking the rules, you'll have a clean slate. I'll even think about letting you come to the Halloween party. But no hitting in school and no hitting girls ever. This is very fair." I patted him on the shoulder and walked away.

As I left him, he punched the wall and cried, "I'm bad, I'm bad, I'm bad . . ."

I walked to the fifth-grade side of the cafeteria to sit with my summer school coauthor Jimmarie. She didn't have many friends in Mr. Krieg's class and preferred to eat alone by the window. I often sat with her for a few minutes; sometimes we talked, sometimes not. We appreciated each other's company, briefly allowing ourselves to forget the people with whom we spent a majority of our day.

That night, I called Marvin's and Tiffany's mothers to tell them about the punch. Both thanked me for the explanation and that was it.

The next morning, Marvin came to school chipper as ever. We did math in the morning, the only subject where he had a fighting chance of holding his own with the class. He understood the rules of place value, but if you gave him a worksheet, he would be lost. He needed every problem started for him. His effort that morning was outstanding and when he told me that the 6 in 12,685 is actually worth 600, I was thunderstruck with pride.

Yesterday, I had promised him a week of lunch detentions, but that felt like a remote world ago. I decided not to enforce the sentence and no one seemed the wiser. Also, a teacher tipped me off to the rumor that for punishment, Mrs. Winslow locked her children in the refrigerator. How could you stay mad at Marvin Winslow?

Meanwhile, trouble was brewing with Verdad Navarez. He had been absent the day before, and now he was silent all day, seething, almost hyperventilating in the back of the room, staring at his desk surface. I took him out in the hall and asked what was bothering him.

Verdad coldly mumbled, "Tomorrow I'm-a bring a gun to school and kill Eddie. I swear to God, I'm-a snuff him."

Wait a minute. Verdad and Eddie were buddies. My skin pebbled with fear. I called the principal. Mrs. Boyd asked for Verdad's mother's phone number, but I knew their line was disconnected. Fortunately, Verdad's mom, Yvette Lara, was in the parking lot to pick him up at dismissal. She said she would talk to Verdad, and we arranged to meet in room 217 after school the next day.

The next afternoon, Ms. Lara and I sat down at group two while Verdad waited in the hall. She was probably my age. Biting her lip, she spoke in a straight voice. "You don't have to worry about Verdad bringing a gun to school. That's not him. He would never do that. He gets very angry sometimes. He's been very different since last spring when we think he found out . . . about his father. His real daddy died when he was a baby. My husband is his stepfather, but we never told him. He does have two brothers and a father with different last names than him."

"Have you talked to him about it after you think he figured it out?"

"No. We should. He's got it tough. Please don't take it out on him, Mr. Brown."

"No, of course not. I know Verdad is a great kid. Everyone likes him. And he's the number one mathematician in the class." Ms. Lara cracked a shining, proud mother's smile. I showed her Verdad's flawless Birthday Bar Graph. "But he needs to bring a bag to school. And he needs to do his homework, especially in writing." I showed her the class homework log. Verdad had completed his assignments decently in September, but in October he altogether stopped.

Her face fell. "He lost his bag. I don't know how he lost it, but it's gone." I started to say something, but she continued, "I kept Verdad home the other day because he didn't have any clean clothes to wear. I don't know if I can get him a new bag. I need to get coats for three kids. They turned off my phone, which you know about . . ." She fell silent.

I didn't know what the hell to say. An idea flashed to give her the cash in my wallet, but all I had was six bucks, and that was the wrong move anyway. I called Verdad into the room. "Verdad, good news. You have a wonderful mom who loves you very much. She and I are going to work together to make sure the rest of the year is going to be better for you than it's been this month. You're a really smart boy, and I'm glad that you're in my class. Can we work together?" I extended my hand and he shook it. His face brightened, and I realized I had never before seen him smile. I think worlds were colliding for him to see his mom and teacher together.

Ms. Lara thanked me for meeting with her and she and Verdad went home happy. I felt good but a little strange. Nothing had changed in their desperate financial situation, but everything seemed sunnier from that day forward. Verdad did his work conscientiously and started bringing a bag to school. His demeanor was cheerful and his writing showed improvement. He was a changed boy for the rest of the year. That is, until his family moved suddenly over Christmas break and I never saw or heard about him again.

Halloween approached. I shut off the lights during Success for All and read from a Mom-supplied *Scary Stories to Tell in the Dark* book, complete with sufficiently creepy charcoal illustrations. I had more leeway for antics with my SFA group, since they were a manageable bunch of half the size and one-tenth the volatility of 4-217. With a whoosh and a leap out of my reading seat at each story's terrible revelation, I drew delighted screams from Kelsie Williams, a polite girl from Ms. Mulvehill's homeroom, and the others. Switching the lights back on brought a chorus of disappointed moans as we beamed back to P.S. 85.

First-year Fellow Trisha Pierson brought in twenty-six pumpkins, one for each of her little first-graders to carve. She said it was the cutest thing she'd ever seen, and the children treated their personal pumpkins like gold. I imagined Lakiya Ray chucking Destiny's hypothetical pumpkin out the window, cackling as it splattered on the asphalt.

Several days before Halloween, I announced that our "Team Effort" board indicated the requisite number of stars over strikes. "Congratulations, we're going to have our first class party on Halloween, this Friday." Unanimous cheers. "*But* I am now creating a list called the 'Not Invited to Party' list. If your name gets on there with two strikes next to it, we will be partying without you!"

The class had in fact not earned a party. My hope, though, was that through some good Halloween cheer and a fun 4-217 party, we could take a step forward as the originally hoped-for "team."

The "Not Invited to Party" list was an effective misbehavior deterrent. Lakiya still did not do her work, but she was quiet all day. Daniel, who obsessed over being on the "Good List," sat with folded hands, which influenced Marvin.

Wild card Eric, however, could not resist pushing Joseph down the steps (a favorite pastime), and Tayshaun slapped Athena in the face, landing the offending pair on the unfortunate list. Tayshaun slammed his fist on his desk and buried his face when he got the final strike. Eric looked totally unmoved.

I could not figure out Eric Ruiz. I was unconvinced his expression would change if I slid bamboo shoots under his fingernails or handed him a suitcase full of cash. Every year his teachers recommended that he be held back, but somehow he always got promoted.

I was sixty-one dollars lighter after arranging a junk food super-buffet, complete with precious Domino's pizza, which greeted the 217 kids when they returned from lunch on Friday. Lined up outside the room, Athena and Cwasey literally jumped for joy. I sent Lakiya to escort Eric and Tayshaun to Mr. Randazzo's office. (Lakiya displayed mirthful diligence in accompanying her peers to meet their disciplinary consequences.)

I had cleared the idea of stashing Eric and Tayshaun in his office with Mr. Randazzo the day before but now his door was locked and he was nowhere to be found. Ms. Devereaux could not be tracked down either, and all of the other rooms were having their own parties. I had ranted all week about excluding disrespectful kids from the party; now my threats proved empty.

I tried to spin my allowing Tayshaun and Eric's presence as a beau geste for better teamwork and class spirit for the coming months. The kids were dead silent during my awkward speech, their eyes fixed on the pizza and sweets.

For the next twenty minutes, everything was aces. I played *Rubber Soul* on Al Conway's borrowed boom box while the kids scarfed the candy and cupcakes with shocking alacrity. Marvin and Daniel found they could mix in happily when everyone was guzzling generic-brand orange soda. Hamisi said it was the best party of his life. Dennis nodded in vigorous agreement. When Lito and Joseph saw Dennis do that, they jumped in to affirm the motion.

Thank you, Mr. Brown, thank you, Mr. Brown. The party was a hit, and now I could use it as a tangible, long-term class goal. Nobody has a great first two months, I thought. But now I'm on track. We're all in this together. I can lead this team of struggling, beautiful kids.

Then the house of cards toppled. Tayshaun, on party probation, reasoned that it was a good idea to take the ice cubes out of his drink, sneak behind Julissa, and jam one in her eye. This happened while I was running a trivia game with some girls to determine who would take home the Domino's leaflet coupons, and by the time I was across the room, Julissa was clutching her face and crying. Lakiya poured her soda on the floor and pushed Verdad over it, causing him to slip. Mr. Randazzo came on the loudspeaker (there he was!) and announced that we were now having a "rapid dismissal," and everyone needed to go directly home to minimize the risk of being hit by flying eggs. The announcement sent the class into a tizzy, scrambling for their coats and belongings. The floor turned into an instant morass of syrupy puddles of wet dirt.

I yelled my head off, but the scene had disintegrated into a wild derby of whirling dervishes. My previous reverie disintegrated like dead roses, and a sober thought passed through my brain: *I have been kidding myself. They were right about me. I have no management, no control. I am a failure. My kids are crying and injured and dirty and screaming, and I can't stop it.* I looked up and saw Principal Boyd in the doorway, deep disgust on her face.

November

Snap

ON HALLOWEEN, I took Jess to a roof party in Brooklyn, but we weren't there more than twenty minutes before I lost track of her. A text message some hours later informed me that she had gone home with Lowell Eldridge, a disc jockey who had come to the party dressed as George W. Bush, the Crawford ranch edition. I spent the weekend throwing up.

A few minutes after midnight on Sunday, my phone rang. I didn't recognize the number on the caller ID. "Dan, it's Karen! Are you asleep?"

"I'm dead awake." I was beautifully surprised to get her call. We effortlessly bitched about P.S. 85 for the next forty minutes. Our profanity-laced gripes were pretty comprehensive: Randazzo, Boyd, Guiterrez, lunchroom fiascos, petty but vicious fights, lack of student interest in academic achievement. She told me about her student Dequan's rubbing his penis against a female classmate's jacket during their Halloween party.

A brief silence passed. "You looked pretty dark leaving on Friday," she said.

"Yeah. I think I might be going under."

"I felt the same way all last year. What the hell are we supposed to do when they just won't cooperate?"

"I don't know."

"I try to think about something, and I hope you don't think I'm some kind of asshole trying to give you cheesy advice," she said.

"No, of course not. I need it."

"This is the thing. You might be the *only* good person in their lives. Some of them just go home and fight and have no space and see terrible things and everything is fucked up. The only time all day, or all year even — because summer is horrible — that they're with someone who is generous and good to them could be when they're with you. Something comes across just by being there, even if they're too young or immature or emotionally crippled to express it. They do appreciate you. It's a long year, and something will come across. It *has* to."

I still called in sick on Monday.

Tuesday, November 4, was election day, and a full day of Professional Development for all teachers. I still felt ill, but I was incredibly thankful for this fourth day of respite from my students, following the Halloween disaster.

I received a predictably terrible report from my Monday substitute, Ms. Richardson, a tall, middle-aged Nigerian woman who had been bouncing around P.S. 85 as a floating sub the past few weeks. "That mean girl is *so* fresh, that —"

"Lakiya," I finished for her.

"Yes! Lakiya. Terrible attitude. And we had a problem in the front with —"

"Deloris."

"Exactly right. She is *mean*. And the boys don't care about their work one bit. No respect for school or themselves. *Quite* a class you've got. This is your first year? Unbelievable."

The focus of our Professional Development day was encouraging nonfiction reading and writing. Almost immediately, a heated grievance-venting session ignited, centered on the question of how teachers are expected to squeeze in extra time for literacy skills, when we do not even teach our own homeroom students during the ninety-minute SFA block. Everyone seemed to agree that achievement plateaus out in the second half of the teacher-proof Success for All program, but we were handcuffed to this time-eating literacy curriculum.

The faculty's points were strong but I stayed out of the discussion, not because I was a rookie but because I secretly and selfishly relished Success for All. For those ninety minutes every day, my regular twenty-six left, and only fifteen plus Fran Baker entered. The new personalities were cut from a similar cloth as my homeroom kids, but the smaller number made life exponentially easier. I could deal with a momentary distraction from sneaky Dequan or talkative Victoria without losing the whole group. Also, I got to meet perpetually sunny Kelsie, Maria, and David, and they were joys.

I got excited when literacy coach Marge Foley talked about walking field trips to the neighborhood public library on Bainbridge Avenue. I also hatched an idea to take the class to nearby St. Barnabas Hospital to learn about health and nursing. Gladys Ferraro and Tiffany wanted to work in medicine, something I learned from their autobiographies. Lakiya did not write an autobiography, but I had her specifically in mind for the hospital trip. She showed surprising compassion for sick or injured classmates. When Fausto strangled Eric back in the first week of school, I entered the lunchroom to find Lakiya's arm protectively around Eric while he retched. I also remembered her rubbing Dennis's back and keeping gapers away when Dennis got upset over an insult Cwasey cracked about his old-looking clothes. Lakiya Ray might hate elementary school, but maybe she could be happier if she had some educational experiences outside the iron-barred windows of P.S. 85.

Later, Marge Foley politely told me to put the field trip ideas out of my head. "I wouldn't risk it with your group," she said. "It's just not safe." She was right.

In the search for ways to break the cycle of misbehavior through more stimulating in-class activities, my hands were not tied but lopped off. No trips. No games, because all of my boys, except timid Evley, were incredibly sore losers. No hands-on work, because of inevitable throwing or destroying. If I cut independent work time short, kids would not finish and would get discouraged. If I gave extra independent time, the lag produced shiftlessness and loss of interest. I could not be humorous or affable because a light moment was license to make noise and, unfailingly, the class subverters leapt on it. My rewards seemed ineffective, and my punishments were so limited and so often undermined that I looked like a chump dealing out empty threats.

Hope existed only if I could get them to behave themselves. My bathroom mirror was getting an earful these days. "It's a long year. *Something gets across!*"

I thought Cat Samuels could use a bit of Karen Adler's verbal medicine. Cat taught a prep lesson in Karen's room on Mondays, but they had never had a conversation about anything outside schoolwork. I suggested the three of us go out for a drink. We rode the Manhattan-bound D train south, traveling from the country's poorest congressional district to one of the wealthiest in just twenty minutes.

We walked into Kennedy's, an Irish old-timer haunt on West 57th Street, with big mahogany tables and a record player more likely to turn the Chieftains than U2. Karen and Cat hit it off, and Morris, the white-haired barkeep, put several rounds on the house. We cursed our jobs and laughed, munching on the complimentary onion-and-potato pancakes.

I got a call from a friend who was with some girls at a bar on Rivington Street in the Lower East Side. They were talking about me, and he encouraged me to get down there despite it being a school night. Of course I'll be there! I was twenty-two and tired of feeling dead.

Soon I was guzzling Jack Daniel's and emphatically recounting the inflammatory exploits of Fausto Mason to a rapt audience when the room started to bend. For some reason, the ancient antiseptic smell of the P.S. 85 second-floor faculty bathroom floated into my head and stuck there. After a second round of kamikaze shots, I stood up, intoxication rushing against my eyeballs with unanticipated pressure. I abruptly excused myself and rushed out of the bar, peeling the corner onto Essex Street to revisit my onion latkes.

Reeling on the sidewalk, I remembered that it was election day, and damned if I wasn't going to cast my ballot! I stumbled three avenue blocks to my polling place at the corner of Allen and Stanton streets.

Inside at the table, I gave my name and address and was directed to a booth. Behind the privacy curtain, I felt sudden tranquility. Just for a moment, I allowed my eyes to relax. I don't know if ten seconds or ten minutes passed, but, from outside, an impatient slap to the metal wall of the booth jolted me back into the world. *"Buddy!"*

I flipped a few switches, then walked straight out of the building, staring at my shoes. I leaned against a parking meter, spit, and wiped my watering eyes. At 8 a.m., I would have twenty-six children expecting me to teach them, and I had gotten smashed the night before to forget about it all. I fell into bed. This was dangerous.

I hit the snooze bar four times before rolling out of bed at 5:36. I couldn't discern whether my nausea was a hangover or just the usual dread, exacerbated by returning after a four-day break from the students.

My kids cheered when I appeared for lineup, but this time I barely heard them.

"Mr. Brown's here. Yay!"

"We had a mean African lady!"

"I hate subs!"

"Mr. Brown, how are you?" Jennifer asked.

I rubbed my eyes with my palm. "Sick, and I'm still sick."

When everyone lined up to leave for Success for All at 8:45, Sonandia pranced over to me. "Mr. Brown, are you sad?"

"I don't know, Sony."

"I see. Is your birthday more than two days away?"

I nodded. "Yes. It's February ninth."

"I know it's February ninth. That's why this is for you!" She handed me a piece of notebook paper, crudely fashioned into a bulging envelope.

I unfolded the paper and read her note, written in childish loop-
ing cursive. "Dear Mr. Brown: I am giving you this for good luck. I
see that this can change things for you. Thank you! Love, Sonandia."
She had drawn bunches of stars and hearts near each corner of the
page, with a caption reading "center of the heart and feelings." Enclosed in the paper was a funky beaded necklace with a scraggy
shark-tooth pendant.

The darkness lifted. "Thank you, thank you, thank you, Sonan-
dia! What a cool necklace! That's so thoughtful and generous!"
Sonandia helped hook the thing on me. I had never worn a necklace
in my life, and this was a fine first one. The kids loved it. Even
Tayshaun and Lakiya seemed impressed with the shark tooth, which
I knew had Blazing Hippie written all over it. I wore the necklace
all day, drawing sideways glances from Mr. Randazzo and Ms.
Guiterrez.

Riding the surf of good feelings after receiving Sonandia's gift,
I changed my lesson plan on the fly and brought out the "manipulative" blocks for some hands-on multiplication work. "Manipulative"
is teacher lingo for a material intended to enrich understanding of
math concepts. It seemed a rather sophisticated word to serve as the
catchall for the dusty closet inventory of tangrams, rubber-band
geoboards, spinners, and number grids.

Miraculously, no one brutalized anybody else. (Perhaps I got
some traction with my improvised analogy, "Throwing manipulatives
is like touching poison.") Little lightbulbs popped on all over the
room. Lito Ruiz's moments of epiphany were fantastic to watch; he
would stare at his desk surface, look up, look back at the desk, and
nod progressively faster until he had a smile that would eat his face.
Jennifer gave me our daily hug in the parking lot and I sent them
home for the first time without thinking I was verging on collapse.
Maybe it's not the elaborate behavior systems that determine our
flow, I thought. Maybe it's the way I carry myself. When a teacher is
happy, the kids are happy.

I stopped at Crif Dogs, a much-beloved East Village hot-dog

joint, on my way home and grabbed two Philly Tube Steaks as a present for this renewed school spirit. And I kept the toothy necklace on.

On Thursday, November 6, 4-217 scored its first perfect "4" in Mr. Randazzo's daily lineup inspection.

At 8:55, I was perched on the edge of my rocking chair by the reading rug, making crazy faces at a troop of children entranced by an enthusiastically requested encore performance of "The Ghost with Bloody Fingers," a particularly delicious selection from Mom's *Scary Stories to Tell in the Dark*.

"Mr. Brown, I need to speak to you now."

Mrs. Boyd stood by the blackboard, her face clenched in seriousness. I hesitated, ripped suddenly out of the delicately constructed climax of the lamenting, oozing ghost. "*Now,* Mr. Brown."

I handed the book to Fran Baker. A collective sigh of disappointment exhaled from the group. Mrs. Baker was a wonderfully generous and intelligent teacher, but she was a self-admitted novice when it came to leading an exciting read-aloud.

I assumed Mrs. Boyd wanted to talk to me in the hall, so I headed for the door. Her hand reached out and caught my forearm, not letting go for an uncomfortable interval. "We can speak here. What can you tell me about" — Mrs. Boyd looked down, referring to her paper — "Sonandia Azcona?" She pronounced Sonandia's name very slowly, as if she had never said it before.

My anxiety lifted. I thought this meeting was finally going to put words to her murderous glare from the Halloween party disaster. Calmed, I instinctively reached for my right pocket where the sharktooth necklace now resided as a lucky charm. "Sonandia is my best student. She's the best behaved and the most academically advanced. She's mature and a good leader; she's always my line leader. She grasps concepts quickly and is able to apply them to solve problems. She always volunteers to —"

"Show me her portfolio," Mrs. Boyd commanded.

A flow-tide of queasiness rose up in me. The *portfolios.* I had fallen desperately behind in keeping them current with multiple-draft pieces of completed work. Piles of student papers covered my desk, but I was remiss in getting them organized into the important red folders. Major paperwork surgery was penciled in my planbook for Tuesday night, but I had gotten wrecked instead.

I led Mrs. Boyd to my desk and began madly riffling through compositions titled "Why We Write" as she fingered my crate of virtually empty portfolios.

"Forget it," Mrs. Boyd said. "Sonandia's mother is a paraprofessional here in our cafeteria."

"Yes. Ms. Tavarez."

"Right. Ms. Tavarez approached me with concerns that this class might be a little too out of control to be the best environment for her daughter. She asked me to transfer her to Ms. Adler's class, and I'm going to do it, effective after report cards next week."

Mrs. Boyd looked at me to respond. I had nothing to say. "Oh," I fumfered.

"Okay, good. And Mr. Brown" — Mrs. Boyd tapped twice on the anemic red folders and made a laugh-snort — "we have a lot of work to do, babe."

My first thought was simply, Ms. Tavarez's idea makes sense. I would not want my kid in my class either.

I stood dumbly and alone by my desk. I realized I needed to resume the reins of the SFA group. I moderated Meaningful Sentences practice, Treasure Hunt review, and Adventures in Writing first drafts, all the while feeling a growing lump in my throat.

I spent my prep in a long line for the downstairs copy machine, listening to a small cluster of veteran teachers discuss their jobs.

"Ungrateful, *disgusting* little fuckers. Don't they know by now that I don't give a damn if they cry? Cry all you want, Tyrell. I don't see an extra ten dollars in my paycheck for being your friend."

"Seriously."

"I don't play. They know I don't play. I've had it with these brats."

"Forty-seven more till winter break. Then twelve whole days out of here."

"Jesus Christ, give it to me *now.*"

During our math lesson, Sonandia raised her hand for every question with her usual exuberance. I realized: *She doesn't know.*

Karen was absent, so I ate lunch alone. Sitting in the silent classroom, mechanically shoveling tasteless things into my mouth, my numb melancholy hardened into anger. I would be dead without Sonandia. Not only was she a funny and lovable kid to have around, but she was the crucial litmus test of my ability to teach. She was now proficient in graphing, place value, and basic multiplication, concepts to which she had only been vaguely exposed before September. Her writing showed the seedlings of a unique voice that I was eager to cultivate. Apparently unobstructed in her progress by the other issues in the room, Sonandia was the best proof that I wasn't a tailspinning hack, as Bob "I-don't-want-to-give-up-on-you" Randazzo seemed to think, though he had never come into 217 to watch me teach. I *needed* her!

On Tuesdays and Thursdays, I had a morning prep to go with our Extended Day schedule, which meant I carried the entirety of the dreaded after-lunch teaching periods. Across the school, Extended Day afternoons were the most stir-crazy, misbehavior-prone times of the week, and Thursdays were always the worst.

I had planned to combine a social studies and writing lesson to introduce our unit-culminating Iroquois-perspective journal pieces, but when I showed up in the cafeteria to pick up the class, I could tell it was going to be dicey. Jennifer and Athena ran over to me immediately.

"Everyone hates Deloris because she's saying nasty things!"

Deloris suddenly appeared behind me, evidently from wandering outside the cafeteria. "Shut up, you slut."

"You a slut!"

"Hey!" I shouted. "Get in line!"

Another wave of complainants barraged me. "Bernard and Daniel got into a fight!" I looked at the table and saw Bernard sitting cold-eyed, cheeks puffed, hyperventilating. Daniel faced the corner, crying. Tayshaun Jackson was dancing around the middle of the cafeteria with the industrial broom.

"Tayshaun!" I called. He heard me, looked up, and leaned all of his weight on the broom handle. The wood snapped in two. The lunchroom supervisor, Len Daly, was nowhere to be seen.

After three minutes of yelling, only twelve of my twenty-six kids were in line. Daniel was still crying, Destiny was now crying too for some reason, and Marvin Winslow was plain missing.

"Where's Marvin?" I shouted frantically at Dennis.

Dennis shrugged. "He left."

"He left? On his own? Which way did he go? Did someone give him permission? Was he alone?" My eyes darted around, as if Marvin might be lurking just beyond my periphery.

Dennis was clearly rattled by my interrogative onslaught and held his palms up. "He left."

The kids tramped into 217 seventeen minutes late and without Marvin Winslow. I called security and a building-wide search began. Marvin did not turn up. Meanwhile, still-fuming Bernard, labeled on his blue card as an "extremely temperamental child," took out his anger by toppling Hamisi's desk while I was on the phone with security. Hamisi went nuts, attacking Bernard like a clumsy mongoose. I ripped them apart, tossing Bernard into Mr. Randazzo's office. I continued to battle the tide via rhythm-clapping, shouting, moving seats, and subtracting points. After fifteen minutes of this, the class settled, like a shaken soda can after its pressure-induced eruption. I picked up a marker to make a chart-poster and asked my first introductory review question, calling on Ms. Guiterrez's recommendation of employing the five senses in prewriting. "If I were living four hundred years ago in an Iroquois longhouse, what is one thing that I would *see* when I woke up in the morning?"

"Marvin!" Dennis cried.

With total nonchalance, Marvin Winslow swaggered through the 217 door and took his seat like someone returning to a dark movie theater from the restroom.

"MARVIN! Where have you been? I called security! I thought you were dead. I was worried sick!" I became an official grown-up when I said that.

He did not look at me. He always tuned out when people yelled at him. I was incensed, though, and later wished I had controlled myself.

"Answer me! Where did you go! Talk!"

He folded his arms on the desk and buried his face. "Leave me alone," he mumbled into his shirt.

Suddenly, Deloris was having a crisis. "My skin! Mr. Brown, my skin!" She rushed over to me (breaking the out-of-seat law), clutching her inner elbow. I saw nothing wrong with her arm and told her to sit down.

"Oh my God, *mah skin*! I got bumps on my skin! Send me to the nurse, please!"

I wanted her gone. I scribbled a nurse's pass on a torn-off corner of a scrap of paper that had missed the wastebasket. "Go!"

She left, and I restarted the stillborn lesson. Eight minutes later, Deloris reappeared, escorted by the frowning nurse. "This girl has *nothing* wrong with her," Nurse Tina said tersely. "Please don't send me frivolous things again. It's a waste of my time." I nodded, a little miffed at her tone. I turned back to the group, asking the class again about hypothetical olfactory stimuli for Native American farmers and artisans when an unmistakable voice shrilled out.

"*My eye*! Oh my God, Mr. Brown! My eye!"

The class erupted in a mix of disdainful yells and laughter.

Lakiya and Eric fell off their chairs. When Joseph and Lito saw, they fell off their chairs too.

I looked at Sonandia and her half page of notes about Iroquois ways of life. A string snapped inside me, and I lost it.

I lifted cackling Tayshaun Jackson's desk above my head and *wham!* smashed it to the floor. *"SHUT YOUR MOUTHS!"* My voice shook with convulsive intensity. The room went dead silent and motionless at my paroxysm, like a record scratching to a halt in some terrible game of Freezedance.

"Do you have any idea what you are doing to me? Just shut your mouths!"

"It wasn't me —"

"SHUT IT, CWASEY! I don't care. I don't care!" I was kickball red. "Do you know that all I want to do is teach you? *That's all I want to do.* I don't have any other job. This is it. And you make me yell and scream *all day!* Do you know how sick that makes me? *Do you know how sick I feel right now?"*

With the last phrase, I snapped my body hard to the right, punching the blackboard with my closed left fist. The chalkdusty surface splintered and gave, and I saw my hand in a six-inch cranny between the board and the cement wall. Lakiya Ray's face froze in a crazed openmouthed grin, but the rest of the kids looked appropriately petrified. My eyes bulged, and I brushed sweat from my temple.

"Mr. Brown, you wiped a little blood on your face."

"Thank you, Destiny." I dabbed at the red wisps on my forehead and glared at the back wall's "Iroquois Longhouses" bulletin board, safeguarding my eyes from meeting those of any terrified children. *Especially Sonandia.*

"I'm thinking about not being your teacher anymore," I said gravely. Several stunned gasps escaped from the mute gallery. I righted Tayshaun's slammed desk and sat on it, feeling weary and spent. "None of you deserve to experience fourth grade like this." A long silence passed. The quiet made it feel like a different room, and even though I had unforgivably just lost all composure in front of ten-year-olds, I briefly relished holding the uncontested floor of 4-217. If only everything could be different.

"Class is dismissed. Groups one, two, and six, get your coats."

They lined up solemnly, and we marched into the hall. As we passed Mr. Tejera's room, site of the infamous face-grabbing, Wilson stuck his head out of the door. "Brown! What are you doing, man?"

"Dismissing."

"It's only twenty to. We've got eighteen, twenty minutes till dismissal."

"I'm doing it now."

"Don't do it. Seriously. They'll call you on the carpet for that. It's a big mistake, man." Mr. Tejera turned back to his own class. The halted line looked to me for direction.

"About-face, 4-217. We're going back."

Everyone milled around for fifteen funereal minutes. I collected Bernard from Mr. Randazzo's office. Destiny handed me an illustrated card that read:

Dear Mr. Brown,

We dont mean to make you yell like that we are sorry we dont mean to. We are sorry. Love, Destiny and Tiffany

Daniel gave me a paper that said:

Mr Brown I no how you feel Dot feel sad I feel sad tow Bot otdr techrs have towo com. wen I see you I feal like god Bless me The and.

"Thank you for these nice letters," I deadpanned.

"You're welcome," the three writers said in unison.

"Everybody get in line."

I finally sent them scattering on 187th Street and stomped back upstairs to assess the damage. The good news was that the blackboard was broken away and gone only in the top left corner of the center segment of the three conjoined boards. The empty area was off-center enough that I could move my "Mr. Brown's Words and Phrases" poster over it, obscuring the mess completely, save for a few skinny spider-cracks, and still have my main board space free.

I sat down in the Teacher Center and breathed for a few minutes, holding a brown paper towel to my cut knuckles, remembering our perfect score at morning lineup. I confessed everything to coach Marge Foley, who nodded in sympathy through the whole account.

"Do you know Mr. Rose?" she asked.

"Mr. Rose and I go way back. Summer school."

"He has a brother who used to teach here, one of the lower grades. He was a wonderful man, a really good teacher. But his class had some *monsters* that drove him crazy. One day he punched the glass window in the door and cut himself really badly. It was terrible. He doesn't teach anymore, but everyone remembers that."

Thursday meant Mercy College night class. This day refused to end. All eleven new Fellows at P.S. 85 were assigned to the same course section, which served to create a group therapy vent session, despite our facilitator and administrative trainee Charles's fierce intentness on limiting discussion to the course packet readings.

We were in haggard form. Everyone had a kid whose every move seemed to spell disruption and destruction. Trisha Pierson talked about Theo, my pronoun buddy from Mr. Rose's class in June, who was in his second year in first grade. Theo's eyes often rolled back in his head and he violently lashed out without warning. (In March, Theo was moved to special ed.) Corinne Abernathy had a second-grade boy named Devon who swatted at butterflies that were not there, and threw hysterical fits when he had to sit in his seat for extended amounts of time. (Devon was transferred to special ed in May and given a full-time personal paraprofessional.) Elizabeth Camaraza talked about Raymond Prince, who kicked a girl in the mouth as hard as he could. Tough Marnie Beck was already in special ed, so she had some really good ones. There was Michael, who had a penchant for slipping past "security" and out of school during prep periods to wander the streets. She also had Tenasia, who had burned her family's apartment to cinders last year and occasionally brought matches and lighters to school. And finally there was Lorenzo, who couldn't read and hated everyone, especially teachers and girls.

I kept mostly quiet. It was a grim night.

The next day I woke up on autopilot, brushed my teeth, and guzzled my new over-the-counter cocktail of two Sudafeds to battle a constant cold, a multivitamin horse pill, extra-strength Tylenol, my newly acquired hair-loss med, and three echinaceas, washing them down with Dayquil. I walked to the bodega, picked up a butter roll, an orange Vitamin Water, a *New York Times,* and boarded the train.

The day passed in blurry streaks. Our morning do-now was "Why Today Is Going to Be Better Than Yesterday." I gave free reading time for a very long block.

Barbara Chatton, my assigned mentor, visited me at lunch. "You don't look well," she said. I shook my head slowly. "Do you want to talk?" I thought about it for a long pause.

"They're taking Sonandia out," I said.

"I know."

"I've heard some rumors, and I hope you can clarify them."

"Okay?" Barbara asked with pained eyes.

"Is it true that Casey Hibbard and at least one other cluster teacher saw my roster in August and refused to prep my class?"

"Yes."

"Is my class a dumping ground for the kids that no one else wanted?"

Barbara paused. "Yes —" She broke off, as if she had only said the first word of a longer thought.

"But what?"

"But it wasn't meant for you. It was for Adele Hafner. The Queen doesn't like her. But you asked for it." My blood went cold. "Without knowing you were asking for it, of course." Barbara softened. "It's unfortunate all around."

So this was not a black eye. It was a terminal internal hemorrhage.

This wasn't an unfortunate situation. It was an abusive relationship.

The worst class in the worst school in the worst neighborhood.

"You have what it takes to be a really good teacher. It's very rough that there are all these circumstances to contend with," she said, touching my shoulder.

I nodded in a daze, aware that my last two months had just been aptly summarized in two sentences. Then as a coda, she added, "It's never as good as you think it is, and it's never as bad as you think it is."

Besides sighing, there are few ways to respond to that elastic maxim. I imagined that carrying on without Sonandia there to learn would be like trying to play a violin with your strings ripped out and replaced by rubber bands.

I watched ESPN in sweatpants all weekend, eating little except cereal. A friend, who knew a thing or two about the condition, said, "You're depressed." Greg told me I looked demented.

I wanted to get undepressed, but how? My class was a rotten hand dealt from a stacked deck. I had come at them with everything I could think of: praise, bribes, withholding rewards, elaborate systems, common sense. Four-two-seventeen was a mess. It wasn't even safe. Mr. Brown was going down. I called in sick on Monday, my fourth absence, now over the one-per-month allotment.

I sat alone in my cold apartment and felt my frustration sublimate into molten fury. How dare they hang me, or Adele Hafner, out to dry? I'm a young teacher, not the sacrificial lamb of Public School 85! I began to type with rage.

Dear Mrs. Boyd,

Teaching is hard. The fact that P.S. 85 is labeled an "extended hours" school feels like an ironic understatement. Since the first moment I began filling out my NYC Teaching Fellows application in

February as a senior at NYU Film, I resolved to dedicate myself fully to this challenging and rewarding profession. However, I am writing you this letter because I feel that certain formidable obstacles are preventing me from adequately doing my job. Fortunately, I do believe the obstacles are surmountable with some assistance.

The 4–217 class roster is an intimidating document. This list contains well-documented chronic discipline problem children Lakiya Ray, Deloris Barlow, Eric Ruiz, Asante Bell, and Tayshaun Jackson, as well as violence-prone Marvin Winslow, Bernard McCants, Hamisi Umar, Cwasey Bartrum, Manolo Ruiz, and transient nonreader Daniel Vasquez. Additionally, impulse-control-free Fausto Mason was in my class for the first four days of school. In 4–217, the task of teaching is put aside 90% of the time in the interest of Classroom Management.

Since September 8, I have been studying, implementing, and reinventing my classroom management systems. As a new teacher, I know it is common to struggle with classroom management the first year. I have received support and ideas from numerous colleagues, particularly Ms. Chatton, who helped arrange a day-long visit to Ms. Claxton's third-grade class. However, 4–217 is still in poor shape. We are the last class out of the cafeteria at the end of lunch period and a perpetual embarrassment while seen walking in the halls.

I have taken what I feel are drastic steps to curb students' acting out, but have discovered that their deep-seated disrespect and hostility are not directed so much at me but *upon each other.* This group is a violent mix day in and day out.

On Thursday November 6, I learned that Sonandia Azcona, my highest ELA-scoring and most well-behaved student, is to be transferred out of 4–217, because the volume of misbehavior in the class has excessively debilitated the learning environment. This was disappointing, but understandable news when looking at it from Sonandia's mother's perspective. 4–217 is simply not a good place to learn.

It has been my suspicion that as the sole rookie teacher in fourth-grade general education, I was inserted into a class overloaded with "difficult kids." This idea has been encouraged by several colleagues. Though nothing was ever said to me, I heard about two enrichment teachers who approached the administration prior to September 8 with refusals to teach my class. During a November 7 meeting with a faculty member with reliable sources, it was corroborated to me that 4-217 is in fact a consciously designed "dumping ground."

I feel no shame in disclosing that trying to teach and manage this "dumping ground" has brought on an accelerated physical, mental, and emotional deterioration in me. I've lost my appetite, developed insomnia, and have lost a personal relationship as a result of the job. Previously, I have tried to chalk most of this up to having signed on for a difficult profession. However, now that the administration has officially acknowledged that 4-217 is not a healthy learning environment (with the transferring of Sonandia), there must be some substantive help and change accompanying the move. Here are my ideas.

1. Give 4-217 a second teacher that I can collaborate well with, as Ms. Chatton and I have discussed. This will help immeasurably with management and planning, both of which are overwhelming me. Twenty-six of them are too many for just me.

2. Take Deloris Barlow, Lakiya Ray, and Eric Ruiz out of my class. The rest of the group is still very challenging without them, but those three in the same room are impossible for me to control simultaneously.

3. Take me out of 4-217 and make me an enrichment teacher.

My current despondence that has come with the news of the last week has impaired my ability to be the best teacher I can be. I believe this year can still be a positive educational experience for the students of 4-217. They deserve it. However, right now, I feel overwhelmed.

More than anything, I want to teach children in P.S. 85. The "objective" part of my résumé reads, "Teach and model accountable character and citizenship while maintaining high expectations for helping students to become stronger problem solvers and self-motivated learners." I still believe in and attempt to live by these words every day. However, I feel tightly handcuffed by my current situation.

Though I may be a new and young player in a longstanding educational establishment, the Great Expectations School, I think it would be unfortunate for a young, dedicated, energetic yet inexperienced teacher to be left to twist in the wind. I can't twist that much longer.
Sincerely,

Dan Brown
4-217

cc: Mr. Randazzo
Ms. Guiterrez
Mrs. Chatton

I e-mailed a condensed version to Barbara to give her the heads-up that I would be coming in blazing.

Before lineup Tuesday morning, I stood in the office holding the signed letters and staring at the narrow mail cubbies. One, two, three, four. I methodically slid the papers into the boxes, oddly aware that while this paper could spell the end of my brief teaching career, my head was clear and my pulse was normal.

I peeled out of the office toward 217 and ran into Barbara, who wore a doleful look. "Dan . . . how are you?"

I shrugged.

"I spoke to Kendra [Boyd]," Barbara said. "She wants to meet, the three of us, in her office during SFA. Did you give her the letter?"

"I just put it in her box."

"Take it out. She's going to help you, but . . . you have to let her think it's all her idea."

"Okay," I mumbled. "See you there." I turned back to the office and yanked out my letters.

Mrs. Boyd and Barbara sat at opposite ends of the meeting table. I was told to sit next to Mrs. Boyd. I held the folder containing my letter in my lap, noticing a ceramic bowl on the desk inscribed "Excuses."

"Mr. Brown, I am putting an official letter of warning in your permanent Department of Ed file. Do you know why I'm doing this?"

My clueless expression indicated I did not.

"You have taken four sick days." She consulted the paper in front of her. "October 3 and October 20 . . . November 3 and yesterday, November 10. This is a serious problem because all of those days are Mondays or Fridays, the two days of the week that teachers are *not* allowed to take off. Monday is our important Professional Development day, and we can't condone teachers skipping out on Fridays to make a weekend of it. Why have your actions demonstrated that you think it's okay to do that?"

This was not the way I had hoped to start this help-me-or-I'm-out ultimatum meeting.

"Do you think it is okay to proceed as such?" she pressed.

"I was too sick to come to school those days. I was not making a weekend of it."

"Can you produce documentation from a doctor?"

"No. I didn't see a doctor."

Barbara winced. Mrs. Boyd leaned back in her chair triumphantly.

"It's not easy being a teacher, Mr. Brown. Sometimes it takes a little toughness."

I ground my teeth in silence. You wouldn't last ten minutes in 4-217, I thought. You know it, and that's the reason you've never come to my classroom to meet my students. Then I checked myself; showing anger or offense would be a death sentence.

"I know you're having problems. Why don't you tell me what's going on."

I swallowed. "The good news is that with practice, I am now feeling more confident in planning out my units and lessons. Also . . ."

"Can I see your planbook?"

"Right now?"

"Yes. Let's be real here. Let's see what we're talking about. You say you're improving, but as we say, 'Fail to plan, plan to fail.'"

I excused myself and picked up the planbook from 217. When I returned, Mrs. Boyd and Barbara abruptly stopped their conversation.

The principal leafed through the ragged spiral-bound box-planner. She made a face of tepid acceptance, as if she had just ordered some expensive platter that tasted lousy but had to be eaten because it was already paid for. "I see that there is some evidence of an attempt at planning," she said. "Continue with what you were saying."

"My problems are rooted in classroom management. I've tried and adopted many different approaches, but all of them have yielded only the most ephemeral success." I had learned in high school that using the word "ephemeral" can impress people and alter the conversation dynamic.

"Ephemeral," she said, taking the bait. "That's a good vocabulary word. I hired you personally because you're a smart young man. Because, as I've told you before, you have the teaching gene." With a smile, she digressed into a tangent about her early years as a teacher, holding unofficial classes during a strike in the early seventies. When the story was over, it was time to cut to the chase.

"Mrs. Boyd, I have a few specific kids that are severely weighing me down in my ability to work with the whole group. Deloris Barlow and Lakiya Ray alone can —"

"When students misbehave, it is because we, as their adult guardians, have enabled them to misbehave. Do not blame the kids for your shortcomings, Mr. Brown. They are just children."

That was it, I thought. The end. *Fin*. I wanted to whip out the letter so at least I could read her the snappy ending. What a lousy way to bow out: ingested alive while getting berated by spectators.

"I'm going to help you," she said. "Ms. Chatton pleaded your case admirably and we've decided to give you one of the ATRs to support you with management. Ms. . . . "

"Richardson," Barbara finished. I knew Ms. Richardson: the tall Nigerian lady who covered my class the Monday after Halloween!

"I'm going to have Mr. Randazzo try to arrange it so you'll have her starting tomorrow."

"She should be with you at least till Christmas. Hopefully longer," Barbara added.

I exhaled, glad the letter never made an appearance. No matter how true my allegation about the conscious creation of a "dumping ground," Mrs. Boyd would have taken mortal offense at it. I would have burned the bridge for sure. I picked up my planbook from the table. "Thank you," I said.

Cordelia Richardson and I met in the Teacher Center during my prep period. She was elated with the arrangement; coteaching with me sounded infinitely better than her current setup of random K–5 substituting spots.

"You just worry about teaching, and I'll handle the management at first," she said. "We'll straighten them out together!"

The next morning, Ms. Richardson was waiting in room 217 when I ushered in the line. "Who that?" asked mystified Marvin Winslow.

"Why we got that mean sub here?" Lito demanded to know.

"Silence and I'll explain everything. Eddie, Joseph, Tayshaun. I'm about to speak. Thank you. Today, 4-217 is the luckiest class in the school. From now on, you have two teachers, Ms. Richardson and me. We're running the show together. Stop moaning and groaning like kindergartners. Take out your homework so I can see it, and groups one and two use the closet."

As I began roving around the room to check homework, Ms. Richardson's voice resounded like an airhorn. *Take off that jacket! No jackets in school!*

Tiffany looked confused and terrified. I had always let her wear her hooded sweatshirt in class as long as the hood stayed off. All of the kids knew I wore a gray hoodie over my shirt and tie instead of a regular autumn jacket.

"Get rid of it now!"

Tiffany looked to me. "Do it, Tiffany," I commanded.

"Sit up straight in your chair, Tiffany!" Ms. Richardson boomed. *"You're still slouching. No slouching in school, Tiffany! SIT UP STRAIGHT!"*

Tiffany straightened her posture and sniffled, staring at her desk. Nobody moved.

"School is not fooling-around time. That's over!" Richardson was a powerhouse.

The next two days contained my smoothest lessons of the year. Even Eddie participated; he was really getting multiplication. When Deloris called Lakiya a "crack ho," Ms. Richardson immediately took them both out of the room, and I kept rolling along with math.

Ms. Richardson's privately shared criticism was constructive and actionable. "Your homework-checking system creates a lag and you need to be on them *every* second. I can introduce a new system tomorrow, and if you like it, you can keep it." Her system involved leaving a numbered folder on each group before the day began. As students enter, they insert their homework in the folder. I would collect the folders and find a few minutes during independent work time to check the work. Ms. Richardson also recommended making a publicly displayed grid, charting completed and missed homework. This would foster healthy competition to get the most checks and give recognition to conscientious students.

She was right on both counts. Once my "Homework All Stars" chart went up, homework completion went up over twenty percent, and I had more control in the tone-setting mornings.

Thursday, November 13, was Report Card Day. Classes were dismissed at 11:30 and walk-in parent-teacher conferences were slated for 1:00–3:00 and 5:00–7:30. No report cards went home unless they were directly handed to a parent or guardian. Ms. Richardson stayed by my side through the first afternoon session.

Grades were given in the same one-to-four rubric as the state standardized Tests.

1 = far below grade-level standards
2 = approaches grade-level standards
3 = meets grade-level standards
4 = exceeds grade-level standards

Ones failed; everything else passed. Teachers were discouraged from giving threes and flat-out restricted from fours in the first marking period. Mr. Randazzo told us this was so the report cards would show improvement over the year.

Lakiya, Deloris, Marvin, Daniel, and Eric got nearly straight ones. Everyone else hovered around twos except Sonandia, who got straight threes. Her mother was first to arrive for a conference.

Our meeting was short and sad. I said I understood why she had asked to transfer Sonandia and that Karen Adler was a wonderful teacher. I extolled Sonandia's virtues, recommended more nonfiction reading at home, and said I would miss her daughter. We shook hands and parted. Good-bye, Sony.

A line of parents and families formed outside my door, waiting to see Mr. Brown. It was a reality check as to how many people had a stake in the embattled 4-217 experience.

Lito Ruiz brought an entourage of his Spanish-speaking grandmother, his twenty-year-old sister who acted as translator, her boyfriend, another young man whose relation was not explained, and an infant who reeked of an unchanged diaper. We all lamented the September glasses-breaking incident, but Lito's smile lit up the room when I showed his grandmother his small stack of successfully completed "A+" work. Maimouna's father came in, eyes bloodshot and smelling thickly of marijuana. The whole time I talked to him, I could not shake the memory of Maimouna writing about how she gets whipped. Lakiya Ray's calm mother assured me Lakiya would complete her work, as long as the boys stopped harassing her. When I explained that Lakiya was hardly a victim of harassment during class time — quite the contrary — Mrs. Ray very clearly tuned out. Cwasey's mother and stepfather looked truly stunned when I told them about Cwasey's propensity and lack of remorse for hitting girls. They told me it would *never* happen again, but I recalled his blue card had said, "Mother is supportive but her interventions seem to roll off his back." I discussed work samples with every parent. I talked about strengths, opportunities to become stronger, and how crucial it is to read together at home.

Deloris's mother came in reeling from savage reports from Deloris's Success for All teacher, Ms. Cole, Mr. Daly (regarding lunchroom behavior), and the gym teachers, with Deloris's younger sister Ladeisha and older sister Lakeisha's teachers still to visit. She began our meeting with a preemptive speech about how "some girl named Destiny" was always picking on Deloris, and how this intimidation was probably the reason for all of the ones on her report card. The tirade lasted several minutes.

I looked directly at her. "First of all, Deloris has not fully completed one assignment all year. Often, she doesn't even write her name on her paper. She has had a few arguments with Destiny, but now they are sitting in opposite corners of the room, and that has absolutely nothing to do with Deloris's grades being what they are. Deloris has an intelligent mind — she could probably be a great lawyer with her ability to argue — but she is not doing fourth-grade work and is blaming everyone else for it. The time to make excuses is over. The *only* way for Deloris to pass fourth grade is for her to take responsibility for her own schoolwork. That is it." I had never spoken so forcefully to someone I had just met.

My speech seemed to connect. By the end of the conference, Deloris said, "I promise I'm going to really do my work and try hard all the time."

Athena Page's mother (also named Athena Page), whom I knew

relatively well already, nodded vigorously when I talked about Athena's chattering at inappropriate times. Athena sat silently, nervous and fidgety.

Ms. Page told me, "Thank you for the good news about math, but you *will* see an improvement with the talking. Athena, tell Mr. Brown what punishment you're on."

"No TV."

"And?"

Athena's face fell. "No Christmas."

Eddie's and Tayshaun's parents were the only no-shows, giving 4-217 an excellent percentage of attendance. Karen and I dragged ourselves out at 8 p.m., cotton-mouthed from setting personal talking records. Progress was happening, though. I could feel it. And dammit, Athena Page was going to have Christmas.

The next morning I expected two things to happen, and neither did. First, I thought Mr. Randazzo would approach me at lineup to transfer Sonandia to Karen's class. He didn't, and Sony led the 4-217 line as usual. The second thing I counted on was to see Ms. Richardson in my classroom when I arrived with the group, but she wasn't there. Mr. Randazzo swung by at 8:30 and said, "Heyyy, Dan! Cordelia Richardson's out, back problems or something. Okay?"

Not okay, Mr. R. There was no way I could keep the strict-discipline momentum going by myself.

Surprisingly, the day went fine. Kids adapt quickly to some things, and they behaved as if Ms. Richardson were still in the room, save for a few minor scuffles and disruptive insults. My spirits were also buoyed by having a bonus day with Sonandia, and simply that it was Friday, day of anticipatory, limitless tolerance.

Walking down the hall for dismissal, Sonandia wrapped her hand in mine and said, "Mr. Brown, will you please be my daddy?"

"I'm your teacher, Sonandia." And not for much longer.

"Please be my daddy!"

★　　★　　★

I felt lonely all weekend, even though I was surrounded by friends. I couldn't explain what I was feeling and didn't bother to try. My parents encouraged me to resign to salvage my health. Twice I dialed several digits of Jess's phone number before hanging up. I talked to Karen for a long time on Sunday night.

Monday morning, Sonandia was in my line, and, thankfully, Ms. Richardson was in my room. She said she had back problems and might soon need an operation. With her around, the week sped by swiftly. We neared our big multiplication test. Half of the class understood the concepts and knew the times tables inside out. The other half might as well have been playing their Game Boys during all of our lessons.

Sonandia stayed in my class every day, and no one said anything. On Friday, November 21, the other shoe dropped.

Ms. Richardson was absent, and I got word that she was undergoing back surgery. She would never coteach with me again. I had hoped for a collaborator for the rest of the year, or until Christmas at the bare minimum, but I wound up with one for just six school days. When I announced that Ms. Richardson was gone, the class reacted with genuine groans of disappointment. Their sadness took me by surprise; I thought they hated her for her ultratight discipline. In six days, they had gotten attached.

I was eating lunch in 217 when Jennifer jogged in. "Mr. Brown, they need you in the lunchroom right now. You have to come down!"

The scene in the cafeteria was not what I expected. Sonandia had separated herself from the class and was sitting by the window, her face buried in her arms on the table. She was crying hard. Sonandia *never* cried in front of the class. Her pals, Gladys Viña and Julissa, patted her on the back.

"Sonandia, what's wrong?" I asked frantically.

She shook her head, not looking up.

"She's upset," Gladys V. explained.

"Tell me what happened," I said to the support crew.

Sonandia lifted her head. "I don't want to make the change. Please. I don't want to make the change."

My pulse quickened. *She hadn't known about the transfer.* Or had she? I thought she did. What was going on?

"It's all right, Sony. I'm going to miss you too. But Ms. Adler's a great teacher and I'm going to check in on you all the time."

Olga, Sonandia's mother, left her post between the two lunch-rooms and relieved Julissa and Gladys V. of back-patting duty. Sonandia continued crying. "I don't want to leave Mr. Brown. Please!" She and her mother spoke in Spanish, and Sonandia cried harder.

Everything happened quickly. I dashed to Mr. Randazzo, who was supervising the fifth-grade cafeteria.

"Dan, what's up? You okay?"

"Mr. Randazzo, I know I'm a new teacher and I've been knocked around a bit. But I'm on my feet now, and the class is really improving . . ."

"I know. I'm hearing the screaming through the wall less and less."

"I know that both of us were kept out of the loop in the decision to move Sonandia. Her work has been excellent with me, though, and she's improving . . ."

"I just told her she was going to Karen in the afternoon."

"I know. But she doesn't want to move. She's crying her eyes out right now."

"What?"

"Can we give this some more time? I want some more time. A couple weeks."

"Let's go see what this is all about."

Mr. Randazzo and I walked to Sonandia and her mother, making an impromptu summit of the four key players in this crisis. Randazzo said, "Ms. Tavarez, if Sonandia doesn't want to make the switch, going to the new class could actually *hurt* her. She's not going to do her best work if she's unhappy." Sonandia nodded in concurrence. "Maybe we should let her stay with Mr. Brown if that's what she wants."

Ms. Tavarez, put on the spot, pursed her lips. "Okay," she said.

I wanted to burst into a wild touchdown dance, but I kept a straight face and nodded slightly and gratefully. Sonandia's reaction surprised me. Her tears stopped, but she said nothing and stared blankly ahead. Then she put her head down again. I think she was ticked at all of us for putting her through this.

On the D train home, tears trickled from me for the first time since I became a teacher. What a turnaround! My emotional swell soon gave way to a heartening realization. I no longer needed lofty aphorisms to propel me. My concrete reason to stick with it was gloriously clarified. Every day from here on I owed to Sonandia for standing up for me, for wanting me to be her teacher. She brought me back.

As of Monday, the SFA cycle was over, which meant Fran Baker and my ninety-minute midmorning respite from 4–217 were temporarily gone, and I would miss them terribly. Now I had to plan for three-and-a-half- and four-and-a-half-hour blocks and I wasn't used to it.

My Success for All group had produced some bright moments. On the last day, Kelsie Williams attempted (with moderate success) to recite Robert Frost's "Fire and Ice," which I had read and photocopied for them. When Mrs. Baker and I made a big fuss over Kelsie's performance, she timidly asked if she could read a poem that she wrote. Of course, Kelsie! She read a Halloween poem that I was sure she had composed as an assignment from her homeroom teacher, but our group showered her with applause, motivating other kids to write their own poems. I told the kids that I would always read and give performance time for any poems they would ever write in school or out, whether I was still their teacher or not. This led to several poets sporadically swinging by 217 throughout the year.

On Tuesday afternoon, a bubbly Ms. Richardson waltzed into my room, ostensibly free of crippling back pain, igniting a sea of cheers. "I've got a great new position down in East Harlem," she said, smiling. I was surprised and confused, but it was good to see Ms. Richardson one last time to let her know how much I appreciated her help.

At 3 p.m. on Wednesday, the day before Thanksgiving, P.S. 85 breathed a massive gasp of relief. I booked it to Port Authority to catch a Greyhound home for the holiday weekend. I fell asleep as the bus inched down the traffic-swamped Jersey Turnpike, thankful for a nine-year-old Dominican girl in the Bronx.

December

Courage Bear

NEW YORK CITY CAN GET VERY COLD very fast. Thanksgiving weekend had whizzed by, with my teaching stories being the star attraction at the big family dinner. No one could believe the insanity in P.S. 85. I raked leaves and watched football with my dad, had long talks with my mom, and snuggled with our little Chihuahua-Pekingese, Mac. But in a blink, I was back in 4-217.

"If I am planning a trip from California to Idaho, which country's map should I use?" I asked. Several kids consulted their individual maps, but no hands went up. I called on random students, who shrugged blankly. I held up my placemat-sized North America map and pointed crazily at California and Idaho. "What country am I looking at?" Still nothing. "Sonandia, help me out." Sonandia didn't know. "It's the U.S.A.!" I boomed. "It's our country!"

A few reluctant nods happened around the room. I pointed more. "If I travel from Texas to Louisiana, what *country* am I in? Julissa?" Julissa looked down at her worksheet.

"It's not on your paper. Just look and listen." I pointed at Dallas and traced my way to New Orleans. "What *country* am I pointing at?

"The U.S.A.!" I exclaimed. "Who knows what U.S.A. stands for?" No reaction. I wrote "*United States of America*" on the board. "How many states are in the U.S.A.?"

"Fifty!" two dozen kids chimed in unison.

"Correct. Can anyone tell me which one of those fifty states we are in right now?"

Silence. Jennifer and Sonandia slowly raised their hands. I called on Jennifer. "Is it New York?"

"Yes! We are in New York State, and we're also in New York City, which has how many boroughs?"

"Five!"

"And which one are we in?"

"The Bronx!"

"Good. Back to the whole country, *all* of this area is the U.S.A. See? These are the fifty states making up one big country, the United States of America, with one president. So look at my finger. If I drive from here, Florida, to here, Georgia, what country am I in?"

No answer. "The U.S.A.!" I exploded. "This is all the U.S.A.! This is what our country looks like on a map. U.S.A.! If I travel from Florida to Georgia, what *country* am I in?"

"U.S.A."

"Yes. If I travel from Wyoming to Colorado, what country am I in?"

"U.S.A."

"From Virginia to North Carolina, what country?"

"U.S.A."

"Now look *very* closely. If I travel from here, Rosarita, to right here, *Mexico City,* what *country* am I in? Look carefully."

"U.S.A.," the class chanted.

I wanted to chalk up the scene to the post-holiday morning sleepies, but I couldn't. How could none of them know these things? I found out that the third-grade social studies curriculum is "World Cultures," focusing on foreign continents. Second and first grades, depending on the teacher, often gloss over social studies in the interest of a math and literacy fundamental skills blitz. Without substantive discussion about civics at home, these inner-city kids had never learned their country, state, or, as I soon discovered, what planet they lived on.

I believed that knowing one's planet of origin was prerequisite to most other fourth-grade tasks. We had to get back to basics. As a class, we made a large poster titled "Where Am I?" and mounted it on the door.

On Wednesday, I led my students to the third-floor computer lab for our second-to-last session. First-year Fellow and Menzel underling David de la O cracked the door open. "Ms. Menzel's out today. I'm real sorry."

My students heard him and looked distressed. "That's fine," I said. "I'll run the class."

"I don't know, I don't think Ms. Menzel would like that. This is my lunch period, so I don't know if I can —"

"David, I'm an expert. I'll run the class. It's okay. We're going in."

He nodded tentatively and I sent my kids in. To cheers, I proclaimed, "We're going on the Internet!" I directed them to a youth search engine, and from there, instructed them to look up some ideas from our Drugs & Alcohol unit.

The kids discovered a bunch of excellent educational sites, complete with full-color gross-out photos of cirrhosis-ravaged livers and emphysema-addled lungs. At the end of the period, Jennifer told me she used to think computers were boring, but now she was going to ask her mom to teach her how to use them.

My attempts to get help for Marvin Winslow met brick walls. The tutors who pulled out six of my students for a daily fifty-minute session would not take him because his skills were too low. Marge Foley sat and read with him for twenty minutes here and there when her erratic schedule allowed. Because of the unwritten rule explained by Dr. Kirkpatrick at the September meeting, I could not refer him for full-time special ed.

In the parking lot, Marvin's mother assured me that every night she told Marvin he was "the little train that could," and whenever he feels he can't do something, he just needs to try harder. I responded that it was lack of fundamental skills, not lack of effort, that was keeping Marvin down, fueling his low self-esteem and violent outbursts. I told her to read with him at home. She grimaced.

"I'm trying, but it's hard, Mr. Brown. I got four other kids and no husband, no job, and we're all staying with my mother. You understand?"

Some things were turning around. Although Bernard had begun the year fistfighting every day or two, he showed significant progress. With some stern words from his parents and my positive phone calls home and wild fits of praise for his self-control, he had not fought since the mid-November conferences.

Kids began understanding division and loving it. We learned long division through the traditional "DIVIDE MULTIPLY SUBTRACT BRING DOWN" method. I showed them the mnemonic DMSB = "Dear Mrs. Sally Barbour" that I learned from my magnificent third-grade teacher, Mrs. Barbour, back in Johnson Elementary. That nugget from my background lodged in their memory banks and prompted a renewed assault of personal questions for me to duck.

At dismissal on December 10, Hamisi told me, "Mr. Brown, the class changed. We were bad and now we're good!"

"Yes, I'm very proud of all of you. It's more fun this way, isn't it?" Everybody smiled, but I was skeptical of Hamisi's assessment. Just a day earlier, I had dealt him a lunch detention for sneaking Fritos and cursing and throwing the bag when I called him on it.

Four-two-seventeen was a giant ocean liner, with changes in course difficult to feel or measure. My energy high from retaining Sonandia, from keeping my head above water, had quickly dissipated in the daily grind. That ordeal had made me feel tempest-tossed, treading waves overboard, thrashing wildly for a life preserver. Now I was rescued from the violent drowning, but I still had a long way to go.

Elizabeth Camaraza was at the end of her rope with her third-graders. "They are *so* petty," she said. "I need Christmas or pills and neither is coming fast enough."

Trisha Pierson looked pale and shattered every time I saw her. First grade was no picnic. "Theo will be the death of me," she said. "I will be a dead person. I won't be alive. I need to get back in a real grad school."

Cat Samuels projectile-vomited into the second-floor faculty toilet after a full-day coverage job with Evan Krieg's fifth-graders. I went into Krieg's class during my prep to babysit the class crazies, but that wasn't close to enough to salvage her relentlessly chaotic seven hours.

Not counting computer man David de la O, Marnie Beck was the only first-year Fellow who resembled herself from pre–September 8. This was amazing, since she took her lumps as hard as anybody, working special ed down in the sequestered basement. She stoically told me, "Right now, it's all about maintaining. Just maintain till the holidays. Then it's a new year."

Eddie Rollins won a districtwide art contest. Ava Kreps, a lower-grade art teacher, had pulled Eddie out of 217 almost daily through-out the fall to work on a gigantic holiday-themed collage, which now earned him a day trip to the borough president's office for a photo opportunity and cake. He came to school on the day of the celebration wearing a dirt-splotched dress shirt, with a striped rayon necktie in his hand. He and Mrs. Kreps didn't leave for the borough president's building until 10 a.m., so Eddie sat silently at his desk, embarrassed at his unhip clothes. Three years older than his class-mates, he found his physical maturity already a scarlet letter to bear; having to wear this square outfit was more of a punishment than a reward.

When the kids shuffled out of the room for SFA, I stopped Ed-die on his way to the door. The tie was now draped around his neck. "Let me help you with that," I said, tying him a smart Windsor knot.

"Oh my God, that's adorable! I need to get a picture of that!" Marge Foley enthused, spotting us while passing in the hall.

The photo of Eddie and me was enlarged and mounted near the

office, where every fourth-grade class walks on its way to lunch. The next week, I heard Dennis say in the line, "Eddie, you look good with Mr. Brown. He's tying your tie!"

"Mr. Brown's the man," Eddie replied.

I positively hadn't been "the man" according to Eddie before that picture existed. After its display, his somnambulistic demeanor changed, and he became one of my most engaged, trusted "teammates."

December 11 looked like it could be the first Thursday to pass without any major incidents. My newly invented "Twenty-Five-Second Challenge" proved an immensely effective vehicle for expediently moving the kids from their seats to the line. I told them my secret tabulation of successful Twenty-Five-Second Challenges would determine whether we would have a holiday party. For the dismissal line, I ticked down the seconds aloud in slow motion. The girls' line was perfect. Even Lakiya stood shoulders straight, looking dead ahead, amused by the swift uniformity. The boys looked good except for Marvin and Tayshaun, giggling about eight feet off the line.

"Five . . . four . . . three . . ."

"Get in line, yo!"

"Come on, get in line!"

Athena's voice towered over the other pleading hisses. "Tay-shaun!"

Tayshaun wheeled suddenly and flew at her. "Shut yo' mouth, bitch!" he shouted, clearly imitating something he had seen, and landed a sharp slap to the face. Athena burst into tears instantly, crouching down and holding her cheeks.

"Tayshaun!" I drove him against the chalkboard, my head suddenly light with rage.

Happening past in the hall, Linda Devereaux, stormy keeper of the Alternative Education Strategies in-school suspension room, caught the gist immediately. Tayshaun was one of her regular customers. "YOU LITTLE PUNK! YOU THINK THIS SCHOOL

WILL TOLERATE YOUR DISGUSTINGNESS? LOOK AT ME! YOU'LL BE WITH ME ALL DAY TOMORROW AND EVERY DAY UNTIL YOU STRAIGHTEN OUT YOUR ACT!"

Tayshaun looked past her and laughed. Ms. Devereaux laughed right back with pure fury. "YOU'RE GOING TO WISH YOU NEVER DID THAT. I'll get him at lineup tomorrow."

Athena's face was not bruised. I told her mother, Ms. Page, the whole story in the parking lot five minutes later. She shook her head, more sad than angry. "I feel bad for that boy. He probably has no parents to teach him right from wrong. It's a shame these kids aren't safe in their own school."

Tayshaun was not in the morning line the next day. Or the next week. He cut school six days in a row. On Monday, Eddie told me he had seen Tayshaun from a distance that morning. He said, "T-Dog called over to me to go with him, but I didn't. I need to be in school." I dialed Tayshaun's mother, but the number was now disconnected. I told the office I had a truant student wandering the streets. School security said they would send someone to check it out.

Meanwhile, problems with Deloris hurtled out of control. She told me the woman who came to our parent-teacher conference was not her mother and that she was not allowed to see that woman ever again. Deloris and Lakiya locked horns over nothing substantial as far as I could tell, but neither would let the other alone. "She bothering me!" both yelled several times a day, instigating denials, arguments, and fights. At lunch, Deloris threatened Destiny that the older Barlow sisters would follow Destiny home and jump her. I got so sick of Deloris's terrorizing ways that the sound of her voice repelled me.

On Tuesday, December 16, while I was at the weekly fourth-grade meeting during my prep period, the class went ape on mild-mannered Ms. Samuels. She deducted all kinds of group points and scribbled numerous disturbers of the peace on the Detention List, but they would not settle. When I returned, Cat looked ready to walk out of the Great Expectations School and never look back.

Later, I brought out the coveted Tarheel-blue Economy Candy

bag, full of treats from the famous Lower East Side junk food outlet. I had bought twelve two-dollar Spider-Man chocolate bars to reward my consistent Homework All-Stars, but now the bag felt light. Four bars were missing. The class immediately caught my consternation.

"It was Deloris! She was in your desk when Ms. Samuels was here!"

"I saw her! It was Deloris!"

"Deloris was beasting!"

Deloris exhibited shock at her accusers. "I didn't do nothing!"

Everyone started yelling that Deloris was guilty. I silenced them. Maimouna raised her hand. "Deloris was eating them at lunch. She asked me if I wanted a piece, but I said no."

"You lie, bitch!"

I sent Maimouna, along with the first two accusers, Bernard and Joseph, to Mr. Randazzo's office. Randazzo was usually willing to play detective and judge for a kangaroo court, and students often left his office puzzled but satisfied over his attention to the matter. However, this time I had lowballed the kids' passion for proving Deloris's guilt. Half of the class rushed out in the hall, anxious to contribute testimony against her. A small melee erupted outside Mr. Randazzo's door. He looked at me as if to say, "What the hell is this?" I ushered my students back into 217 and stared longingly at the clock. Deloris upended her desk, claiming innocence. Marvin Winslow was the only one who did not come out against her.

Deloris had crossed a new line by stealing from me. This violation of my belongings struck me like a personal affront. It nauseated me to picture her opening my desk drawer and riffling through my papers until finding the chocolate, then gleefully showing off her plunder and offering Maimouna a taste.

I left school disgusted and went shopping for my Secret Santa recipient, math coach Al Conway. Chocolates, a classic rock mix CD, and VHS copies of *The Dirty Dozen* and *Rio Bravo* would have to suffice.

A minute after midnight on Wednesday, December 17, the third and final *Lord of the Rings* movie was loosed upon the world. I was a bona fide Rings fanatic and *Return of the King* had always been my favorite book of the trilogy. Samwise Gamgee was my hero. Six friends were catching the first screening, and there was no way I was going to miss it.

I stumbled out of Middle Earth at a quarter to four and reached my apartment at 4:12 a.m., sixty-three minutes shy of my alarm beep. I couldn't even sleep, though, still charged up from the movie's perilous adventures. I knew I would crash at some terrible point in the coming school day, but I didn't worry about it.

Mr. Randazzo greeted me in the office with miraculous news. "I'm taking Deloris out of your class permanently, starting today. You're beginning to pick things up and she's brutal." I silently exulted. Then came the rub. "I'm going to throw her in with 4-111."

Karen's room.

No, I thought. No, no, no. Karen's class is going well. She has her three musketeers (Dequan, Dontrell, and Arthur) relatively contained and a healthy community dynamic. She plays games and holds "Class Council" meetings that could never happen in my room.

Should I stand by for the destruction of Karen's hard-earned positive classroom culture to lighten the burden on myself? I thought about telling Mr. Randazzo to forget about it, and, while he was in the class-switching mood, to send me back Fausto. I could see Pat Cartwright struggling every day. Someone had to teach the sacrificial crazy class. Mr. Spock said, "The needs of the many outweigh the needs of the few," and he was always right, or at least logical. Then I thought about Sonandia, Jennifer, Athena, Evley, and Destiny, and said nothing.

"Dan, you okay?"

I nodded and went to my room. Karen came by fifteen minutes later. She had already gotten the news. "Deloris's behavior is *terrible*," I said. "Do *anything* you can to get Randazzo to put her in another room."

"There's nowhere else for her. Fiore would bitch and moan till she got her way. Mulvehill just got two new kids yesterday, and Cartwright's class is already horrendous. It's all right."

"No. I'll hang on to her," I said.

"No. We'll try it out. I'll take her till winter break, and we'll see how it goes. It's okay, trust me." She said the words, but I don't know if she believed them.

Karen saved my life. With Deloris out, the new 4-217 was a comparative dream. I was able to spread Lakiya, Marvin, Eric, and Bernard to the four corners of the room. Tayshaun was still out of school roaming the streets.

At lunch, Karen said Deloris was silent and polite all morning. "It could just be a honeymoon period, but at least I know she's capable of doing work and being quiet. I sat her far away from Dequan. They seem to be okay with each other." We both knew Dequan and Deloris had started their third-grade year in Ms. Claxton's class, but got separated when Dequan brought a knife to school to, in his words, "stab her in the titty."

In the afternoon, I was leading a review of division with remainders when a distinct fart ripped across 217. "What the hell was that?" Bernard shouted.

"Hey!" I countered. "Watch your language." My voice tripped, and I laughed. In a moment, I recovered my straight face. Gigantic smiles instantly swept the room.

"That's nasty, Athena," Lakiya mumbled, loud enough for everyone to hear.

I moved to defuse the issue. "Relax, Dr. Ray. It is a perfectly natural —"

WHAM! A second, exponentially more powerful encore thundered out of Athena Page's group two. She pressed her palms to her temples, elbows on the desk, with a tiny smile of guilty amusement on her face.

"You crazy, Athena!" Lakiya screeched.

I couldn't help it. I laughed. Then I couldn't stop. I had one of my dad's signature hysterical fits. Tears trickled down my face. The whole class burst into weird laughter.

"Mr. Brown taking the laughing gas!"

"Mr. Brown gone crazy!"

When the dust settled, it was dismissal time. I was working on no sleep and no over-the-counter meds, but the mix of no Deloris and some maniacal laughter felt better than just about anything else all year. I went home and fell into bed.

Marvin's mother had said in October that he was blind in one eye and that was the reason for his deficient reading skills, but that she could not get him glasses because she was unemployed. I told Ms. Guiterrez about the situation, and she immediately arranged a conference and submitted paperwork to get Marvin state-subsidized eyeglasses. My early encounters with Guiterrez were strange and disconcerting, but when it came to dealing with parents, she was an effective human tornado.

At lineup on Thursday, December 18, Marvin tugged on my sleeve. He looked terrified. "Mr. Brown, I got glasses," he whispered, his right hand fingering the new soft case in his jacket pocket.

"That's great news! Let me see them!" He shook his head. "Okay, you'll show me when we get to class. I'm sure they look very sharp. I need to get glasses myself," I said, putting my hand on his shoulder. He smiled.

At the beginning of the math lesson, Marvin silently slipped on his new glasses. For a moment, he did not look like a lost little boy.

"Marvin has four eyes," Julissa said.

"*Julissa!* Marvin looks extremely good right now and can see sharper than any of you! I'm jealous of how well he can see and I want to get glasses for myself. Group two loses three points for that rude, mean comment!"

It was too late. Marvin had already buried his face in his folded arms, sobbing. His new glasses were on the floor under his sneaker. I picked them up; they were destroyed.

Edith Boswell and Cheryl Berkowitz had invented the Performing Arts Class program as a fourth- and fifth-grade honors class with some music and drama added in. Both sections (thirty-plus students each) were housed in the same extra-large classroom, separated only by a bookcase. The main event on the PAC calendar was the Holiday Show, a seventy-five-minute singing and dancing extravaganza.

My kids looked forward to the latest annual "2B Production" with fervent anticipation. Aside from Mr. Randazzo's monthly announcements of the lineup rubric winners, they had no assemblies and certainly no music.

Four-two-seventeen sat in the back. I couldn't decipher much of the action since the actors worked without microphones, but Santa was in trouble and Harry Potter, Spongebob Squarepants, and Beyoncé Knowles were contestants on some kind of game show that could get him out of his scrape. Sonandia whispered to me that this seemed like the same show as last year. After a half hour, my kids started to writhe. Eric Ruiz got shushed nine times. The performance closed with a rousing singalong to "Crazy in Love." Standing by the rear doors, Boswell and Berkowitz radiated embarrassment at their creation.

A man named Professor Darling came to P.S. 85 on Fridays. I had heard things about him: he taught painting at Barnard, he was a close friend of Mrs. Boyd, he did brilliant art lessons. Occasionally I saw him in the hall with his broad leather portfolio.

On Friday, December 19, I asked Mr. Randazzo if Professor Darling could come to 4-217 that day. Randazzo threw me a look that I read as, "How do *you* know about Professor Darling?" He said skeptically, "Do you think they can really handle it?"

"Yes. I think they need it."

Mr. Randazzo paused, thinking. "All right, you got it. Ten-thirty to twelve."

Professor Darling had a soft voice and short, curly hair. The kids watched enthralled as he pulled out large photographs of the Empire State Building, the Sears Tower, and the Chrysler Building, which I taped to the board. The professor wrote "SKYSCRAPERS" in large block capitals.

With a blank sheet of oversized drawing paper, Professor Darling illustrated the fundamental elements of a skyscraper from the broad base to the top spires. He passed out notebook-sized sheets and walked the students through drawing their own skyscrapers, step by step. They had never done anything like this before.

After about forty minutes of steady instruction, the professor handed out oversized sheets, like his, for each student to create an imaginary cityscape. Eddie Rollins drew a brilliantly inventive sky-line, complete with the Twin Towers, in three-dimensional perspec-tive. Lakiya showed some drawing talent as well. I was sad that Tayshaun, my mad sketch artist, missed it.

I decided to be extra-lenient on enforcing the stay-in-your-seat rule because the kids were so excited to show and talk about each other's creations. At the end, Professor Darling wanted to read Langston Hughes's short poem "City." I wrangled everyone back to their seats, but they wouldn't stop talking. They had just had their most exciting classroom experience of the year and it was Friday lunchtime, less than a week before Christmas.

Professor Darling had to wait much longer than he wanted to get through the poem, and when he finally read the words, he hur-ried through it, still without the undivided attention of the full group. Several times he said, "If you can't settle down, I won't be able to come back to this class for another lesson." When the poem was over, he picked up his portfolio and sadly shuffled to the door with-out saying good-bye. I chased him outside.

"Professor Darling," I said. He turned. "That was really a great lesson. I know the kids really appreciate it." He made a kind of grimace and nodded. I could tell he was disappointed about the poem. "There are some very disturbed kids in this class. It's a really tough class. But this meant a lot to them, and it would be really great if you came back."

I extended my hand. He shook it. But never came back.

Tayshaun Jackson reappeared at morning lineup on Monday, December 22. During my prep, I brought him out to the Teacher Center, where he stared at the table. "I like you, Tayshaun," I said. "I want good things to happen to you and for you to be happy." He looked up. "But I can't help you when you skip school six days in a row." He looked down again. "You hit Athena and that's unacceptable. You have to face what you did. No more running away. You have to act like a man."

I made an awful decision saying that last sentence. I had hoped to curry some kind of macho favor, but instead I probably invoked angry memories of an abusive father who ran away from the family. Plus, the kind of gender stereotyping in phrases like "act like a man" was the opposite of the ideas I wanted to present to my students. Tayshaun scowled.

"This afternoon I am going to announce that we're having a class holiday party tomorrow afternoon. At lineup tomorrow, you will be picked up by Ms. Devereaux for the whole morning. If she gives me a good report at lunch, you will come to the party. If I get a bad report, forget it. Does that sound fair?"

Nothing.

"Tayshaun!"

"Yes," he hissed.

The next morning, Ms. Devereaux told me, "I'm so sorry, I can't take him. I forgot they're having the Secret Santa–revealing parties in my room. I'll come by in the morning and scream at him."

At 11:30, the fourth-grade teachers gathered for the last common prep meeting of the year. We had made it to the desperate, final hours before the coveted break, but Marge Foley ran the meeting with gravity in her tone.

"I know we're all excited to get out of here, but we need to talk about ELA [English Language Arts]. The Test is the first week of February, and, for the several of you who are new, this is a very, very serious, very high-security test. There will definitely be monitors from the state watchdogging our every move when we administer the Test. P.S. 85 effectively sinks or swims on the fourth-grade Test scores. I'm just giving you the heads-up that while it feels far away, because we're about to have this break, it really is breathing down our necks. Expect to do little else in January besides preparation. Are there any questions?"

My mom gave me a box of books from Scholastic, a class set of homemade holiday goody-bags, and three teddy bears with medals labeled Courage, Hope, and Love.

During lunch period, I scrambled to set up the junk food buffet (with food the *kids* brought in this time — and no ice) and a book display, where each kid could pick one to keep. As I scurried around my childless room, Chantal, one of Evan Krieg's fifth-graders, showed up. Krieg was a young second-year teacher, but his eternally mellow demeanor and suave handsomeness had earned him the title "the Tom Cruise of P.S. 85."

Chantal had spent several days in my room when Krieg was absent and the administration had broken up his class. "Mr. Brown, we're having a celebration! You gotta check out some of my white rice, it's slammin'!"

Mr. Krieg was throwing a potluck party for the culminating activity from a two-month Author Study unit he had created. Every student had orally presented a research paper about his or her author in the morning, and now they were feasting and laughing and talking about books. It was a classroom scene of dreams. Krieg had told me he felt like a failure his entire first year as a Fellow. Now, less than four months into his second year, he exuded an unstoppable force of positive teaching energy. I wanted to run my class like that. Like the Tom Cruise of P.S. 85.

Our second stab at a 4-217 party was much more successful than the first, even if Tayshaun spit in the soda and washed the board with erasers soaked in apple juice. Lakiya and Gladys Ferraro surprised me with gifts. Lakiya gave me a gold-painted ceramic bear, and Gladys gave me an ashtray, an amusing choice in the midst of our antismoking health unit. I flipped out with thanks on both of them. I made a brief speech about some phantom raffle and presented the three bears to the "winners." Hope Bear went to Athena, Love Bear to Sonandia, and Courage Bear to Marvin. Their faces told me I had made the right decisions.

"Now I know my mom will let me have Christmas," Athena said, embracing Hope Bear.

The kids could not seem to believe that they could really and truly keep the book they picked out as I called them up one at a time to receive their goody-bags. I felt pretty good, and I felt even better when they all went home.

I was alone in 217, picking up trash, when a woman I did not recognize came to the door. She looked very sad. "Mr. Brown," she said.

"Yes."

"I'm Jimmarie's mother."

"Oh, hi! It's so nice to finally meet you." I dropped my trash bag and walked to the door.

"I just wanted to come and say thank you for everything you've done for my daughter. That book is so beautiful. You made her and my mother so happy."

"Jimmarie is a wonderful girl and a great writer. She's given me a lot of happy things to think about too."

"We're moving south. Next week. Things are . . . things are bad here."

"I understand," I said.

Jimmarie and her younger brother appeared in the hall.

"Hi, Mr. Brown," Jimmarie said.

"Hi, Jimmarie."

"We're moving to Florida."

"I know, your mom just told me. That will be a good thing."

She did not look assured.

"I want you to remember," I continued, "no matter where you go, or what happens, that Mr. Brown will *always* know what a smart and loving and tough girl you are, and he'll be thinking about you. And we'll always have *From the Floor to the Moon*. Okay?"

Jimmarie said okay. I hugged her and shook hands with Jimmy.

"Merry Christmas, Mr. Brown," Jimmarie's mother said.

"Merry Christmas. And I know the new year will be better than the last."

January

The Dentist Is In

Extend your hand to a black and white creature
Often confused with koalas in my mind
Not eucalyptus that this one wants to be eating
He's only interested in watching you die
(Oh . . . no . . . I . . . am . . . toast!)
I'm in danger! You're endangered!
I'm in danger! You're endangered!
Droplets of blood coursing down my neck
How I wish the khaki hunter had left you in Tibet —

— MAN VS. PANDA
(Music by the Hygienists/Lyrics by Dentist)

UNBEKNOWNST TO MY P.S. 85 COLLEAGUES, I had been leading a double life. Most days and nights I was Mr. Dan Brown, struggling rookie teacher who, every venture in public, saw his name stamped on a particular ubiquitous best-seller about secret messages in the Louvre. But occasionally, I shed this straitlaced skin and assumed a more colorful, musical persona: the Dentist, lead singer of the rumpus-inducing rock sextet the Hygienists!

During his senior year, my roommate Greg had secured the job of social chair at Princeton University's Terrace Club, his responsibilities consisting chiefly of booking live entertainment for drunken college hipsters. One time in October, a band canceled on him a week prior to a show. Greg called fellow road-tripper McKenzie and me, offering us the time slot. We had no band, no gear, and I had no musical abilities, but we instantly agreed to the gig. After gathering several high school pals to fill out the instruments and assigning costumes and personas (Ninjar on keyboard, Gun Politician on drums), we threw together a few garage practices and played the show.

The crowd went berserk for us. The irreverent songs, incorporating references to Donald Sutherland, the Boston Tea Party, and *The Canterbury Tales,* struck a chord with the loosened-up house. Doing my damnedest to channel David Byrne and Johnny Rotten, I danced and shouted while my bandmates rocked with raw, punk rock verve. After the show, Greg bought a sampler and a chainsaw (for dramatic effect during "Canterbury Tales") and joined the band, rechristening himself Business Casual. We played at CBGB and a bunch of other downtown clubs, billing ourselves as an "avant-clowncore extravaganza from Reverse Calcutta!" People actually showed up. This is something I love about New York City.

During lunch periods, I'd sometimes compose Hygienists lyrics in my brain, occasionally jotting them down on my lesson plans. Once in the fall, during a visit to my desk, Tiffany caught a glimpse of my scribble. "Man us panda?" she asked.

"Forget it," I blurted, grabbing our blue, stuffed class mascot from the shelf and offering it to her. "Want to hold Mr. Lizard for the rest of the day?"

A raucous New Year's Eve soiree starring the Hygienists at a University of Pennsylvania frat house brought me into 2004 with a cleansed grin on my mug. (My perpetual 4-217 laryngitis even worked to my vocal advantage at the show!) I was still on a cloud from the fiesta when I found myself back in the P.S. 85 cafeteria for morning lineup.

"Mr. Brown! What you did on Happy New Year, you was crying?"

"What? No. Why would I be crying, Asante?"

She grinned. "I don't know. Some peoples was crying!" Must have been some party. "Well what did you do, Mr. Brown?"

Cavorted in a lab coat while screaming about snakepits. Made out with a stranger on a freezing Philadelphia rooftop. (She insisted the lyrics to "Canterbury Tales" touched her deeply.) Realized that loud and fast music could temporarily cure the P.S. 85 blues. Passed out on a random couch. I was Dentist!

"I watched the ball drop on TV," I said. "I never miss Dick Clark."

Mr. Randazzo showed up at my door several minutes after I walked the class upstairs for the first time of the new year. Loud enough for everyone to hear, he said, "Mr. Brown, I have wonderful news. You have two new students coming in, and one just moved to the United States from *Antigua*! They're both terrific readers, and both need some help in math. They became friends, just sitting there in the office signing in. They asked if they could be in the same class, so I said sure!"

He handed me two orange slips. Seresa Bosun and Epiphany Torres. I had lost Verdad Navarez, namesake of truth, since he never returned from Christmas break, but now every day I would appropriately have an Epiphany.

There had been many changes in 4-217 personnel since the first week, eons earlier in September. Angry Marvin Winslow had come into my world. Asante Bell had appeared, still commuting alone from a shelter in Queens, but only showing up once or twice a week. Daniel Vasquez had come in from one-on-one special ed in Detroit, and after a painful three months was finally sent to an appropriate school for his needs. Reynaldo Luces came and went one day with a crying fit. Mischievous Fausto Mason and Deloris Barlow had wreaked disaster before being transferred to other fourth-grade rooms. My coteacher, Ms. Richardson, came and went in a flash, and Verdad had disappeared with no fanfare. Jimmarie had also left town, but she came to me to say good-bye. This rampant transience could not be healthy. I looked at the two new girls and wondered if they would be gone the next week.

Seresa was from Antigua. Fortunately, English was her first language, and she spoke beautifully. When Randazzo told me her nationality, I had immediately thought of Elizabeth Camaraza's student Omar, who had moved from Paris to the Bronx in November and spoke only French.

Epiphany did not make a peep her first day, although I got the eerie feeling she was silently judging me because of my circus classroom. We did a writing activity titled "You Are the Teacher," and her paper was all about changing her classmates.

On Monday, second-year Fellow Randy Croom came sixteen minutes late to teach a lesson to 4-217 during my out-of-class prep period, apparently held up covering a kindergarten class. I improvised through the she'll-be-here-any-second lull with map trivia, which went over well. Every kid now knew in which country we all lived. After a flurry of apologies, Ms. Croom wrote several long sentences on the board about "Note-Taking Strategies" and then played Seven Up for the remainder of the period. I often heard Randy talk in the Teacher Center about how physically sick she was, and I felt bad for her, although I was positive no one learned anything during her prep lessons. When her period ended, I inherited a class full of fired-up kids, still juiced over controversies from the intense Seven Up game. I thought, how can this time be better used?

I spent my lunch period in my mentor Barbara Chatton's minischool office, giving her the idea that I had everything under control, my kids adequately motivated into submission. She seemed to buy it. Barbara subtly divulged that the consensus of the Randazzo/Guiterrez/Boyd administrative triad was that after the big Cordelia Richardson intervention, enough time had been spent on me. In truth, I felt overrun with doubt about the future of 4-217. Were these kids learning anything? By June, would they have eaten each other alive?

When I stepped out of Barbara's office, Trisha Pierson called out to me from down the hall. "Mr. Brown! Could you help us investigate something for just a minute?"

Despite being a new teacher, Trisha taught first grade like a genius. Her room was meticulously organized, her lessons sharp and well-communicated, and she ruled over her children with love and intimidation. Besides Theo, her discipline problems were minimal. She had submitted a proposal to Mrs. Boyd for starting an after-school dance club. To me, Trisha exemplified the best qualities of a young, intelligent, dedicated teacher.

I walked into Trisha's thickly foul-smelling first-grade classroom. "I think there's a dead animal in the vent shaft, but I can't tell," she said. "Can you place it?"

I treaded slowly around room 1M8, sniffing and weaving my way through the intensely curious seven-year-olds. The stench was dense and powerful, but I could not detect its point of origin. I apologized for being of little help and left. Then I had an idea and came back.

"Ms. Pierson, what are you doing Mondays at 11:30?"

"Teaching."

"No prep or anything? I think that's the time to launch Plan X," I said.

"Excellent. I'll get my things ready. Next Monday. How many have you got?"

"Depends on how many you want. Six?"

"Six is perfect."

"I'll bring my A-team," I said, and walked out.

When Ms. Croom showed up on time the following week, I announced, "Evley, Athena, Sonandia, Jennifer, Tiffany, and Destiny, get your coats. We're taking a little trip."

The children breezed down the hall, breathless with excitement. Athena Page clapped her hands and grinned. *"Where are we going?"* she asked. We walked outside into the frigid January air, crossed the blacktop, and entered the minischool lobby.

"We're going to Ms. Pierson's class. You are going to be tutors and help the little kids with reading."

"Oh, boy," Sonandia said, as if she had just turned on a scary movie and couldn't wait to watch it.

The tiny first-graders stared in awe as the towering Big Kids entered their realm. My students looked to me for directions. They were not used to being stars.

Trisha calmed nerves by dishing out instructions in a welcoming and organized manner. She paired one preselected student of hers with one of mine and gave each duo a book, a pencil, and a specially labeled Tutor Notebook. The first-graders would read the book to their fourth-grader helpers. If the reader stumbled on a word, the tutor would jot the difficult word in the notebook. At the end of the story, they would review the story content and the tricky vocabulary words together. The first-grader would make up a meaningful sentence with the tough word and print the word five times. Trisha taught a math lesson on the carpet to the other three-quarters of her class, and I strolled around the room, witnessing magic.

We had conceived Plan X, our intergrade reading buddy plan, at the semester's final Thursday-night Mercy class back in December, when the group discussion snowballed into a galloping gripe session on overwhelming academic and emotional deficiencies in our students.

Trisha had curbed the negativity by offering, "Almost all of my first-graders get picked up at dismissal by their older siblings in eighty-five. I know a lot of kids have to look after their younger brothers and sisters. These kids are definitely screwed in a lot of ways, but one area where they probably have an accelerated amount of expertise is in taking care of little kids."

Now, here in 1M8, Athena Page had her arm around little Dustin, helping him sound out "where." Evley gave William S. a high-five when he finished his first sentence. Big Jennifer and Little Jennifer giggled as they read a book about turtles. I ran down the hall and grabbed Barbara Chatton to show her the scene.

Too soon, I had to drag my students, and myself, away from this cooperative, stress-free learning haven. The promise that we would do this every week for the rest of the year finally coaxed the fourth-graders to the door. Trisha gave Hershey's Kisses to all of the participants. Athena tugged on my sleeve and said, "I think I want to be a teacher when I grow up."

I asked Trisha under my breath if she had ever solved the case of the horrendous smell.

"William S. took a dump in his pants and sat in it all day," she said. "Gotta love first grade." I glanced at William S. absently smearing his chocolate kiss on his forehead.

My happy campers and I returned to room 217 to find Ms. Croom reading from Robert Louis Stevenson's *Treasure Island* to an audience of three. The rest of the class was playing with blocks in the back or just marauding around. "It's so much easier with less of them," she said.

The Test proved to be the ultimate trump card. By fourth grade, the kids had endured so many threatening speeches that the Test's fearsome reputation well preceded me. Lakiya Ray sat up straight. Dennis's face went solemn at the mere mention of it.

Following our division assessment, I dropped math from my planner for January. I thought this was an extreme move, but the veteran teachers were dead serious about it. Wilson Tejera taught the bilingual class only English Language Arts from September to January, and then only math from February to May.

Four-two-seventeen quickly developed a dry daily routine centered on mammoth stacks of Test preparation materials. We practiced identifying and explaining main idea, setting, sequence, note-taking, scanning for details, making inferences, drawing conclusions, main and supporting characters, conflict and resolution, cause and effect, fact and opinion, context clues for vocabulary words, making predictions, parts of speech, and author's purpose. These concepts are important, but I thought framing them so intensely within the context of the multiple-choice Test worked menacingly against enduring comprehension.

I never revealed to my students any inkling that I thought the weight of the Test was overemphasized. (During a prep period, Adele Hafner actually barked, "These scores go on your permanent record, which will follow you for the *rest of your life!*") We practiced, practiced, practiced. I brought out the "Thriller" claw-dance almost every day as a reward for getting through the skills activities.

Marge told us, "The scores are going to be low. Try not to get too disappointed or take it personally."

"They're clueless," Catherine Fiore seconded. "And don't look at their papers when they take the real Test. It will only make you want to jump out the window."

Proctoring the Test was super-serious business. I taped blank newsprint paper over all in-class posters, charts, signs, and anything else containing words. Teachers were not permitted to sit during the Test, but we could not stand still either. We "casually circulate." No communication with kids was allowed. No one can enter or leave during Testing Conditions. A signal meaning "I need a tissue" is acceptable only as long as no words are spoken. The State would be watching.

At a common prep meeting, we heard a horror story about a teacher who noticed a student had accidentally skipped a question on her answer sheet and was bubbling in the answers for all the wrong questions. A State Monitor happened by the door as the well-meaning teacher alerted her student to the mistake. Loyal to his oath, the State Monitor invalidated all of the Tests for the entire grade and placed the school on long-term high-surveillance probation. The teacher was outcast and, I think the story went, her pay was docked. At the end of the tale, I hoped everyone would laugh and snap out of what seemed to me like an Orwellian trance, but it didn't happen. Only Karen and I shot each other a quick look.

After the meeting, Karen asked if she could vent to me.

"Without venting, we'd all be dead."

"Okay. But it's Deloris. I don't know what to do with her. She's single-handedly destroying my Test prep, destroying everything. She cornered Marilee at lunch, told her she's a lesbian, and asked if she could kiss her. Marilee of course had a conniption and couldn't stop crying. Deloris yelled out that Marilee tried to touch her boob, and everyone believed her. I had to basically call Deloris a liar in front of my kids, even though I wasn't there when all of this happened. I'm falling apart."

"Holy shit."

"She's a wrecking ball. And the worst thing is, as annoying as it is for me to have her in my class, it's nothing compared to how fucked she is for the rest of her life. I don't know if you know about this, but I've heard a rumor that her father . . ."

"MC Onyx."

"Right. I don't even know if I can bring myself to believe this. Apparently, MC Onyx has . . . sex with his daughters when they hit puberty. Deloris just found out."

Midway through her freshman year as an elementary education student at Muhlenberg College, my sister, Amanda, finally agreed to come to work with me. I had been trying for months to persuade her to hop a bus from Allentown to New York to experience an inner-city classroom, but I think my Fausto stories had scared her.

The night she stayed in my apartment, the heat went out at 3:30 a.m. I woke up shivering, and staggered into the common room to find Amanda frozen in the fetal position on the pleather futon. When we hit the street at 6:15, the sky was pitch black. The cutting wind chill dipped to -17°F, the coldest New York City weather in ten years.

P.S. 85 was a ghost town. Fifteen minutes before lineup, two-thirds of the faculty was unaccounted for. Fourteen of my twenty-five students showed up, and I got another five from Pat Cartwright's class. I introduced the kids to "Ms. Brown," my lovely and talented sister, who would be with us for a one-day-only special engagement.

Amanda was understandably timid with them at first. Athena asked her, "Why does he call you 'Ms. Brown'? Shouldn't he call you *sista*?" Lakiya kept throwing Amanda crazy looks, and the whole day was an abnormal mess anyway with half of the class missing. Together, we ran a made-up activity called "Lost in the Jungle," involving a Venn diagram and a writing piece.

Lakiya and Lito started kicking the legs of their desks. Testing the new authority figure in the room, Lakiya shouted out, "Ms. Brown, Lito's bothering me! Lito, you *touch* too much!"

Amanda was sharp. "I don't know, you're sitting pretty close together. It looks like you like each other, not like you're bothering each other. Do you have a crush on him?"

"Eww!" And that was the end of that.

Midway through "Lost in the Jungle," Ms. Devereaux appeared at my door, holding an unhappy kid by the wrist. "This one was giving Ms. Fiore a problem," she fumed.

I nodded and in my best cop voice, assured, "He won't be a problem in here." I sternly led the pouting boy to a back-corner desk, quietly thrown by the supreme role reversal. I was glad Amanda saw that.

Every 4-217 kid wanted to hug Amanda at the day's end. Later, over chocolate-and-banana milkshakes at the Waverly Restaurant in the West Village, she said, "I'm not sure the Bronx is for me."

I lived in a converted tenement on the corner of Rivington and Allen streets in the Lower East Side. The pizzeria on the ground floor had been gutted for renovations over Christmas week. When I got back to my apartment building after dropping Amanda off at Port Authority, trouble awaited.

Six or seven men in rubber pants stomped around a shallow pool of freezing water, where the pizza place's seating area used to be.

They looked at the exposed pipes and wires in the ceiling, shaking their heads in bewilderment and dismay.

"What's going on?" I asked.

One worker shook his head sympathetically. "Muchas problemas," he replied.

Upstairs in my frigid apartment, the kitchen faucet did not work. The toilet refused to flush. The restaurant renovators had accidentally cut the heat to the whole building. Attempting to fix their blunder, they burst the pipe insulation, causing a minor flood in the pizzeria and, more importantly, exposing the water pipes to the icy air and freezing up the works.

Greg and I had no running water for the next five days. I showered at night at my friend Kadi's fifth-floor apartment in a walk-up down the street. I used bottled water to brush my teeth and hightailed it over to Angel Bar on Orchard Street, two blocks away, when I needed a toilet. My clothes were ice cold when I dressed in the dark morning. I was going crazy.

I forced Marvin Winslow to wear his second pair of glasses. My Christmas bestowal of the Courage Bear earned some extra traction with him, and I used it. He lasted one full day before Julissa again whispered something right before a Test simulation. Crying, he lunged to punch Julissa, but I got between them.

"Calm the fuck down, four eyes!" Tayshaun contributed. I went nuts on Tayshaun, slamming his name on the Detention List. "I don't care," he mumbled. Angry, I took the power-struggle bait, exploding on him again.

Al Conway walked by. "Mr. Brown, everything okay?" he inquired with concern. "We're about to start a *simulation*."

Tayshaun and Marvin doodled all over their sample Tests, occasionally giving me reason to sharply shush them.

At lunch, I escorted Tayshaun to the detention table. He took out his batch of Yu-Gi-Oh cards, and I immediately confiscated them. His face changed completely as I pocketed the deck. "Can I keep them, please?" he asked.

"No! Prove you can behave like a decent human being, like you did last week, and *maybe* you'll see them again!"

Then something unexpected happened. Rock-hard Tayshaun Jackson fell to pieces, wailing in deep, snotty belly-sobs. His sudden breakdown was scary to watch. Maybe I should just give him the cards, I thought. This kid has *serious* emotional problems.

I did not give him the cards. I turned and left the room.

Gym class was a singular phenomenon. On Wednesdays, I took class 4-217 directly from lunch to the upstairs gymnasium for their once-a-week in-school exercise. The schedule lumped my class with Ms. Cartwright's group (Fausto included), a double dose of excitement for Mr. Zweben and Ms. Friedberg, the two whistle-toting gym teachers.

Gym was hugely popular with my kids, the boys especially, so I occasionally hung around to witness what it was all about. The period generally consisted of twenty minutes of calming everyone down, modeling one athletic move like a volleyball set or soccer pass, and giving lengthy instructions for how to partner up and where to go. The remaining measure of class time inexorably devolved into run-and-tackle free-for-all. Boys from Ms. Cartwright's class usually started the fracas by throwing whatever balls were around that day, and my boys eagerly followed suit. Playtime got whistled short, and it all ended with a disappointed harangue.

Then they couldn't wait to do it again next week.

After school, I swung by disconcerted Allie Bowers's kindergarten room. Before dismissal, Quashawn had stolen her crayons and called another five-year-old a "dumb slut." I asked if she had a prep at 1:25 on Wednesdays, 4-217's usual gym time. "No, I'm painfully here," she said.

"I'm bringing my B-team," I proclaimed.

I experimented with the second wave of tutors, including in the crew Gladys Ferraro and Bernard, both of whom had been stirring up trouble lately. I hoped the experience, with the potential to be an ongoing weekly engagement, would be an incentive to behave themselves in 217. It worked for Gladys; Bernard didn't care. "Those little kids are boring," he whined.

I also brought Epiphany and Seresa, although if I was serious about A- and B-teams, Seresa belonged with the top group. I decided to keep her with Epiphany since they seemed comfortable together. Gladys V. and Dennis, two mostly polite kids, rounded out the team.

Allie didn't have a plan as organized as Trish's for the tutors, but we improvised. The partner-reading was adorable, and the kindergartners were sad to see us go.

The intergrade reading-buddy project got me excited. The first-year teachers had a good idea, and we were making it happen. I decided to pay my first voluntary visit to Mrs. Boyd's office, just to let her in on the good news.

I found Boyd's door closed with muffled adult screaming going on behind it. Outside the office, Paul Bonn wore an I-just-ate-all-the-cookies grin. "Did you see it in time?" he asked.

"See what in time?"

"Oh my God, it's the best thing ever. Did you know Boyd got fired from the last school she was a principal at? I think P.S. 25, maybe? I'm not sure. Someone found an old article in some local newsletter about her getting the boot. They copied it and put one in everyone's box!"

"You're kidding."

"They're all pulled out now. She's on the *warpath*! I didn't get to see it. Solloway did. I don't know who else."

"Wow. Who did it? What a huge risk for some humiliation."

"I don't know who. Nobody knows. No one can stand her, so everyone's a suspect!"

★   ★   ★

On January 26, I received a letter notifying me of my acceptance to the Kodak Student Filmmaker Program at the 2004 Cannes Film Festival. After viewing a rough cut of my thesis film back in November, one of my NYU professors had encouraged me to submit it. Excited by his praise and mired in the lowest depths of my Sonandia-is-leaving depression, I sent off my application. Now I was in, complete with a screening of my film at the American Pavilion, an internship at the *Hollywood Reporter,* and full festival accreditation. The program lasted seventeen days in May, so attending would mean missing twelve school days, or eleven if I skipped the very end. A million scenarios flashed through my head, and all of them involved flying to the French Riviera.

The next day, I approached Wally Klein, P.S. 85's librarian and union rep, to feel out the possibilities. I had curried big favor with Wally early in the year when he learned about my enthusiasm for movies, and he once cornered me in a one-way conversation about Tyrone Power. He was also the only person at the school who called me "Danny."

I asked about the school's policy on leaves of absence. "It's one hundred percent up to the Queen. What do you have in mind?"

I told Wally everything. He grimaced. "Ooh, that's iffy, Danny. I'm meeting with her this afternoon. I can broach the subject, but I don't know . . ."

He did seem to know. I ought to forget about it, I read. "That's all right, I'll just speak to her," I said.

His voice got firm. "No. Trust me. I'll go first." The next afternoon, I received a summons to the principal's office.

"Sit next to me," Mrs. Boyd ordered. "What exactly is this, you're in the Cannes Film Festival?" I explained the Student Filmmaker Program. "So this is something that you took upon yourself to apply to, even though you knew it directly interfered with your professional responsibilities? It's not my job to allow teachers to go on trips during the school year. You realize that, don't you?"

"Yes." I bit down hard. Here comes the guillotine, I thought.

"I went to the first Sundance Festival in the eighties, back before Park City got all commercialized." Her lips curled into a microscopic smile. "We went to a screening in a high school gymnasium with folding chairs, and I actually talked to Robert Redford for a couple minutes, the Sundance Kid himself." She seemed to be looking right through me, as if the ghost of Jeremiah Johnson was just beyond my shoulder. "It's funny that you're bringing this to me now. Not too long ago, I made a list of things I want to do before I die. One of the top ten was to go to the Cannes Film Festival." Now she looked directly at me. "You won't be paid for these days, you understand that. But how could I not let you go to this?"

I thought I would throw my chair in a volatile mix of surprise and jubilation. I thanked her. Mrs. Boyd went into a story about how she taught animation to students in the seventies and a project they made won a New York City award.

"Now talk to me about this," Mrs. Boyd said, taking out my one-page proposal to start an after-school dramatics club. I had copied Trisha Pierson's format from her dance program proposal and submitted mine a week ago, but had not heard anything. I made a brief pitch about extending performing arts beyond the PAC classes, giving students a chance to express themselves through drama and putting on a culminating play.

Mrs. Boyd was skeptical. "Stacy Shanline tried to do the same thing last year with the third-graders. She wanted to put on *Our Town*. It went nowhere." The principal looked straight at me. "You have skills in filmmaking. What do you think about starting a film club? We have lots of remedial intervention programs for struggling kids. This could be something for the more upper-tier students."

I was thunderstruck by Mrs. Boyd's brilliant idea. It was true that the school offered no extracurricular opportunities for gifted children. Until now, P.S. 85's only after-school activity was a thrice-a-week basic skills math review. Trisha's lower-grade dance program launched soon, and if I could start this filmmaking club, maybe we could start a wave.

★   ★   ★

I finally met Asante's mother outside the office when she came to sign Asante permanently out of P.S. 85. At long last, Asante would be going to school in Queens. Mrs. Bell, a young mother, nodded in agreement when I said that this transfer would make things much better. She burst into tears. I scrambled to grab a tissue in the office but all they had were industrial brown paper towels. I gave her a few and Mrs. Bell buried her face. "Thank you, thank God for you, Mr. Brown . . . oh, Jesus, I don't know what to do . . ."

I hugged her, and she cried into my shoulder. "It's going to be okay, it's getting better," I said. I had never felt more like a kid in a costume. "It's okay, it's going to be okay." I had not been any kind of great teacher to Asante. My brief attempts at investigating her dire situation were quickly rebuffed, and I had let it drop in the face of a tidal wave of other problems. Now I was telling this woman that things are getting better?

"Your Rewards List," Mrs. Bell said, wiping her eyes. "You made her so happy when she was on your Rewards List. Thank you so much for everything."

I said good-bye to Mrs. Bell and Asante and walked back to 217, full of a feeling that escaped easy definition. Asante spent most of her time in class chatting, so her name rarely appeared on the Rewards List by the day's end. When it did, I never noticed any exceptional exuberance in her.

Until that moment, I didn't know I had had any impact on her at all. As Karen had foretold, *something comes across.*

Who else had I unknowingly touched? As a student, what had I taken from my teachers, unconscious to them?

My first-grade teacher, Mrs. Tomasso, lost her husband the year I was in her class. The day after the funeral, she returned to school and explained her feelings and told us about her husband's life. At seven years old, I absorbed her grief and love. Did she have any idea how much I grew up in that hour?

My high school English teacher, Mr. Truitt, showed François

Truffaut's *The 400 Blows* to a class of sophomores. Then we had the most honest, far-reaching class discussion I have experienced. Before that week, had I ever considered the idea of poetry in failure? He shined a floodlight on unexplored regions in my brain. Can he know how much that class opened my mind?

In the moment that Asante and her mother turned to leave, the far-reaching influence of teachers upon children took tangible, heartbreaking form. This job was going to kill me.

Test stress reached a critical boil that week, despite the miraculous surprise of Wednesday's snow day. The zero hour was at hand, and the kids were terrified. Four students threw up. Dennis tapped his foot nervously and could not stop.

But they were well-behaved. Also, the repetitive, boring, scary, mandatory Test preparation required minimal exertion on my part. I liked being calm, sharing the room with quiet children. It was a frightening microcosm.

February

Stressed and Assessed

I SHOWERED LAKIYA RAY WITH PRAISE and Juicy Fruit gum for her docile new attitude. Before lunch on Monday, February 2, she handed me an ancient ziplock bag containing her thick dog-eared stack of prized Yu-Gi-Oh cards and asked me to hang on to them for safekeeping.

While finishing lunch with Karen in my otherwise empty classroom, I opened my bottom desk drawer to discover the cards were *gone.* My stomach dropped. Scouring the area, I broke into a sweat. I replayed our transaction over and over. Room 217 had been empty during the ten minutes when I shepherded the class to the cafeteria and stepped out to buy my lunch. No one that I knew of came in the room at odd times. The cards *should* be in the bottom drawer. After Deloris got the boot in December, though, thefts in the classroom had gone from constant to zero. I felt nauseous thinking about having to tell Lakiya what had happened, especially since we were finally making headway together.

When I picked up the class, I gushed apologies to Lakiya and offered to buy her a new deck. She shrugged and said, "Nah, that's okay. Forget it." I detected no passive aggression in her. She immediately turned back to her conversation with Epiphany, as if my news was holding her up from important business. For five months I had been Lakiya Ray's teacher, and at that moment I understood her less than a stranger.

★　　★　　★

The Test is a three-day extravaganza. Part One is all multiple-choice questions regarding basic reading comprehension skills. It is graded by machines (I envisioned Terminator robots) and carries the most weight of all three sections. Part Two involves students listening to and taking notes about a long passage that is read to them in a monotone by their proctor. The students use their notes to answer essay questions. Part Three is all essay responses to passages in their Test booklets.

Before the Test commenced, I gave a brief speech about how I was confident and proud of them. Relax and do your best. I believe in you. I relinquished control to my coproctor, "Big" Mrs. Little, a tutor and twenty-year teaching veteran. Mrs. Little read instructions in the recommended monotone and sharply warned them not to begin an instant before the second hand hit the twelve. I could see Destiny Rivera's pencil shaking.

An hour later, we were claw-dancing the disappointment away. The Test seemed harder than any of the simulations or practice materials we had used. At our 11:30 common prep meeting, the fourth-grade teachers shared arched eyebrows that evinced knowledge of impending disaster. At least I was not alone in thinking that my students had just gotten hammered. Marnie Beck said, "Special ed kids should not be put through this." I agreed, unsure any nine-year-olds should.

I thought the massive cram that led up to this abrupt pressure release on the days of the Test was like jamming ice cubes into a fever patient's mouth in hopes that by quickly checking the temperature, the reading would come out a normal, acceptable ninety-eight point six. The thermometer is not corrupt, but the hospital staff is. If P.S. 85 had more family outreach and year-round, small-group support services for kids struggling with literacy fundamentals, I believed the Test scores would be higher because the kids would be better readers, not savvier multiple-choice guessers.

In terms of support services beyond my instruction of 4-217, only six of my students were pulled out for fifty minutes daily in

September through January. All of that time was dedicated to studying Test-taking strategies. Eddie (who had been held back three times), Lito, and Lakiya received nothing. Keeping with the hospital analogy, this was akin to basing a sick patient's progress on periodic blood tests without substantive treatment between assessments. The hospital can claim without lying that it has the most expensive, state-of-the-art instruments for measuring one's health. However, the appropriation of enormous focus on diagnosis or assessment, not treatment, is disastrous for the voiceless, unwitting patients. Using standardized testing as the sole barometer of students' and schools' achievement is a deeply misguided practice. The sick system cannot get healthy through this means alone.

During Part Three on Thursday, I stood near Eric Ruiz, watching him leave his entire Test booklet blank. He was supposed to write a letter to the principal requesting permission to start a ham radio club, drawing ideas equally from a supplied article about ham radios and his own creativity. Several times I covertly kicked his desk, but he did not pick up my message of "Take the Test." I felt deflated, knowing there was virtually nothing I could now do to move Eric up to fifth grade. He signed his holdover slip that day.

It did not take long after the final booklet was collected for the relative tranquility of Testmania to explode. Midway through our first math activity back on the normal schedule, Epiphany approached me on the verge of tears. "Mr. Brown . . . Cwasey just . . ." She started whimpering.

I gave her a tissue and put my hand on her shoulder, unsure what else to do. "It's okay," I said. "What happened?"

"Cwasey said, 'Bend over and make me money.' "

My mouth fell open as my mind raced to decipher this unfathomably lurid command. Cwasey looked up, infuriated. "She lie!"

"No I don't!" Epiphany wailed.

"Cwasey! Shut your mouth and get out of our classroom! Stand right here in the hall!" I threw the door open.

Cwasey shoved his chair in disgust as he stood up and walked toward the hall. As he passed Epiphany's group, he loudly proclaimed, "Your *mother's* a liar."

Epiphany broke out in tears. She bolted from the room, her face in her hands. Mr. Randazzo was not around, so I couldn't toss Cwasey in his office. Instead of letting Epiphany and Cwasey be out in the hall together, I grabbed Cwasey and yanked him back in the room.

Lakiya whooped, mimicking, "Your mother's a liar!" When Marvin and Joseph saw Lakiya laughing, they cracked up too. The Pandora's box of "your mother" insults was blown open.

At lunch I told Mr. Daly what Cwasey had said and asked for advice on how to handle it. "He's probably repeating something he heard," Daly surmised. "I'll make him say he's sorry. We'll leave the parents out of this one."

At that moment, I spotted Bernard hyperventilating at the table, wearing his I'm-about-to-have-a-rage-attack face. I sat down next to him. "Bernard, what's up?"

Instead of answering, Bernard lunged across the table at Tayshaun. I pulled him back. "He talkin' about my mother!" Bernard screamed.

"No I didn't! Stop lying!" Tayshaun retorted, now walking around the table, toward us. He waved a taunting hand in Bernard's face.

Bernard snapped. I had him in my arms, but he struggled and writhed against me, reaching again and again to punch Tayshaun. Mr. Daly was now at the far end of the room breaking up another fight. "Bernard! He doesn't know your mother! What he says means nothing! You still have a choice to do the right thing and calm down. Take a deep breath!"

Bernard continued pushing against me, but my grip was firm. Finally, he got tired. I sent Tayshaun to fifth-grade lunch detention in the other cafeteria. I gave Bernard to Mr. Daly with instructions to deliver the fuming kid to Ms. Devereaux's room for the afternoon.

After the progress he had been making in controlling his temper, I couldn't let this outburst go unpunished.

The air went out of me when Bernard returned to 217 a few minutes before dismissal, grinning and wearing his forbidden-in-school Yankees hat. "I had mad fun!" he gushed. "I went on the Internet with Mr. Daly and played games!"

That night I racked my brain for a new game plan. I had no choice but to go it alone with discipline. The administration could not be relied upon, and the other fourth-grade teachers were swamped. I had already withheld parties, candy rewards, points, and stickers from the problem causers. I called homes over and over again. They still did not behave for prep teachers or guests. I had sent kids to Mr. Randazzo, Mr. Daly, Ms. Devereaux, and Ms. Guiterrez. (Catherine Fiore had even sent *me* a misbehaving kid on that icy January day.) Nothing worked for the long term. It was like putting Band-Aids on a sucking chest wound. I called Karen.

After venting, I felt a little less crazy and decided to break up the mandated group-seating scheme. Early on the morning of February 6, I rearranged the desks to make individual rows. Maybe if the kids weren't bunched in so tightly, they would stop picking on each other's mothers.

In the hall, before sending the students inside to find their new desk location, I announced, "Anyone who makes a comment about someone else's family is talking about something they know nothing about. That is wimpy and cowardly. *Anyone* who talks about someone else's family is automatically on lunch detention, banned from the Rewards List, and has lost my respect, probably forever! This is *the end of it!*"

Twenty minutes later, Lakiya said to Marvin, "Fuck your fat mother!" Everybody heard. Marvin, despite his significant disadvantage in size, flew at Lakiya with his head down and fists flying. I tore them apart, banishing each to opposite corners of the room. When the dust cleared from the sudden fisticuffs, I noticed something very strange. Tiffany had left her desk and was standing still at the front of the room, right in my usual spot for blackboard-writing. She stared at the floor, no clear expression on her face.

Tiffany was the class space cadet, but she was smart. She was quiet and did well on her practice Tests, so I gave her leeway, particularly in her using our spare bookcase as her personal storage space. Her voice was extremely high-pitched, and she often snuck toys in her desk. She doodled more often than she did her work, but usually had the right answer when I spontaneously called on her. Also, she loved my stuffed blue "Mr. Lizard" more than anybody else, and jumped for joy when I occasionally brought him out of his home in the top closet shelf.

"Tiffany, go back to your seat." She made no acknowledgment of hearing me, so I repeated myself. Nothing. "Tiffany, are you okay?" She looked catatonic. Some kids started snickering, and I immediately shushed them. Tiffany's hands stayed at her sides, completely still. "Do you want to go to the library with Destiny?" No response. Was this a trance? "Tiffany, you *have* to get back in your . . ."

"DON'T TOUCH ME!" Tiffany shrieked, yanking herself away the moment I touched her forearm.

"Tiffany. You must answer me. Who do you want to talk to? If you tell me what you want to do, I can help you." She resumed her original standing position and said nothing. She seemed to be having a psychological meltdown, and I had no idea why.

I called Mr. Randazzo and Ms. Guiterrez, but neither answered the phone. I rang Ms. Devereaux, who showed up in a huff. "What's this, she doesn't wanna sit down?" Devereaux observed, reaching for Tiffany's arm.

"NO!" Tiffany responded with another piercing screech.

"You have to move! This is your last chance!" Ms. Devereaux shouted in her stentorian I-am-serious voice. Still nothing. "I'm getting security." She left and reappeared a minute later with campus patrolman Mr. Joe.

"Are we taking her out?" Mr. Joe asked.

"I don't know. She won't move or talk," I said.

"Let's take her," Mr. Joe decided. He and Ms. Devereaux grabbed Tiffany, who went limp and redoubled her wild screams as the two adults dragged her across the dusty tile and out the door, slamming it shut behind them. In 217, we could hear Tiffany's wrenching cries fading farther and farther away before cutting off altogether. How was I going to teach after that?

Sick to my stomach, I sat down in Tiffany's chair. None of the kids seemed fazed by the episode we had all just witnessed. I remember when I was in fifth grade and Ilene Lambert's knee locked up during our class trip to the Philadelphia Zoo. She cried hysterically in front of all of us, and the rest of the day was creepy and sad. Everyone seemed to feel guilty enjoying themselves if Ilene was laid up in the bus with a chaperone.

I visited Tiffany in the office during my prep. Guzzling a cup of Sprite, she showed no indication of having thrown an apoplectic fit a few hours earlier. I felt like I was walking on eggshells, telling her we were looking forward to having her back in 4-217. I never found out the exact cause of her meltdown, but later in the day, Stacy Shanline, Tiffany's third-grade teacher, told me that Tiffany had had the same kind of episode last year at approximately this time on the calendar.

Just before dismissal, I noticed Seresa sniffling as I called students over to the closet to get their coats. I brought her out in the hall, where she started sobbing hard. "I'm not used to this, Mr. Brown . . . in Antigua, we don't treat the teachers like this. They're so mean to you." She blew her nose.

"I'm okay," I said. "That stuff doesn't bother me."

"But Lakiya was saying you're a bad teacher. She said you don't know how to make the kids act right."

"What Lakiya says means nothing. She's not in charge of your year in fourth grade. You're considerate to think of me, and it shows that you're a good and generous person, and I appreciate that. What

I care about is that I've got students like you and Jennifer and Sonandia and Evley and some of the others. I don't let kids who act mean bug me. You don't have to worry about me, I'm all right. All that yelling is acting anyway. How are you doing?"

Seresa shrugged. "You're still good friends with Jennifer, right?" I asked. Now she started tearing up again.

"I don't know. Sometimes she follows Lakiya, and she says things to me like 'Why don't you have a man?' and they laugh at me."

"Jennifer asks you why you don't have a man?"

"Yes."

"Wow, that's ludicrous."

"Ludicrous?" she asked.

"Ludicrous. It means ridiculous. Silly. Absolutely crazy."

"Ludicrous," Seresa repeated.

"Exactly. Completely ludicrous for Jennifer to say that. She knows you're her real friend. I'll talk to her. You're in fourth grade. None of you have, or *should have,* a boyfriend. Okay? You're a wonderful girl, and I'm very happy that you're in my class."

"Okay. Thank you, Mr. Brown."

Our conversation ended when I saw Bernard and Hamisi near the closet, punching each other in the face. My instinct was to rush in and wrench them apart, but I checked myself, remembering that Bernard's flailing at Tayshaun in the lunchroom had increased when I restrained him. In a kind of surprise at my nonintervention, the two fighters stopped hitting and went their separate ways. In the line two minutes later, they were chatting about *Grand Theft Auto: Vice City* like old pals.

I know that many children reach out for attention and love in strange ways, but after that day, I was thoroughly baffled as to what goes through some of their heads.

Seth Owings, an old college friend of Greg's, came to our apartment on Sunday to watch basketball and shoot the breeze. He was in his second year of teaching freshman English at Central High School in Newark with Teach for America. With each Pabst Blue Ribbon we drank, I became more entranced by his stories.

"My principal doesn't know how to talk to people," he said. "He's always on some weird power trip and is totally out of touch with how it is to try to teach these kids day in and day out. The administration is always having meetings and sending out things about standards and bulletin boards and that kind of crap: basically everything that's cosmetic. But we have no solid curriculum. I just have a vague construct in my head of what we're kind of supposed to teach. It's nice in a way, because no one will ever call me out on giving any kind of unorthodox assignment, but it doesn't matter because almost none of them can write a real paragraph anyway.

"Your expectations go so low that you start praising the shit out of your kids who can just get through something, not 'cause they're really producing anything of any quality. The math teachers have it a little easier, because just by nature math is a little more black and white. You either get it or you don't, and the kids like that. But a lot of them just throw dice in the hall and eat the free lunch." This reminded me of my week of seventh-grade summer school at M.S. 399, when one of the seemingly brightest boys in the class told me candidly, "Seventh grade was out in the hall, man."

Seth went on about gang colors and receiving writing assignments from Crips with gang-mark slashes on every "c" and crossouts through every "b" or "p," since the latter is an upside-down version of the former. The writer would not want anyone looking at the paper — from any angle — to mistake him for exhibiting sympathy for the letter "b," representing his rival gang, the Bloods.

Seth's stories were a little comforting in that I wasn't alone in my desperation, but his comment about lowering expectations made me worry. I absolutely had lowered my expectations from the first day of school when I delivered my "We Are a Team" speech. Now my priority seemed to be eking through the day without anyone bleeding. I didn't even think about great expectations anymore.

Was Sonandia really an exceptional student, or had I attributed so many wonderful qualities to her because I needed something to hold on to? Would other teachers in other schools share my enthusiasm about her? My Sunday-night sleeplessness was worse than usual.

On Monday, February 9, I turned twenty-three. In celebration, I received a new student, Christian Salerno. I also got a note from Ms. Guiterrez about collecting my planbook tomorrow morning, and my name appeared at the top of the list of classes Mrs. Boyd's team would inspect on Friday's upcoming Learning Walk. All interior and exterior bulletin boards needed to be changed for the benefit of Friday's visitors. I received eight handmade birthday cards from my kids, most of them including drawings of flowers and lists of school subjects. Then I taught all day and went to Professional Development.

Mrs. Boyd adjourned our monthly whole-school faculty meeting in the auditorium with the hollow encouragement, "Failure is not an option." Filing out in the aisle, Ethel May Brick, P.S. 85's longest-tenured teacher, tapped me on the shoulder. "I heard it's your birthday. Happy birthday!" Her voice always quivered in a jolly grandma kind of way.

"Thank you," I said.

"It's so nice, just so nice, that young and intelligent people like you come to work at a school like this." Her face saddened. "It's a shame you can't stay."

"Why can't I stay?"

"Oh come on, Dan. This school is a hell. And right now it's the worst it's ever been. This neighborhood is collapsing. I know the area looks bad, but it's really much worse than it seems. You wouldn't believe how drug-infested it is. Do you know the projects next to the firehouse?"

I knew that building well. In front of it was where the September shooting happened and where guidance counselor Mr. Schwesig gashed his head by walking into a Dumpster. "There was a bust there last year, and the police found more drugs moving in and out of that building than any other building in New York City. We didn't know till the bust."

Ms. Brick clearly wanted to chat, and I had one burning question about the children of P.S. 85. "What do you think about the full-moon phenomenon?" I asked.

She answered without hesitation, "Full moons make people crazy. Before I started working here in 1965, I thought it was a silly superstition. But *every* month of *every* year, the tension builds on the full moon. It's especially bad when it's waxing like last Thursday and Friday. Now it's waning. When it's waxing there are more fights, more noise, more aggression. I mark the full moons on my calendar with red circles."

The authority in her tone took me aback. "My class was terrible last Thursday and Friday," I said.

"The whole school was in shambles," she replied. "Really, ask any emergency room nurse about full moons. But it's especially bad right now because of Valentine's Day coming up. We're in the winter doldrums, and that's bad. And the fourth-graders are coming off the big ELA Test and that's really bad. But Valentine's Day is *always* horrible here. Remember that most of these kids are being raised by single women who have been left by men. Valentine's Day has a lot of anger here, and you can feel it. The only worse time of year is Mother's Day. Then everyone's mad at the mothers."

She did not explain the last part.

I met wild resistance when returning to regular lessons after the rigidly structured cram sessions for the Test. The class was becoming more and more academically polarized and the addition of Christian Salerno was no help. I seated him in well-behaved group two, and his nudnik ways quickly awakened the sleeping beast of Gladys Ferraro's mouth.

Gladys was my Student of the Month in October, but the award had had the opposite of my hoped-for effect. She griped loudly and constantly about her peers "bothering her," but she was given to touching other people's belongings, putting her on a collision course with everybody.

Christian and Gladys F. were instantly at each other's throats. I banished Christian to group six, where, before I realized it, he fell under Lakiya's back-of-the-room influence.

Pat Cartwright was absent on Tuesday, Wednesday, Thursday, and Friday. Her class was deemed too rowdy for a sub, so they were split up every day under the direction of Mrs. Hafner. I was sure Hafner still hated me, evidenced by her nonresponses to my "Good mornings," as well as her red-cheeked clam-up in the Teacher Center when I walked in on her emphatically extolling Abba's *Mamma Mia*. She sent me Sayquan (Dequan's brother) and Asonai, two renowned nightmare children. To temper the blow, I also got Kimberly and Mary, two "contained" students.

Asonai and Lakiya had fistfought at lunch the previous week, and their enmity was still in full force. The two slung insults across the room all day. Sayquan asked to go to the bathroom early in the day, and I let him. He returned a half hour later and got upset when I refused his next dozen requests to leave the classroom.

As I walked around during the independent problem-solving part of our adding-fractions-with-unlike-denominators lesson, a flurry of thoughts rushed through me:

1. Destiny is adding the denominators, the same mistake that she made yesterday, even though I conferenced with her for a long time. I'll quietly point it out to her now while I'm circulating, then make sure she's getting it when we do the whole-class review.

2. I should check on Marvin Winslow. Is he calm? No! Pat him on the shoulder. Okay, his head is down.

3. Why is Athena's head down? She loves math. Wait, she's crying! Did something serious just happen? I should talk to her in the doorway.

4. Three kids are holding up their pencils for sharpening. They'll have to wait.

5. How long should I wait to call the class back to order? Three, six minutes? I have twenty-two minutes until my prep. A fifteen-minute review is probably sufficient, but I don't want a lag before or after the review. I'll give them five more minutes.

6. Where's Eddie? He went to the bathroom fifteen minutes ago.

7. Cwasey and Dennis are talking. Have to stop that.

8. Lakiya's not doing her work, but now Jennifer's following her! Need to talk to Jennifer privately about it later.

9. Here's Ms. Devereaux collecting donations for Ms. O'Reardon, whose house was robbed. Five dollars feels sufficient.

10. Damn, I forgot to fill in the backup attendance sheet again. Can't do it now, must remember at lunchtime.

11. Asonai is looking around the room ominously. Give her more drawing paper.

12. My mouth is dry beyond belief.

During my Thursday prep, I mounted my new exterior bulletin board and brought Sonandia and Gladys V. in the hall with me for moral support. They performed cheers and an original song called "Go! Go, Mr. Brown!" I cracked up and became immediately aware that I had not laughed in school in months. P.S. 85 and laughter felt like two familiar but cordoned realms where an intersection was a marvelous and novel occurrence, like swimming and nighttime.

On Friday morning, the Learning Walk paid 4-217 a visit in mid-lesson. Mrs. Boyd and her four helpers inspected my walls for "Clear Expectations," as I sweated through a discussion about Lincoln's quote, "A house divided cannot stand." In fifteen minutes they were gone, and my breath came easier.

At dismissal, gateway to the nine-day midwinter break, Marvin Winslow made a comment about Lito Ruiz's dead mother. Lito slugged Marvin, and wailing Marvin ran down the stairs and out the door. Sayquan and Asonai got keyed up from the excitement and took off in pursuit of the crying boy.

Back in empty 217 after the wild finish, I was organizing clipped bundles of math packets and Lincoln-quote-response second drafts to take home and mark when Elizabeth Camaraza walked in. She listlessly dropped her bag on Seresa's desk. "I can't ever come back here," she said, suppressing tears. She told me about Ms. Guiterrez's refusal to go to bat for her to keep her new seating arrangement, Mrs. Boyd's blistering bulletin board criticism in front of the students, and the catastrophic new RFR situation.

I had never heard of RFR, so Elizabeth explained it to me. An administrator had greenlighted the $60,000 purchase of a new third-grade literacy curriculum called Reading for Results, based on the idea that this program would supplant Success for All. However, Region One signed on for Balanced Literacy as the new curriculum, rendering RFR useless before it was ever used. In order to justify the $60,000 expenditure, or simply to disguise its wastefulness from any potential auditors, P.S. 85's third-grade teachers were mandated to attend weeks of RFR "online module classes," complete with sessions after school and at 7 a.m. Everyone knew the program would never enter a real classroom, and it made the teachers irate with festering disgust.

"I used to empty *bedpans* on the midnight shift with two babies at home and no husband, and this is worse than that," Elizabeth said.

"Yoo-hoo, Mr. Brown!" Mrs. Boyd summoned me from the hall. I answered the call and Elizabeth made a move to leave, but I quickly asked her to stay for a minute.

Mrs. Boyd stared at my exterior bulletin board, eyeing it with a perplexed expression, like someone trying to count jellybeans in a jar. "You've shown improvement, Mr. Brown, but not enough. What I caught of your lesson this morning was superb, but you already know what I think of your ability to communicate. Your classroom environment is bare-bones. The elements are there: the minimal elements. Look at this bulletin board. There's no . . ." She paused, looking for the right word. Not finding it, she moved on. "If you want to stimulate students to learn, stimulation must flow out of every aspect of their experience in school. Do you agree?"

"Yes."

"You say that, but I don't think you understand what it requires of you."

"You want my room to look nicer," I interpreted in monotone.

Mrs. Boyd seemed to take offense at my accusing her of something so superficial. "I want you to put a little more of *yourself* into this job." She walked away.

"Venomous wench," I heard Camaraza mutter from inside the room. "You know she screams into her pillow every night. Let's go, I'll drive you downtown."

Schools were closed the next week, but without any therapeutic Hygienists shows scheduled, I couldn't seem to break out of my mental funk. I looked at the calendar in my room and wished I could fast-forward through time, zipping directly to June.

On one particularly stir-crazy evening, I grabbed one of the new stuffed animals my mom had bought for 4-217 and made a surreally weird four-minute camcorder movie, *Courage Bear*. Featuring only the title character and me, with narration by the bear, the flick follows us as happy roommates (with a highly self-pleasing inclusion of Babs Streisand's version of "Someone to Watch Over Me") until the opening of an unwelcome piece of mail sends me into a rage, during which I launch Courage Bear out the third-story window. Landing on the icy pavement below, C.B. transforms into a creature of the night, drifting ethereally above the dingy Lower East Side snowscape. He ultimately returns to the cold, wet pavement outside our former home. Unheeded by slow-motion passersby, altered Courage Bear mutters his final incantation:

> *I am that bear in the shadow*
> *I am the bear in the cold*
> *I am the one in the rough gray ice*
>
> *If you pass me . . . SAY HELLOOOOOOO!*

When I came back to school on Monday, February 23, my lessons were ready, but I did not feel sufficiently recharged to take on the tidal wave of 4-217. First thing in the morning, I got word that Pat Cartwright would be out all week, meaning I would still have four of her kids to babysit.

Where was Pat? Back in December, she made comments about quitting, saying that Fausto was driving her over the edge, but they seemed like dark jokes. She was raising a three-year-old son on her own and I knew the boy had been sick several times in the fall. I hoped Ms. Cartwright was all right, but my hoping was useless. Now I had to deal with Sayquan and Asonai, two bonus "challenges."

Meanwhile, despite the barrage of crises and cruelty in 4-217, my skills of anticipation and preemption were becoming more and more well-honed. For every time Bernard fought, there were four or five instances when I rushed in to extinguish the fire when it was still just a spark. But, I remembered, it's not how you fall that matters; it's how you land. If I could barely keep them from hurting each other, what would happen when there were no teachers around to check them?

On the way to pick up my paycheck, Ms. Guiterrez waylaid me to say that she wanted to see my planbook first thing tomorrow morning. This would be her second perusal of it this month, despite a satisfactory review last time. Disgusted, I went home and fell into bed, unconscious by 7 p.m. My alarm sounded at 3:30 a.m., and I reformatted the whole book with elaborate form-sheets I made on my computer. I came to school carrying a thick dossier of standards, benchmarks, aims, objectives, Bloom's taxonomy implementations, multistep procedures, and other like information. I hoped this comprehensive showing would get the watchdogs off my back. By now, the consistently glowering inspections really ticked me off. I *knew* I was making progress. Timid Evley, who had broken the ice with me with his mysterious private-part problem, was beating his fear of public speaking. Lito Ruiz was writing creative narratives. Almost all of them could explain multiplication and division inside out. The administration did not see those things. They saw my unattractive board displays, the disconcerted flailing in November, and my young age.

Ms. Guiterrez was nowhere to be found before school, so I retired to my room, the fancy folder tucked under my arm.

At 10:45, a lovely surprise came my way. Julianne Nemet, a social worker from the Montefiore Health Clinic (our privatized nurse's office), showed up to do the last in her series of three monthly lessons on "Friendship and Acceptance." Her first lesson about anger management was taught to every class in the school; the students responded to hand signs and chants of "Baby sleeping! Tai chi!" as a signal to shift from kerfuffle to tranquility.

This time, Julianne wrote "RESPECT" in block letters on the board. She had not done much more when Mrs. Boyd burst into the room . . . *with Dilla Zane!* "Keep going. Ignore us," Mrs. Boyd ordered to Julianne.

Dilla Zane (her first and last names were always said together) was the Region One, Network Five Instructional Superintendent: Mrs. Boyd's direct boss. Her reputation for white-glove-caliber inspections for compliance to city regulations was well-known in the halls of P.S. 85. She came to schools at 7 a.m. and entered empty classrooms with a camera to photograph the bulletin boards for standard-adherence scrutiny. She pulled random notebooks out of student desks and scoured them for proper formatting and content. Dilla Zane zapped people, and the word around the campfire said Mrs. Boyd was in her crosshairs.

The duo descended on me in the back of the room. Dilla Zane riffled through my lesson plans. "Very thorough," she commented. I had picked the right day to tidy up my paperwork. "Show me a portfolio."

I picked out Sonandia's, and Mrs. Boyd frowned. "Not Sonandia's. She's your best student."

"You can look at any one you like," I said.

"How about your *worst* student? Show us that one," Mrs. Boyd said. I didn't like being put on the spot to name my "worst" student to my principal. Dilla Zane reached into the crate and picked out a random red folder.

Deloris Barlow's. She had been discharged from my class two months ago and barely did any work when she was in it. I started to explain, "That girl actually —"

"Just let Dilla look," Mrs. Boyd said with quiet hostility. Dilla Zane closed the folder after five seconds and did not pick out another.

"Mr. Brown is one of our new, very intelligent first-year teachers," Mrs. Boyd said. "He graduated from the prestigious NYU film school and is going to be starting a new after-school film club for advanced students."

Dilla Zane looked to me. "Yes," I said.

"What is the most challenging aspect about being a teacher, Mr. Brown?" Dilla Zane asked.

I was ready. "For me, it's the constant classroom upkeep. I'm getting better, but it's like another full-time job. I've had some issues with management and that's taken the front burner over keeping my displays as current as they should be."

"You can see he has quite a long way to go," Mrs. Boyd chimed.

"What changes do you think could best help you overcome your obstacles?"

This was the real question I had been hoping for. "More allotted time for collaboration and coplanning. We need more sharing of successful practices among teachers. I think the culture of the school could foster that more. We could be more of a team," I said.

"Are you saying you don't feel supported?" Mrs. Boyd asked, aghast.

"No. I definitely appreciate all the help you gave me with the coteacher situation and Ms. Barrow and everything else. And Barbara has been great as a mentor." Dilla Zane and Mrs. Boyd shared a nod. "But the atmosphere in the school is very isolated, and I think everyone could work better with more teamwork built into the schedule."

Dilla Zane shook my hand. "Thank you for your honesty," she said. Mrs. Boyd showed no expression, and they left.

Upon the administrators' exit, hums of chatter instantly ignited. Sayquan and Asonai had already done this lesson in Pat Cartwright's class and started crawling on their desks. Julianne Nemet looked to me to shush the class, and I did several times, but a minute or two later, some kid would naturally start talking. They were actually in much better form than usual, but Julianne Nemet was clearly flummoxed.

"This lesson is about respect, and if you don't show me respect, I'm going to leave," she said through gritted teeth. Sayquan laughed mockingly, and Julianne grabbed her satchel. "Fine. Good-bye."

And she left. I peered out in the hall, thinking this was some kind of joke, but she was gone. I had eighteen minutes until my prep, an awkward amount of time for any substantive activity. I made the kids write apology letters to Julianne Nemet, even though she owed the class and me an apology for hanging me out to dry for eighteen minutes, and reinforcing a pretty lousy life lesson about abandonment.

Tayshaun Jackson grinned crazily as he wrote:

Dear Ms. Nemet,

I feel <u>terrible</u> about what happened. Please forgive us. That was so terrible about how you was mad.

Love, Tayshaun

I collected the letters and, after school, chucked them in the Dumpster.

March

Mr. Brown Can Moo

"Sonandia was in a fight!"

"Where is she?"

"I don't know!"

"Sonandia's cryin'! She was in a fight!"

"Where's Mr. Daly?"

"Mr. Brown, the class gone crazy!"

"Everybody line up! Get in line. Now! Line up! Bernard, Cwasey, Hamisi, line up! Gladys V., come here! Where's Sonandia?"

"The bathroom."

"Go see if she's all right. Line up, 4-217! Where's Mr. Randazzo?"

"Mr. Brown, Sonandia was fighting!"

"Worry about yourself. Let's go, line it up!"

I don't know where Gladys V. went, but Sonandia, alone, stepped slowly out of the bathroom on the far side of the cafeteria. Her face was buried in her hands. I ran to her, and everything behind me went haywire. Several kids bolted in different directions, with Eddie and Lito sprinting up the stairwell. My momentary absence was instantly interpreted as the green light to rampage.

Sonandia's face was scratched, but the skin was not broken. She didn't want to talk. Inez, a paraprofessional, showed up and explained what had happened. Two girls from Mr. Tejera's class, sitting at the lunch table adjacent to 4-217, were mocking a special ed boy about his clothes. Sonandia saw this and got out of her seat to step between the tormentors and their prey. The two girls walked away, and when Sonandia asked the crying boy if he was all right, he attacked her, clawing her face with his sharp nails.

I listened, but didn't know what to do. Olga Tavarez came on the scene, rushing over from her lunch duty post in the other cafeteria. I left Sony to her mother's care and ran back to my class, yanking apart tussling Bernard and Hamisi.

Four minutes later, I had my students in our classroom and demanded silence with a more hot-blooded tone than usual.

"Mr. Brown, you sweating."

"Silence, Hamisi! I want to talk to you all about lunch today. Two different and very important things happened. First, I want you to look at this 'Mr. Brown's Words and Phrases' poster that's been on the board every day since the fall. Words like *empathy* and *random acts of kindness.* You did an excellent job in your writing assignments about these words. But empathy and random acts of kindness don't mean anything if you just think about them sometimes or write about them. You have to *do* them, and you have to do them not when it's easy, but when it's hard. Really hard. That's the difference between really brave people and really lazy people. Today, Sonandia showed what it takes to be brave, to stand up for what she thinks is right. She stood up for someone who probably never had another person stand up for him before, and he got confused and Sonandia got hurt. But even though it turned out that way this time, because of what she did, in that one minute in the lunchroom, Sonandia will *always* have my respect. She's a brave person, and I will always respect someone who has that kind of courage. You are all capable of doing these kinds of things. Whether you actually do them proves what kind of person you are."

I did say all of these things, but not without breaking off between every sentence to pacify at least one out-of-control child. When I first referred to the poster, Cwasey and Lakiya yelled out about my breaking the board and covering it up. Every time I mentioned Sonandia, I received a half dozen callouts offering eyewitness accounts. The Pat Cartwright exiles mumbled audibly to each other the whole time. Toward my driving finale, Athena fell out of her chair and stopped the train. And, of course, my most important listener was not there; Sonandia was off recuperating in some cranny of Public School 85, sipping Sprite from a styrofoam cup.

"The second thing I can't believe is what happened to our line when I left it for thirty seconds. It's sad that I can't trust you not to act like kindergartners. The kids that come with me to Ms. Bowers's and Ms. Pierson's classes know that the kindergartners and first-graders are really better behaved than some people in here." This time I was looking for some verbal assent from the gallery, but all I got was Eric making a fart sound with his mouth. "I can't even trust some people now to be respectful when I'm talking about something that's clearly very important to me. Therefore, until I see more of a positive change, like what we had before Christmas, there are no more bathroom or water fountain privileges. Don't even ask. That is the end. Take out the 'Comparing Fractions' sheets we started this morning." I wanted to call Eddie and Lito on leaving the cafeteria without permission, but publicly singling kids out led to unproductive and momentum-losing denials and power struggles. On the other hand, addressing the group with phrases like "some of you" or "some students in this class" enabled them to pass the buck.

About ten minutes later, with Seresa and Tayshaun as my board helpers drawing greater/lesser fraction pictures, Sonandia walked in, silent and straight-faced, although her pink eyes betrayed recent crying. She opened her math folder, took out two sharp pencils, and quietly followed the lesson.

Pat Cartwright's absence hurt. Rumors circulated about a nervous breakdown. Mrs. Boyd didn't help the swirling unease with the proclamation at Professional Development, "I spoke to her on the phone today and she didn't *sound* sick." Selfishly, I viewed Pat's disappearance as a twisted validation of this job's brutal toll. I wondered if I was a sicko for looking for a bright side to a colleague's collapse.

Steady, informed gripes from the other fourth-grade teachers about the babysitting assignments of Ms. Cartwright's split-up class forced the administration to try something new. The victim was first-year Fellow Tim Shea.

Tim's setup as a coteacher with superorganized veteran third-grade teacher Sarina Kuo was a beautiful thing. He worked intensively with small groups within the context of a solidly preestablished, calm classroom culture. Basically, he was teaching.

On the afternoon of Monday, March 1, the executive decision came down that Tim was to assume the reins of Ms. Cartwright's class, 4-219, starting Wednesday. "You can spend Tuesday preparing," Mrs. Boyd told him.

At Professional Development, Tim looked thoroughly non-plussed. "I have to leave my kids," he said, "because the school won't pay for a sub."

I nodded. "It sucks."

"I've heard they're horrendous."

"Some of them," I said. "If any act like real jerks and you don't want to go through Randazzo, you can send them to me to cool down. Seriously, I have experience with rockheads." Who had I become?

"Thanks," Tim said. "I heard Mr. R. doesn't do jack."

On Wednesday morning, no 4-219 rockheads came to my room, but through the wall I could hear Tim screaming. At lunch he looked crazed, his tie loosed. "I want to hit Sayquan," he raved. "I want to knock him out. I had to control myself. I know you're not supposed to say it, but the kid is an asshole. He's an asshole! He's a flat-out mean kid who tries to wreck everything. I can't stand him. I thought I was going to knock him out. And Fausto is such a bastard. Seriously, that's the most yelling I have ever done in my life. This is fucking ridiculous."

I offered a few suggestions about rewards, realizing that I was essentially looking at myself from six months earlier.

After the second day, Tim marched to the office to reject his corrupt assignment. The administration capitulated, and Tim returned to cheers in his old room. One week later, Sarina Kuo went on leave to be a stay-at-home mom, and Tim assumed the class full-time. Things were as they should be.

Mary, Kimberly, Asonai, and Sayquan from 4-219 returned to my watch indefinitely, but I minded much less, knowing that the alternative would be destroying Tim Shea and his class.

Marge Foley recommended *Phoebe the Spy* to me as a literacy/social studies tool. The historical fiction story features a thirteen-year-old black girl who, encouraged by her tavern-owner father, poses as George Washington's maid to thwart an assassination threat. With few clues to work with and communication unexpectedly severed from her dad, timid Phoebe eventually discovers the would-be assassin's identity (a suspicious employee on the Washington estate) and planned method of murder (poisoned peas). I loved it.

I created a unit called "Spies." To open, I read aloud (with many historically expositional asides and manic hand gestures) the first chapter of our new class thriller. My swing voters in the Cwasey-Dennis-Hamisi clique were taken in by the espionage, and the influential class majority thus agreed with me that the story was worthwhile. Athena, Destiny, and Evley checked *Phoebe the Spy* out of the library before dismissal.

We made a giant list of things we knew about spies, including "gadgets," "secret codes," and "the show *Totally Spies.*" Giant lists reliably made their day.

I told the class we were all going to write our own spy narratives. We would revise our stories together, and ultimately publish a book of 4-217 original works. This was my splashier sequel from last summer's smash hit starring Jimmarie. I improvised to model my own spy-story plot.

"What if, day after day, you kept coming to school, and Mr. Brown wasn't here? When you ask other teachers or Mr. Randazzo, no one will tell you where he is or if he's sick or what. So the class decides to team up and do some spy work! Lakiya and Eddie pretend to fight in the back of the room so the substitute teacher has to go over to them. But Lakiya and Eddie are only acting, getting the teacher's attention on them by creating a diversion! They do this so Evley and Gladys V. can slip out of the class unnoticed and sneak over to the office. When no one's looking, they go through the teacher files and find Mr. Brown's address. They copy it down fast on a piece of paper that Evley brought because he planned ahead. Then they put the file back so no one knows it was gone and they sneak back to class. After school, the class tells Ms. Samuels, who they know they can trust, about wanting to find Mr. Brown. Ms. Samuels rents a bus and drives them to Manhattan. They realize they're not at Mr. Brown's apartment, but at the big Toys 'R' Us in Union Square with the Ferris wheel! When they go inside, Mr. Brown is waiting and they have a huge party. The students are so surprised until Ms. Samuels shows them a note that Mr. Brown wrote to her. It says, 'When they get clever, call my cell phone and take them to the party.' And then 4-217 was the happiest and best-behaved class forever."

For homework, they were each to compose a first draft of an original spy narrative.

The next morning, however, only six out of twenty-four had something to show, the lowest homework percentage of the year. With so few kids to participate, I ditched my peer-revision plans and pushed up our introductory American Revolution social studies lesson, promising my six conscientious writers that I would reward them at lunchtime.

A laminated, full-color mega-timeline, purchased over the February break, aided me in outlining and describing the major themes of imposition, rebellion, and victory. I thought it was going well until Bernard piped up. "Mr. Brown, is George Washington alive?"

I balked, having already mentioned numerous times that these events occurred over two hundred years ago.

"Yes, is he alive?" Athena chimed.

"George Washington is not alive. This was all over two hundred years ago. No one from that time is alive, and none of their children or grandchildren are alive."

"Is Thomas Jefferson alive?" Hamisi, who looked like he was listening, inquired in earnest. I refrained from hanging my head. In a movie, the scene would end on such a punch line, but we still had thirty minutes of this lesson to battle through.

I explained that very few people live to be a hundred. When only Sonandia and Seresa could tell me that 1904 was one hundred years before our current 2004, I realized with similar surprise to the "What planet are we on?" revelation that these kids did not understand elapsed time, be it in minutes or decades. As a litmus test, I asked what time it would be sixty minutes from now. No hands. What time will it be one hour from now? Four volunteers. Thus, my hopes for in-depth, history-based lessons were banished to make way for my new, deceptively simple-seeming campaign for "Time."

I had a shaky history with bringing kids up to the classroom for lunch. The idea was first presented to me in September by Evan Krieg as an isolation punishment, but I quickly learned that spending lunch hour with my hypersocial offenders was more of a punishment for me than for them.

One day in October, Destiny Rivera tugged on my sleeve and in the meekest voice said, "Mr. Brown, I'm having trouble with place value. Could you give me any extra help at lunchtime?" Soon, I had a motley rotation of six extra-helpees, anchored by Destiny. I knew that Destiny got extra math help in the after-school program for ninety minutes, three times a week, covering exactly the same material I reviewed at lunch periods. What she really enjoyed, what they all did, was the intimacy and attention. I couldn't blame them. But my desperate need for a midday respite slowly made "coming up for lunch" a nostalgic thing of the past. On this March day, when I appeared in the cafeteria to bring up my six budding Ian Flemings, I was besieged with pleas to tag along. I smiled at my new leverage, and Seresa, Dennis, Sonandia, Athena, Jennifer, and Evley raced up the stairs. We spent our too-short half hour analyzing Seresa's "Teacher Gone Missing":

> One day a teacher named Mr. Planter had not come to school. But the thing is that he is alwayl at school and he is never absent so the chridren thougth that mabey he is sick. So the kids let that they pass. The next day he did not come so the students say let's investagent it. So the class had a plane to get Mr. Planter address but the office was full. So they made so much noise that all the people that were in the office came to ther class. So the shortes person sneak out of the and went to the office and went though the file and got Mr Planter adrees. So the Class got together and went to his house and when the rang the bell the door opend and then a stremer pup out It was a party for the hole class and They were very surprised and that was the story of the Teacher Gone Missing.

The next day, nineteen kids came to school with spy stories. Most were more awkward renditions of my initial we-have-to-find-Mr.-Brown caper. Tayshaun wrote a five-page epic, complete with drawings of the scene where he and Dennis fistfight my captors. The work reflected enthusiasm for the material, now flowing once the seal had popped.

I marked up each composition with longer-than-usual comments, questions, and recommendations. Since the kids were psyched about their subject matter, this was my opportunity to zero in on clarity. I didn't need a class full of O. Henrys; coherent written thought was a major victory. They wrote second drafts in class, which I again marked up. On Friday, I tabled the spy stories to finish *Phoebe the Spy* and write book reviews.

I felt reinvigorated over the weekend. I set Monday aside for exchanging spy stories with peers and making comments, using the model from my lunchtime workshop. As soon as we began, though, I sensed problems.

I had been following — and feeling good about — the progressive draft model recommended for portfolio work, but the kids were out of steam. Three days had passed since our last tinkering with these papers, and they had already written three drafts. I should have anticipated that peer-revising wouldn't work. Many of them had a hard enough time stitching two logical sentences together, let alone giving or receiving substantive feedback. Frustration boiled over immediately. "Dennis the Spy" was dirtied on the floor, thoughtlessly pinned beneath an impaling desk leg. Gladys F. got upset with her partner Bernard and ripped his paper, so he ripped her paper. Cwasey scribbled all over Tayshaun's opus, so Tayshaun tore it up and cried.

The folder containing all of Seresa's subsequent drafts of "Teacher Gone Missing" disappeared forever.

I didn't know what to say. My train derailed, all in one minute, while I was talking to Evley about making sure that his readers understand the setting. I collected the surviving stories and put them in the portfolios as they were. No 4-217 spy book.

When Ms. Croom showed up for my prep period, I shepherded my six tutors to Ms. Pierson's class in the minischool. On our way to Trisha's room, we passed K–1 assistant principal Diane Rawson's office. She called out, "Yo, Brown! I want to talk to you." I delivered my tutors and answered the request.

"Mr. Brown, I've noticed you've been taking some of your fourth-graders to the lower-grade rooms, like right now. How is that going?"

"Extremely excellent," I said in a somber tone, still raw over the spy fiasco.

"Great. We've noticed, and we think it's a very positive thing for the school," Ms. Rawson said.

Who was *we*? Did *we* include anyone who was considering "giving up on me" several months ago? I noticed Diane Rawson's gray, cigarette-stained teeth, and they somehow made me angrier.

"Thank you," I said.

"We had an idea. This month is Dr. Seuss's hundredth birthday. We're planning a special celebration for the lower grades, and we want to have groups of upper-grade kids going around the school to read Seuss stories to the little ones. We thought you might be interested to do it with your class as the readers. Some parents are going to whip up some green eggs for everybody. No ham, though. Too complicated. What do you say?"

"It sounds great."

"Great! We're going to do it next Tuesday, on the parent-conference half day. You know, a nice thing before we give out report cards. I'll give you more details tomorrow."

"I have something to ask, though," I said. "Or at least, something I'd really like. Art. I want Mrs. Kreps to come to my class for a period to make paper Cat in the Hat hats. The kids would love it."

"Um, we'll see. I'll have to talk to Kreps about her schedule." Rawson's reluctance was evident.

"Okay. Thank you for the offer. I think everything will be terrific." I wheeled out of the office on an instant mission to track down Mrs. Kreps before Rawson got to her. I was successful, and we made a morning date for Friday.

Off the cuff, during our social studies lesson on Wednesday, I mentioned that as a fourth-grader, I did a report on the state of Pennsylvania. Sudden and overwhelming interest in doing state projects of their own caused me to change gears and tabulate the interested students (everyone, even Lakiya) and their selected states. I did not have state projects in my plans, but I didn't want to stanch this unexpected geyser of academic enthusiasm. The next day, Maimouna (Missouri), Seresa (Florida), Jennifer (Ohio, her home state), and Destiny (Texas) brought in lavishly decorated construction-paper folders containing information printed from the Internet. I had underestimated the hunger for projects and looked to the upcoming Seuss-fest as an opportunity to execute a more structured whole-class adventure. I decided to tuck away the state projects as an ace for next year.

Meanwhile, I sought to salvage writing lessons by focusing on a fresh concept: figurative language. I brought back my Robert Frost poems and focused several lessons on passages from Louis Sachar's *Holes*. Sony wrote a poem called "Touching the Sky":

Up! Up! So high
People look like ants
I see this all over town
Why is this?
I am touching the sky
With its baby blue color
Tippy-toeing on the top of a skyscraper
Tryin' not to fall.
This giant sky which I'm tryin' to reach is tryin' to pull me and hug me
How much more can I reach the sky? Hmm!
Who knows?
Up up and away I go?
Into the sky blooming into a beautiful sky and being together.
Oh I have reached
the sky.
It feels great!

I announced the coming Tuesday's event, giving special highlight to 4-217's exclusive participation, and received the hoped-for enthusiasm. I let them choose their own reading teams (a mild circus), and modeled dynamic Seussian possibilities by performing *The Foot Book* as a rhythm poem. Lito Ruiz's face showed life that had not been there since before the ELA Test. "Mr. Brown, I can't wait till Tuesday!"

Mrs. Kreps's art project was a massive success. The kids were giddy with their new paper hats, giggling throughout the one-two-three-step process. The remainder of the day proved a better than usual Friday, with art catalyzing the upbeat mood.

Over the weekend, I caught a Greyhound back to Jersey to collect my mom's comprehensive roundup of Dr. Seuss books and paraphernalia, including eleven giant red felt bow ties with safety pins, several Thing One and Thing Two dolls, and a full-body Cat in the Hat mascot suit, hat and footies included.

Our rehearsals on Monday forebode disaster. Inhibited by their peers' glazed-out stares and occasional mocking comments, the groups turned *Marvin K. Mooney Will You Please Go Now!* into indecipherable mumbles. Realizing the 217 stage was a deterrent for performance, I separated the groups for private practice time. Whatever was going to happen on Tuesday, it would at least be out of the ordinary.

At the end of the day, I brought out the special rewards bag to bestow packs of Starburst to last week's winning group. My hand felt frantically around the bag. No Starburst. I opened and closed my desk drawers. Gone.

Who had stolen from me? *From my desk?* I mentally riffled through the primary suspects' imaginary dossiers. Deloris, my previous offender, had been banished. Lakiya, I didn't peg for a thief. Marvin had been very happy lately, and he only seemed to misbehave when he was upset. If Tayshaun had stolen the candy, he would have bragged and word would have gotten back to me. Eric did not have the guts to pull off such a risky move. I felt guilty for suspecting specific children, all of whom, or at least all but one, were innocent. I got angry at myself for not learning my lesson after Lakiya's Yu-Gi-Oh stack disappeared a couple months ago. I didn't *want* to lock my things away from my students. I wanted us to share a basic trust, to be a team. Reality socked me in the face; it wasn't working.

At the back of the Professional Development room, I seethed. The fourth- and fifth-grade teachers leafed through three-inch-thick red binders, our new bibles for the coming transition from Success for All to Balanced Literacy. With the new literacy curriculum, homeroom teachers would deliver daily Writing Workshop and Reading Workshop lessons in a ninety-minute "golden block" of time. As Marge Foley explained the new flow of the day, set to begin April 13, I tried to slow my raging pulse.

As I mulled over how I could not trust my kids, Ms. Guiterrez took the floor and gave a speech about how immensely critical the first days of Balanced Literacy would be in setting good routines that would last for the rest of the year. When the floor opened for questions, I raised my hand. "I agree that getting the routines going the first day is crucial. I have two kids [Marvin Winslow and Lakiya Ray] who I absolutely know, I am absolutely positive, will not be able to follow the workshop model and independent reading schedule. I'm worried they could throw off the dynamic for the whole group, especially in the new program's infancy when we're setting the tone. Could we set up, just for the first few days, with Ms. Devereaux or someone, a preemptive pullout of sure-fire problem kids, like we did for the Test last month? Kind of like a Balanced Literacy jail."

The jail comment drew some bland chuckles, and Ms. Guiterrez proceeded with her speech without acknowledging I had said anything. "We have a tough job changing gears in the middle of the year. It's going to be hard, but I have confidence . . ."

Being ignored, especially after making what I felt was a reasonable and actionable suggestion, pissed me off. Ironically, I had been the only fourth-grade homeroom teacher not to send any of my kids to take the Test in Ms. Devereaux's circus room when the option was given. I waited a few minutes, raised my hand again, and made the same suggestion. *I will be heard!*

Ms. Guiterrez did not look at me. "Mr. Brown, if you cannot control your own children, then there are larger problems than Balanced Literacy. Look at Ms. Mulvehill. She has Horace to deal with, and she's doing fine."

Melissa Mulvehill visibly cringed when Guiterrez dropped her name, forcing a weak smile out of politeness. She had been interviewing at other schools since January, and talked openly during my occasional lunches in her room about her disdain for every administrator in the school. In December, when she received a voice-mail message during lunch that a close aunt had suddenly passed away, Mr. Randazzo would not let her go to her family until the end of the day, because he could not find someone to cover her room.

I'm finished with you, Guiterrez, I thought. You don't believe in me, and I don't believe in you. No one knows how this is all going to end, but it's probably going to get ugly. And breathing does not equal being fine.

I opted against marring the start of our Dr. Seuss/parent-teacher conference half day with accusations about Starburst. Instead, I bought new packs at the corner deli. The uncharacteristic morning candy distribution fueled excitement for our big day.

Each group got a schedule listing four K–1 classes. The kids put on their hats and I selected eleven lucky bow tie wearers. I persuaded Mr. Randazzo to clear Cat Samuels's morning so she could cochaperone the festivities, and we went to work pinning on the red felt ties. For my final trick, I slipped into the Cat in the Hat outfit — surprise! — and lined up my delighted children. Ms. Rawson greeted us excitedly in the minischool lobby. "Oh my God, you have to get a picture in that costume with Kendra [Boyd]!" she bubbled.

With a vote of faith, I sent my groups on their routes. Cat and I darted around the school, checking in and occasionally commandeering the readings. I put on some frenzied performances of *The Foot Book* and the aptly titled *Mr. Brown Can Moo, Can You?*, modeling for my 4-217 performers as much as entertaining the little ones.

The whole thing felt good. When I appeared in a room, I felt a proud "Yeah, I'm with him" vibe radiating from my students. And after one or two goes, they really got into it. Soon the slated itineraries were exhausted, but everyone wanted to keep the activity going. The Lakiya-Hamisi-Eric *Foot Book* contingent worked fast and hit every kindergarten and first-grade class. The minischool corridor echoed with shouts of "I need a *Green Eggs and Ham* in 1M9!" or "KM1 needs *The Cat in the Hat Comes Back!*" I exhausted a disposable camera, and, with the exception of Cwasey knocking Athena's green eggs to the floor, the event was a love fest.

Mrs. Boyd and I smiled at a camera, and she gave me a vague nod, putting her hand on my forearm. "Come to my office during the break. Ms. Guiterrez and I need to speak to you."

Students were dismissed at 11:30 from the lunchroom. On a

high from the Seussian success, I made an in-costume star turn in the packed cafeteria. Children flocked to the five-foot-nine Cat in the Hat. "Yo, Mr. Cat in da Hat man, wassup!" offered Tyree, the most famously recalcitrant of Mr. Krieg's overgrown fifth-graders.

With a ninety-minute break before conferences kicked off at one o'clock, the Fellows lunched at the Splendid Deli on Fordham Road, but I stayed behind, standing outside Mrs. Boyd's closed office door. When it opened, Mrs. Boyd directed me to sit in an awkward position between herself and Ms. Guiterrez at the meeting table.

"First of all, good work on the Dr. Seuss event. That was beautiful," Mrs. Boyd began.

"Thank you."

"Unfortunately, we have a pretty big problem." I noticed my class stack of report cards under Ms. Guiterrez's palm, to my right. All teachers had submitted their student report cards on the previous Friday for a perfunctory check-over. I had spent probably twice as long calibrating and commenting on this set than I had in the first marking period back in November. Now that I had more of a grip on what I was doing, I felt my assessments were more thorough and accurate.

Guiterrez cut the silence. "Why are your children not improving, Mr. Brown?"

"They are improving."

"No. They are not." She took the top report card from the stack and opened it. "Manolo Ruiz. All twos. No improvement."

My heart pounded. Out spilled words, not sufficiently composed for a cogent rejoinder. "Lito's one of my most improved students. He's really come a long way."

Ms. Guiterrez and Mrs. Boyd looked at me like I was an imbecile. "Apparently not," Mrs. Boyd said with a laugh-snort. "His grades indicate no change. Mr. Brown, you *begged* me for a classroom in the summer, and I gave you what you wanted. I took a chance on you. But I have to tell you, the proof is in the pudding."

Lito Ruiz came to 4-217 in September as a low "one," to view him in terms of the scholastic achievement rubric. He was an orphan who smashed his classmate's glasses. But by December, he was working hard. He scored much higher on my division assessment than he had on the previous unit's multiplication test, which indicated that he finally did get a grasp on multiplication concepts, since you can't divide without them; it just took him longer. In February, after I read a book to the class about colonial-era religious-tolerance seeker Roger Williams, Lito asked if he could write a story in which he got to meet Roger Williams. His penmanship and mechanics were terrible, but his ideas had teeth. I wish I could reproduce the story, but when it was nearly complete at two pages (by far his longest ever composition), the work vanished from his desk and was never found.

For this second round of report cards, teachers received explicit instructions that the students' grades should be accurate projections of their scores on the Test. Lito Ruiz was a poor taker of standardized tests. My twos for him in the second marking period were hugely optimistic. As for the first marking period, I elected against giving him the "ones" that his academic-rubric-based output reflected because I knew that seeing a full slate of the lowest possible grades would crush him.

I didn't say any of this because I was frozen, off guard, and Ms. Guiterrez was on Mrs. Boyd's heels with the next victim.

"Gladys Ferraro. This student has actually *decreased* in the 'personal and social growth' categories. Hamisi Umar, same marks as the first period. No improvement."

I cringed, realizing I was in for a full audit of all twenty-five of my kids. Mrs. Boyd took several from the pile. "Lakiya Ray. We can skip her; she's an idiot. Okay, Marvin Winslow. He actually has a little improvement in math. A few twos. Will he get a two on the Math Test?"

"Probably not," I said. My principal had just called my student an *idiot*. Ms. Guiterrez shook her head at me.

"So we have two problems," Mrs. Boyd announced. "Number one, we need to see some improvement, and number two, we need that improvement to be real. Mr. Brown, everybody teaches. The school day is a long day for everyone. But whether we get tired from being here is not the measure of being a good teacher. Your classroom is often a mess, and your bulletin boards just don't illustrate real caring. I don't want this to be a lost year for those children. I have to consider giving you a U rating unless you can really show us something. Do you have anything to say?"

After being called an incompetent, loafing liar, there were many things I wanted to say. I swallowed them all. "The students are learning and I apologize for not reflecting it better in the report card data. I will do everything I can to improve my methods and my management. I would really like to ask, though, to officially start the Visual Arts Club. It will energize me and the kids, and, at the worst, it will be an interesting no-loss experiment." I could feel myself veering out of coherence with the last sentence and abruptly stopped speaking.

Mrs. Boyd's demeanor changed so completely that it seemed the past five minutes had not happened. "I've told you we have money in the budget to pay you overtime for after-school work, right?"

I nodded cautiously.

"Okay then, it's a go," she said.

I gave another solemn nod, my blood still up.

Ms. Guiterrez snapped back to business. "Sonandia Azcona, we know about her. Joseph Castanon, no improvement. Tiffany Sanchez, no improvement except in 'shows evidence of understanding text,' but she went down in 'builds on the ideas of others in conversation.' Eric Ruiz, oh boy . . ."

No parents showed up to conference with me, so I brooded over the U threat. At the year's end, teachers are rated with either an S (satisfactory) or U (unsatisfactory), the latter spelling the end of your teaching career if you get zapped with it before gaining tenure. Considering New York City's severe teacher shortage, U's were reserved for dire, intolerable circumstances. *Am I unsatisfactory?*

Two parents came just before the three o'clock break: Sonandia's and Jennifer's mothers. Some teachers still had none. I had better traffic at the 5:00–7:00 session, although Lakiya's and Cwasey's mothers did not make the return trip, probably smelling trouble.

I told Christian Salerno's mother that he was in deep danger of repeating fourth grade, because he did not take his work seriously. She responded that Christian told her the work at P.S. 85 was too easy for him after transferring in from a tougher parochial school. I stifled my shock at the enormity of Christian's sustained lie and bluntly told her — and Christian, who was sitting there — that Christian was struggling with fundamental math concepts and writing basics. "He needs to cut the laziness and lying and get *serious* about school," I asserted.

Mrs. Salerno sighed. "All he does is close the door to his room and dance. He listens to disco jungle all day. *Disco jungle.* Can you believe it? He's always moonwalking." Christian tried unsuccessfully to suppress a sheepish smile. I had a sudden, bizarre desire to see Christian Salerno do the moonwalk. He vigorously agreed to an impromptu performance between groups one and six. What kind of teacher was I?

Tiffany Sanchez's chiseled father wrote "Tiffeny" on my sign-in sheet. Smelling strongly of cologne, he was exceedingly affable and nodded understandingly when I brought up last month's in-class breakdown. When I recommended talking to Tiffany about alternate ways to express her anger, he closed off. "That's how she is," he said flatly. "She'll be fine." He scared the hell out of me.

Both of Bernard's parents came, lugging him in tow. This was the meeting I was waiting for. I thought Bernard had the greatest swing potential, that this conference might actually impact his behavior and his life. I opened by praising his creativity and enthusiasm to participate. Everyone was smiling.

"But there is something holding Bernard back from being the best student he can be, which would be one of the top students in the class," I said. A sharp, anticipatory silence hung in the air. I fumbled for my first lower-the-boom words, prolonging the expectant pause. "Bernard explodes when he gets angry. I know we've talked about this before, and I'm grateful that you came to me back in September to talk about it, but it's getting worse, and as Bernard gets bigger and stronger, it's getting more dangerous for him and his peers. I can't tolerate fighting in the classroom, so when it does happen and when Bernard's involved, I have to call him on it and punish him. I think this has led to Bernard resenting me. I need him to understand that I want to help him. I am not the enemy. Bernard has shut down during lessons and is constantly talking and moving around, which causes disruptions, and isn't fair to the other kids. He *needs* to check himself when he feels himself starting to get upset. He can ask to leave the classroom, and I will always let him if it's to cool down. And he *needs* to be respectful in the classroom. He should be one of my leaders, but lately he's been causing problems."

Bernard's parents were stunned that this speech could follow my glowing introduction. Anticipating what was to come at home, Bernard started quietly to cry.

Students with at least one parent who worked academically with them at home could read well. Students with no help at home could not. The difference was never more starkly apparent than after meeting with a succession of parents at the conferences.

Allie Bowers reported the same findings with her kindergartners. "It starts when they're born," she said. "Once they get to school, that gap widens so fast, because the kids who know the alphabet excel, and the kids with deadbeat parents just get discouraged."

I came up with an idea for City Hall: free literacy-based parenting classes with attendance incentives, like Huggies and books. If your kid is anywhere from in the womb to five years old, you can come to a weekly meeting to learn ways to raise a literate, empowered child. The evening classes would be moderated by community members, which would create jobs and foster a neighborhood culture of learning.

At home, I pitched the idea to Greg. "I don't know," he said, grimacing. "You'd need a lot of money to start that up, and I don't think people would come. The parents who would need the literacy training the most are probably illiterate themselves and don't want to get exposed and look the fool. People are also touchy about being told how to raise their kids. Maybe they'd show up once, take the Huggies, and never come back."

My idea died. I had enough mountains to climb without writing probably doomed proposals for social programs. The next week, Greg got accepted to the University of Chicago school for public policy.

Pat Cartwright came back. I hugged her at first sight in the cafeteria during lineup. Most of the faculty treated her with distant politeness, eyeing her with the masked but acute awareness of a celebrity in the room. The administration said nothing to her beyond Mr. Randazzo's "Good to have you back, Pat," and in fifteen minutes everyone was sequestered in their classrooms as if she had never left.

The P.S. 85 Visual Arts Club launched on Wednesday, March 24. The regular school day ended on a frenzied note, with Athena's desk toppling right before dismissal. Carol Slocumb, the second-year Fellow who ran her third-grade class with boot camp intensity, agreed to help me out by leading 4-217 down the steps to the parking lot, so I could remain upstairs to greet the after-school participants. I had nine girls and two boys, ranging from third to fifth grade. Olga Tavarez agreed to let Sonandia come, even though it meant that Olga had to wait in the auditorium until 4:30 to drive Sony home. (This was when I learned that Sonandia actually lived outside the P.S. 85 neighborhood, but her mother kept her enrolled there to avoid disrupting her school experience.)

Cat Samuels and I made a circle of chairs in the back of the room. When the apprehensive, well-behaved lot settled into their seats, Cat and I congratulated them for being handpicked to pioneer this groundbreaking new club. I wrote the words "image" and "frame" on the board and invited the students to think of pictures outside the context of family photos or book illustrations. I showed them a selection of photographs I had taken over the years, spanning from a Fourth of July backyard barbecue to sunrise at the Joshua Tree National Park. Cat's photos were more unconventional than mine, experimenting with extreme close-ups of subjects like her pet rabbit's eye or a single blade of grass. She also had some great rock-and-roll concert shots. We discussed controlling the frame and picking out just the right moment to shoot the picture.

Then I announced, "Put on your coats. We're going outside!"

"What?"

"We're going on a neighborhood walk. With this!" I produced a disposable camera from my pocket. "And everyone is going to get to take pictures. Then I'm going to send you home with your own camera to shoot whatever you want. You'll bring them back to me, and I'll get the film developed so we can all look at your photos together."

"Oh my goodness!" Jodi, one of Karen's star students, enthused.

Snow had fallen on New York the previous night, coating the sidewalks with glistening powder. We walked up the Marion Avenue hill (or Murder Hill, as some locals know it) and around the block, passing the camera to whichever kid yelled out that he or she had an idea for a picture. Matthew made a snow angel, which Lilibeth wanted to shoot from a high angle. Joshua arranged Corrina, Ivana, and Sonandia to stand in front of a parked car and look curiously at each other, while a chained dog on the roof of the auto body shop went nuts in the background. After forty-five minutes, we returned inside and I handed out the cherished personal cameras. Before that day, none of them had ever taken a photograph.

The next day at lineup, Jodi, Lilibeth, Corrina, and Jennifer gave me their already-spent cameras. I tossed them in my bookbag.

I counted the minutes until three o'clock, when Carol Slocumb took the 4-217 line downstairs and my Visual Arts kids entered the room with excitement, this time arranging the circle themselves. I talked about and illustrated the idea of reordering, or editing, moving pictures. This was something they had never heard of. We discussed how a director can pick out exactly what he or she wants the audience to see and in what order they will see it, using music videos by Spike Jonze and Michel Gondry as models. Jonze's "It's Oh So Quiet" Björk video was a particular hit.

"We are going to make one of these before the year's over," I announced. "We're going to make our own music video." The thrill in the room was palpable. Sonandia's and Corrina's mouths were wide open. This is my best Thursday of the year, I thought.

Instead of heading home, I hopped off the D train at West 4th Street and strolled through Washington Square Park. The weather was very chilly, so only the die-hard pushers loitered by the fountain.

I had patronized the downtown photo lab at Waverly and Greene since I first arrived in New York, and I always appreciated the complimentary white borders they put on the pictures. As I came in from the cold, the lab man greeted me, "Good to see you, my friend. How is everything?"

"Extremely excellent," I said, swinging my bag off my shoulder to unzip it. I reached inside. *The cameras were gone.* My Discman too.

I emptied the bag, hunting through the side compartments. I was positive I had put the cameras in there. Positive.

"Are you okay?" my friend asked.

"Yeah," I said, drifting out the door. I walked to the northeast corner of the square and sat on a cold bench. A sharp chill shot through my chest. *Someone went through my bag.* Someone had stolen the cameras. Jennifer, Jodi, Corrina, and Sonandia's first rolls of film. The cameras were irreplaceable, and worthless undeveloped.

I vegetated for ten minutes, pins and needles all over. My Visual

Arts Club would have been better off never existing. I had hoped to build something new, but now the foundation was pulverized to ruin. I wanted to talk to someone, but I had nothing to say. I called my mom.

"Danny, hi!"

"Hi, Mom."

"Are you okay?"

"I don't know."

"What's wrong? Did something happen? Where are you?"

"Four kids from the club gave me their finished cameras this morning. I just realized they all got stolen out of my bag. And the roll from the whole club on Wednesday and the Dr. Seuss day pictures. I don't know how it happened. I don't know what to do."

As I spoke, my mom said, "Oh no" about six or seven times.

"I don't know . . . it's like everything gets swatted down. It's a hell. I can't stop them . . ."

"Danny. Look . . . Danny." She was using her crisis voice, grasping for comforting things to say. "Can you try to find out who did it and get them back?"

"I don't know. They're gone. That's it. I shouldn't have called."

"No, no, no, you can *always* call us. But what a *shame.* You can make it. You've got less than three months left. And one more week till spring break. You can hang on."

"I don't know. Guiterrez and Boyd keep telling me I'm a failure. Now this happens . . ."

"Have you given out the new bears?" my mom asked, trying to change gears.

"Bears?"

"The new Courage and Hope Bears. And the other, the Love Bears."

"No. I still have them," I said.

"Try to give them out. Maybe it will motivate some of them to behave better."

"I don't know . . ."

"Maybe you'll be surprised. Just give the bears a chance. They'll *want* to behave better."

"The bears don't matter, Mom. I can't . . ."

"Danny? Danny?"

I crumpled into a crouch on the pavement. The sound coming from me could have been mistaken for constrained laughter, but tears and snot gushed out. I moved the cell phone away from my ear, trying to breathe.

I came in on Friday with a singular, cold-blooded mission: my thief would be revealed. At lineup, I ordered my students around with ice in my voice. I hated this school.

Once inside 217, I began my mentally rehearsed speech about cowardice and truth, but I had barely started when Ms. Devereaux barreled in the room. "I heard about someone *stealing* from Mr. Brown! WHO DID IT?" Devereaux roared.

No one made a peep.

"Say who you are *now*, or we'll have the police look at the tapes from that camera up there, and yes, that is a real camera!" She pointed at a black fixture on the wall that was part of the fire alarm system and absolutely not a camera. "We've got you on tape. If anyone saw anything, say something *now*!"

Utter silence. Even in this furious moment, I still recognized and appreciated the relative luxury of a quiet moment in room 217.

Julissa raised her hand. "It was Marvin. I saw him in after-school."

Marvin Winslow had his head down.

"Marvin! Did you take the cameras?"

"It wasn't me," he whispered.

"Did anyone else see Marvin with the cameras?" Ms. Devereaux asked. Three hands went up — all kids in the after-school program.

I scribbled off a note to Andrea Cobb, the after-school teacher. Sonandia delivered it and returned minutes later with written corroboration that Marvin had in fact been playing around with several white disposable cameras yesterday.

"Step out in the hall, Marvin," I said.

The class remained silent, partially in relief of their collective exoneration, but mostly in perverse excitement to see a classmate get nailed. Standing in the doorway, I grilled the hapless boy while Ms. Devereaux watched.

"Where are the cameras?"

He looked at the floor.

"Marvin, answer me, or you'll eat lunch alone for the rest of the year. Where are the cameras?"

"I don't have no cameras."

"Did you have any cameras yesterday at after-school?"

"No."

"Ms. Cobb says you did. Is she telling the truth or is she lying? Marvin, is Ms. Cobb lying?"

"No."

"So you did have cameras in after-school, yes?"

"One."

"What color was it?"

"Black."

"Where did you get it?"

"My uncle."

"Your uncle who?"

"My uncle from Manhattan."

"What's his name?"

"Killer."

"Uncle Killer from Manhattan gave you one black camera and that's what you had yesterday, not six white cameras from my bag."

"Yeah."

Ms. Devereaux interjected, "We're getting your mom in here to see about this nonsense. Get in Mr. Randazzo's office *now!*"

Devereaux ushered Marvin away. I turned back to the class.

"Okay, let's talk about elapsed time. Who can show me they're listening?"

Forty minutes later, my in-class phone rang. Ms. Guiterrez told me that Mrs. Winslow was here and I should come to the office to meet with the two of them and Marvin. Mr. Daly agreed to cover my class, and I rushed out of the room.

"Mrs. Winslow, thanks for coming in so quickly," I said. "The main issue is that I don't know where they are, but yesterday, in the after-school program, Marvin had six of my disposable cameras. It is very important that I get these back."

"I'm sorry, but I *have* to speak," Mrs. Winslow seethed. "The issue here is people in your class, that *Lakiya,* are picking on Marvin and that's why he has to fight back. And I want to organize the parents of Mr. Brown's class because he don't give no homework. I send my son to school to learn and he come home with no homework *every day.* Marvin needs homework to learn. And I want to talk about that Ms. Devereaux. I don't want her touching Marvin. When I see her, I will knock her down and she will not get up. Yes, this is a parent saying this. Yes, I am aware that I am a parent saying these things. Don't let me near that Ms. Devereaux, because I am not a little boy like Marvin. I am a grown-up, and I will *hurt her.*"

Silence. Ms. Guiterrez and I looked at each other, unexpectedly united for the first time. I turned back to Mrs. Winslow.

"I give homework every day for math and literacy. Maybe one day out of every two months, there will be no homework. You can look at the chart in the classroom or another student's homework planner if you like. If Marvin is telling you that I don't give homework, he is saying something he knows is not true. Marvin, do I give homework every day?"

". . . Yes."

"Do you have time to copy it?"

"Yeah."

This refutation of Mrs. Winslow's first emphatic countergrievance made her angrier. "Where is that Ms. Devereaux? I need to tell her something about me and then she will not be knocking my Marvin around."

Guiterrez finally stepped in. "Mrs. Winslow, please relax. We will deal with that very soon."

The conversation turned to the stolen property. Marvin denied everything until his mother assumed the role of interrogator. Then the waterworks really turned on.

"I will not ask you again. Did you take Mr. Brown's camera?"

"*Cameras,*" I corrected.

"Marvin, I will not ask you again," Mrs. Winslow pressed. "Stop crying. Be a man. Did you take Mr. Brown's cameras?"

Marvin wiped his face with his shirt and left a streaking mark of runny mucus.

"*I will not ask you again!* Did you take the cameras?"

Marvin put his head in his hands and confessed, but said he did not know where the cameras were. Ms. Guiterrez sent them home, after I gave them Marvin's homework packet, of course.

Ms. Devereaux stopped by my room twenty minutes later, her cheeks bright red. She monotoned, "I can't take Marvin Winslow anymore." I learned that, on the way out, Mrs. Winslow had peeled over to Ms. Devereaux's room and began hollering and cursing. Security came and escorted her out of the building. Less than a minute later, Mrs. Winslow barreled back into P.S. 85 on a beeline back to Devereaux's room to continue her tirade. Surprised, the security officer was not able to get her out for several intense minutes.

After all of the drama, the cameras were gone. A wave of lightness hit me, as if I had been twisting and struggling to hold my grip on ninety thousand helium balloons while running a marathon and now, hopes thwarted, had let them all go. I carried on with the second part of my elapsed-time lesson, my chest empty.

I dropped my kids off at lunch and bolted back up the steps, barely reaching the faculty toilet in time to vomit up my morning bagel and cream cheese. I thought about the future. The Fellows commitment was two years, but I could not do this again. I fought the Bronx, and the Bronx won. Another winter here and I would be where Pat Cartwright was.

My senior thesis project would be premiering over the upcoming spring break week at the NYU First Run Film Festival. Maybe I should move to Los Angeles to find entry-level work in the movie industry and write on the side. My college buddy, Neal, drove out there right after commencement and raved on the phone to me all the time about his sunny West Coast life.

A few minutes before dismissal, Marvin Winslow showed up at the 217 door. "Marvin, I thought you were sent home," I said.

He opened his fist to show six rolls of film, roughly extracted from their disposable-camera shells. They were unexposed. I put the rolls in my pocket. "Thank you. Go home," I said. He nodded and went away. The administration agreed to keep him out of my class until spring break and to expedite his special ed referral.

I looked at the students in the room and told them again to copy their homework assignments. Gloria Diaz, a shy new student who had appeared last week and fit right into Sonandia's group two, obeyed studiously, looking up at the board and then down at her paper in between writing each word. Evley wrote with his usual solemn expression. Dennis raised his hand.

"Yes, Dennis?"

"Mr. Brown, you didn't laugh today."

"No, you're right, I didn't. We'll laugh after spring break."

"Okay," Dennis said.

The all-consuming disgust of the last twenty-four hours dissipated. As I learned over and over that year, sometimes it's a victory just to keep the house standing.

The pictures were incredible. Sonandia documented her home with still-life shots around her window. Joshua employed his younger brother as a model and snapped art-directed scenes of a stuffed-animal avalanche. Jennifer explored minutiae with close-ups of a bare light bulb or cracks in her building hallway's tile floor. I flipped through them in Pizza Mercato on Waverly Place, my jaw agape in amazement. Jodi, a star in Karen Adler's class, took a picture of footprints on a desolate snowy sidewalk that belonged in a gallery.

On the last day of March, the Visual Arts Club reconvened to look at our work. By that time, every kid had returned his or her camera. I had doubles processed for each roll; one set for the kids and one for me. In our circle, I examined and praised each picture before circulating it for everyone to see up close.

"This picture of Gabriela's mother really makes me feel like I know her," I said. "Look at her face. It's not a pose, it's real life captured. She has documented her home in pictures. It's a glimpse for us into Gabby's home life, one image that Gabby has *picked* to show us, and I love it." We only got through half of the kids' work because of the amount of discussion and analysis each picture received.

I felt strange on the subway home. Some of my efforts were dovetailing into success as others were splitting apart at the seams. Three months remained in the school year, and I had no idea what new twists awaited me. I recalled an apt bit of guidance from a screenwriting professor in my previous life as a college student: "There are two nonnegotiable conditions for a satisfying ending, and in this, life imitates art. An ending must be simultaneously *unpredictable* and *inevitable*. Fulfill these and your characters may rest."

April

Teacher Dance Party

"First of all, my real name is not Mr. Brown. It is Dr. Claudius Zornon, and from now on, that is what you will call me: Dr. Zornon. When I was a baby in Vancouver, it didn't take long for everybody to realize I was a prodigy, which means a child super-genius. When word got out of Vancouver that the Zornons had a prodigy in the family, I got invited all over Canada on the lecture circuit, giving speeches and sitting on panels in front of *huge* groups of people. I made some powerful friends and earned more than a little political influence in the Yukon Territory. Penn State also gave me an honorary bachelor's degree.

"Along with all the money my parents made off of me, the Canadian government granted me an around-the-world hot-air balloon pass. Everyone knows what that is, right? Okay, good. I got to take my four best friends with me, and we traveled to every continent, including Antarctica, and we swam in every ocean in the world. We had to hurry, because our balloon pass was only good for eighty days, but the whole trip came to an early end when our balloon popped over Tokyo, Japan! We were falling so fast, everyone was sure that would be the end of us, but calling on a few ideas I picked up on the lecture circuit, I used scientific knowledge to turn the popped balloon into a hang glider. News cameras filmed us when we touched down, and it was very exciting. A few music groups even wrote songs about it, and one called 'Man vs. Panda' went to number 2 in Germany. It was a little too techno-y for me, though.

"Anyway, at age ten, I got my own apartment back in Vancouver and picked up a job teaching fourth grade, although it was a little bit strange at first, because I was the same age as all the students. This lasted five years until I wanted to travel again.

"An old buddy of mine named Rex, who was living in Italy, called me up and asked me if I wanted to help him. I said sure, so I got on a superjet to Rome. We went out to lunch near the Vatican, where the pope lives, and Rex asked me to drive his car. I like driving so I agreed. He gave me directions to a big bank and told me to park in front and wait, leaving the engine running. He put on a mask and ran into the bank. A minute later he ran out, carrying a huge bag of money and screaming at me to let him in and then drive away. Rex was a bank robber! I was so surprised that I froze up and couldn't move, and the next thing I knew, Roman policemen were slamming handcuffs on us and yelling in Italian.

"And then I went to *jail*. I know it sounds crazy, but it's true. I used my one phone call to ring a lawyer friend, and he got my charges dropped. This meant I was out of trouble and had to go back to North America. On my way out of jail, I saw my old buddy crying in his cell. I said to him, 'I know it was you, Rex. You broke my heart.' I still visit him in prison whenever I go to Italy. He's only got eighty years left on his sentence. Crime doesn't pay.

"So I moved to New York City and got a swell apartment on the 107th floor of the Empire State Building. You all know my favorite author is Dr. Seuss, of course. Well, I decided to try my hand at writing books just like Dr. Seuss. I spent two years working on a book called *Dr. Zornon and the Wornons*. I went to every publisher in New York, but no one liked my story. I was about to give up when one editor at Julius Erving University Press loved my illustrations of the Wornons and showed them to his brother, who happened to be the curator at the Museum of Modern Art, or MoMA, as they call it. This curator guy, the boss of the museum, gave me a big showcase that got written up in every important magazine, and I became the toast of the art world. You've probably seen my pictures of the

Wornons before and just didn't know it. They are big purple crea-
tures, probably as tall as this ceiling. They have three arms, two heads,
but only one brain, which makes them excellent . . . farmers. Sound
familiar? Awesome.

"Around this time, P.S. 85 called me up and offered me a job,
but I told Mrs. Boyd, 'Thanks, but I have something very important
to do before I can ever teach fourth grade again.' And that very important thing, kids, was to join the circus.

"I linked up with Ringling Brothers in Pittsburgh, and even
though I was still kind of used to my luxury Empire State apartment,
I got into the idea of sharing a train car with the chimpanzees pretty
quickly. We drew a line in the middle of the floor; I stayed on my half
and they stayed on theirs, so we made it work all right. I stayed with
the circus for six months until everything came to an abrupt end with
the Great Clown Fiasco in Memphis, which I'm sure you've all heard
of. Wait, you haven't? Really? Should I tell you about the Great
Clown Fiasco? Okay.

"Well, we had a fire-eater in the circus named Lazarus. For the
grand finale of every show, Lazarus would eat a gigantic bouquet of
fire and the ringmaster would yell, 'Send in the clowns!' Eight
clowns would come charging out and gang-tackle Lazarus, who
would get up, brush himself off, and then *burp out flames and smoke!*
It brought the house down every time.

"One night in Memphis, we had a new clown named Crumbles, who was real jumpy and nervous because it was his first circus
show ever as a clown. Crumbles was so nervous about missing his cue
at the big finale that he actually started running to tackle Lazarus too
soon, before Lazarus had eaten the whole fire bouquet! Have you
ever seen someone's eyeballs on fire? Okay, Eddie has. So he knows
how crazy it looks. Lazarus's face was burning up. I ran out from
backstage and blew the fire extinguisher in his face to put out the
flames.

"Since my part with the chimpanzees was at the beginning of
the show, I was allowed to ride in the ambulance when they rushed

Lazarus to the hospital. I held his hand and talked to him, but what he said back to me didn't make any sense. It was all about exploding rainbows.

"The doctors at Memphis General Hospital made me wait in the waiting room for five hours before I could see Lazarus. When I finally saw him, he spoke very quietly and told me he was *blind*. The last thing he ever saw before everything went black was my face looking down at him in the ambulance, and now that image of my face was burned in his brain. All he could ever see, for the rest of his life, was the face of me, Dr. Claudius Zornon!

"I had to drop out of the circus after that. Crumbles served two years in clown prison, but got out early on funny behavior. I moved back to New York and asked P.S. 85 if they still had a job for me. Mrs. Boyd told me I had the teaching gene and of course I could work here. And that's the story of my life."

Thirty seconds of dead silence.

"That's the weirdest story I ever heard," Tayshaun said.

"That's the best story I ever heard!" Gladys V. cheered.

"Yeah!" seconded Jennifer and Destiny, grinning.

"Is that real, Mr. Brown?"

"Please call me Dr. Zornon."

"Is that real, Dr. Zornon?"

"Of course it's real, Dennis! Do you think I could just make all of that up?"

"I don't know."

"How old are you, Dr. Zornon?"

"Everything is true. Oh, except I forgot one detail. April Fools'!"

"DAAAAAAAAAA!"

Later in the day, cold-faced Marvin Winslow walked into 217 and sat down at his desk. He had been banished down to third grade since the camera crisis. "Marvin, you're supposed to be with Ms. Claxton."

He shook his head.

I called Ms. Claxton's extension. "I'm sorry," she said, "but he hit two girls. Hard. I can't keep him up here."

"I understand," I replied. Then I called Mr. Randazzo and Ms. Guiterrez, but neither picked up the phone. The guidance counselor, Mr. Schwesig, and his occasional reading pal, Ms. Foley, couldn't take him. I couldn't put him with Ms. Devereaux. He had to stay in my room. There was nowhere for him to go.

When Marvin broke Tayshaun's pencils a few minutes after coming in, I moved him to the back of the room, where he pounded his knuckles into the desk. He buried his head in his folded arms and seemed to fall asleep for a while.

The next morning, Marvin was all smiles. "Mr. Brown, Mr. Brown," he said, tugging on my sleeve at lineup.

"What is it, Marvin?"

"Good morning."

At math time, he really tried hard to understand the mixed-skills word problems. I was able to come to his desk and work with him through one, an issue of how many ten-cent candies can be bought with three quarters, and he got the right answer! I instantly thought to put him on the Rewards List for that kind of effort, but then remembered that just yesterday, he had beaten up third-grade girls. What do you do with a kid like that?

On Friday, April 2, the last day of SFA, Kelsie read the class her latest poem:

My SFA class is great and I don't hate
It's fun and I like to get things done
My teachers name is Ms. Baker and Mr. Brown
They probably like the town
Mr. Brown likes Lord of the Rings and a lot of things
I like the way he reads books because it's like he's really there
I like how he cut his hair
He probably went to the barber shop to take a stop

Ms. Baker is a nice lady
She probably gets paid maybe
I like her hair it's nice and flare
So that's my poem about my SFA class
And my SFA teachers are the best

At 10:15, P.S. 85 quietly achieved its much-discussed curriculum transition from Success for All to Balanced Literacy. No more changing students from 8:45 to 10:15. On April 14, when we came back from spring break, it would be Mr. Brown and the regular 4-217 crew, all day, every day.

Everyone broke up with everyone. Allie Bowers moved out of her shared apartment with her long-term boyfriend, Clay. Trisha Pierson, Elizabeth Camaraza, and Tim Shea saw relationships turn to dust. Cat Samuels was on the rocks with live-in Rob. Karen Adler's long-distance boyfriend did not empathize sufficiently with her P.S. 85–related emotional strains.

I didn't have anyone to break up with me. I spent most of the break laid up with what I thought was mono but turned out to be exhaustion. Books and television kept me company through my convalescence. I read Ron Suskind's compelling *The Price of Loyalty,* which painstakingly documents Paul O'Neill's journey from megasuccessful chief executive of Alcoa to George W. Bush's first treasury secretary and, ultimately, to his resignation from that post in 2003. Bush politics aside, O'Neill's affable, hands-on management style resonated with me. He put a premium on personal relationships between employees, and he relied on good research and analysis to guide his policy.

Calling on analysis and group input to find solutions seems like an obviously logical methodology for both troubleshooting and constructing a long-range vision, but this was precisely what was lacking at P.S. 85! The decision-making administrators were locked in a war of resentment with the teachers, who, in many ways, were just as culpable in poisoning the community spirit. (The nasty distribution of Kendra Boyd's unflattering news article was case in point.) Blaming it all on the massive overarching bureaucracy wouldn't wash. I willed myself out of my morose mood. I'm going to think solutions!

Despite my manufactured bright-side epiphany, on the morning of P.S. 85's return from spring break, the faculty looked more like zombies than rejuvenated teachers. Evan Krieg, formerly a rock of idealism in action who had orchestrated the magical potluck author celebration at Christmas, moped from the hot food line to the cashier in Lee's Deli on 188th Street. "I don't want to see them," he told me. "I've got three girls who determine the mood of the whole class, and I've got to appease them. I want to tell them, 'You're ten.' I don't know if I can do this another year."

Balanced Literacy afforded far more decision-making than Success for All. Guided only by a lesson format, I chose the content we would cover. Some grumbling teachers even complained that this was *too much* freedom and wanted more ready-to-use materials handed to them. Fran Baker, my wonderful SFA coteacher, still joined my class from 8:45 to 10:15, which was like a Ms. Richardsonesque boost, just having another responsible body in the room with the 4-217 crowd.

I borrowed Karen's class set of *Pocahontas and the Strangers* books and handed one to each kid to write his initials in the inside cover. Thrilled to possess their own book, the kids listened intently to my introduction to historical fiction. I also discussed the idea of "themes" in literature, and previewed the theme in this book of "freedom and imprisonment." Every day we spent thirty minutes on a round-robin reading and discussion, tearing through the nearly two-hundred-page book. Most students had never read a book so lengthy and would never have gotten through it without our team reading and steady, thorough analysis. I sucked the text dry for writing prompts, having the kids write journal entries from the perspectives of four different characters, as well as papers on predictions and text-to-self comparisons. Everyone got excited when I announced it was time to take out *Pocahontas and the Strangers* and groaned when we had to put them away.

Several times a day, a student asked me, "What book are we reading next?"

I had dreaded Balanced Literacy because of its time commitment, but the curriculum switch turned out to be the most academically beneficial change all year.

Mr. Randazzo delivered another new student to my room. "This is Clara Velez. She's going to be with you for the rest of the year." Clara craned her head to stare at the ceiling.

"Does she speak English?" I asked.

"Oh yeah. She was with Fiore, but Catherine asked me to take her out. Just a personality conflict. They didn't mesh."

I had a few characters I did not exactly mesh with either, but there was no point getting into that now. Think solutions! "I don't have a desk for her," I said. "I guess she can sit at my desk."

"Great," Mr. Randazzo replied, already out the door.

At our next common prep meeting, Catherine Fiore gave me a rundown on Clara. "She does nothing. And she's a bitch. She needs to get left the hell back."

Fiore's shortness ticked me off. She and Jeanne Solloway interacted with the other teachers with a sense of entitlement since they were ostensibly being groomed by the administration as the heirs apparent to the gifted Performing Arts Class. Rumors abounded that the veteran PAC teachers, Ms. Boswell and Ms. Berkowitz, were preparing to retire.

True to her reputation, Clara avoided schoolwork and irked classmates. She was a chronic finger-pointer, reigniting the blaze of 4-217 tattling. She had sticky fingers when it came to pencils and small change. At this point in the year, I didn't even get upset about the petty conflicts anymore. Clara showed occasional bursts of empathy (an unsolicited apology letter for her "big mowth" to Gladys Ferraro), and I liked her. Maybe wishfully, I thought if I could have worked with her for the whole year, her attitude toward assignments might be different. Fiore had written her off in September.

When the Probable Holdover forms came around, Fiore directed me to write Clara's name, so there it went next to Eric, Marvin, jungle disco fan Christian, and Lakiya. I knew Lito's Test marks would be on the fringe of passing, but I wanted him to move up so badly that I kept his name off even the Potential Holdover list.

On Tuesdays and Wednesdays, the Visual Arts Club was dessert after a long meal of overcooked cabbage. In the first week of April, we reviewed each kid's roll of pictures. Following that, I brought in several short films from my NYU days. The club members got a particular kick out of the ones where I appeared onscreen.

Jodi gave a story pitch for our P.S. 85 music video. "What if Mr. Brown is teaching the class and everybody's bored, but then he has to leave to do something, and right when he leaves, the whole class starts dancing?"

Everybody loved it. I had instant visions of a surreal choreographed number to Tiffany's version of "I Think We're Alone Now." We honed the plot and drew up storyboards to include Mr. Brown's sudden exit resulting from a secret note delivered by Ms. Adler. After the students' celebratory dance, they sneak into the hall on a mission to find their missing teacher. Slinking down the corridor, the kids stumble onto Ms. Adler's mysterious note, crumpled outside the closed door of a classroom. Every kid looks on expectantly as Jodi unfolds the paper to find the words *"Teacher dance party NOW!"* Lilibeth cracks open the door, and all mouths drop in shock to find cavorting teachers who, suddenly caught, freeze as a record scratches to a halt. After a mutually mortified moment, Sonandia leaps dancing into the fray, breaking the ice and instigating an all-ages dance fiesta.

Shooting the movie went far worse than expected. We set two

April dates for filming and both were aborted because of club-member absences. I was also having a difficult time recruiting teachers to dance. Instead of making our movie, I showed the present participants how to work the camcorder and let them film each other in simple scenes that I arranged. Everyone clamored to hold the camera. Using the patch cable for video input, we immediately screened their work on the TV. Sonandia and Jennifer framed some especially interesting close-ups. I set a May 5 D-day for principal photography. Since I was headed to France for the Cannes Festival on May 7, this was the last chance to shoot and quick-edit something to submit for the mid-May Region One Literacy Fair. I had promised Mrs. Boyd we would be ready.

I called Bernard's home to give a positive report about Bernard's behavioral progress following our parent-teacher conference. Mr. McCants thanked me for the news.

"Just one thing I need to ask you about, Mr. Brown. This boy Marvin. Bernard says that Marvin is instigating with him and trying to steal his things. I'm trying to teach Bernard not to fight, but he has to defend himself if this boy Marvin is really trying to hurt him. Have you seen any of this?"

"Yes. Marvin has . . . a lot of problems."

"It sounds like he does. I feel bad for that boy, but Bernard has got to defend himself when it comes to it."

I could not promise Mr. McCants that his son would be safe from thieves and instigators in my classroom. Every time I sent Marvin away, he always came floating back to 217. No one wanted anything to do with him, so he was my responsibility. This was not the first time a 4-217 parent had voiced a grievance about Marvin's behavior. What would Paul O'Neill do?

"I think if you wrote a letter to the school," I said, "that could probably be an effective way to separate Bernard and Marvin. The school is very sensitive to parents who make their concerns known."

Bernard came in the next morning with the letter, which I

forwarded to Mrs. Boyd. Within an hour, she called me to the hall, leaving Fran Baker to supervise 4–217.

"Mr. Brown, I have to wonder what exactly you're doing to manage your kids, specifically this Marvin, when I receive a letter like *this* from a parent!" She showed me Mr. McCants's page.

"Marvin Winslow's misbehavior is not my fault. He has severe, *severe* problems, and I have tried every avenue of discipline known to me to control him, but he continues to return to my room and continues to terrorize his classmates, mostly at lunch when I'm not there. And his mother assaulted Ms. Devereaux."

"Whoa, whoa, whoa, Mr. Brown. Nobody has *assaulted* Ms. Devereaux. It could be very detrimental to you and the school if you throw around loose words like that."

I plowed forward. "Bernard's father voiced a legitimate complaint to me, so I encouraged him to voice it directly to you."

Mrs. Boyd was shocked. "This letter was *your* idea?"

"Yes."

"Mr. Brown. I *cannot believe* you would do something so unprofessional. Do you have any idea what it means to be professional? When you tell" — she consulted the letter — "Bernard McCants's father to start writing letters, you are saying to him, 'We can't take care of our own.' You undermine the entire school. You're going over Mr. Randazzo's head, which is rude and . . . *unprofessional*. Do you think Mr. Randazzo does nothing? Is that what you are implying in your actions?"

"No. Mr. Randazzo has been doing this for over thirty years, and I'm a rookie. What I am saying is that many people more experienced than me, including Ms. Guiterrez and Dr. Kirkpatrick, agree that Marvin should not be in a regular classroom. But he still is, intimidating and beating on kids and ruining the fourth grade."

Mrs. Boyd delivered an oral treatise on professionalism and stormed away, warning me not to encourage parents to write letters. Marvin spent a couple weeks in a second-grade class before a bloody punch-up with an eight-year-old spurred his inevitable return. Meanwhile, Bernard had a great two weeks.

The February English Language Arts Test might have been the be-all and end-all of life as we know it, but the May Math Test was not far behind. I officially put away my neglected math pacing calendar and cleared the schedule for a drab recipe of one part Balanced Literacy and four parts Test prep.

Like every other fourth-grade class in P.S. 85, we had a lot of catching up to do, particularly in probability, logic, time, geometry, and measurement. These conceptual surveys and mandatory Test-taking skill reviews were easy on me for their minimal preparation, but the monotony (despite my continuous insistence that this was fun *and* important) took a toll on everybody. One day without warning, I brushed my teeth in class and passed out toothbrushes and tooth-paste, compliments of my family dentist in New Jersey. We discussed and wrote about dental hygiene, making for a snazzy bulletin board display. Then back to business. Including sporadic Mr. Lizard and claw-dancing time, I had approximately two days to cover mea-surement in mass, weight, length, volume, area, perimeter, diameter, radius, and conversions for English and metric systems. Two days for logic and probability questions. Two days for geometry with poly-gons, vertices, angles (acute, obtuse, right), and parallel and perpen-dicular lines.

After the frantic pre–ELA Test cram, all complaints about the futility of these crash courses were exhausted, and now the disgusted teachers and bored students just knew to deal with it, to limp to the finish line. My Paul O'Neill thinking failed me here for a way to spin this vortex into a positive experience.

At the monthly assembly, Mr. Randazzo called Maimouna Lugaru to receive the 4-217 Student of the Month award. Every month as the names were read, I watched Maimouna with her eyes shut tight, praying in her auditorium seat that she would be a winner. When her name really was called, she made no noticeable reaction, dead-fishing me on a handshake and sauntering blankly to the front of the room.

After the Students of the Month were promised that their personalized certificates would be printed up and distributed in the future, Mr. Randazzo read the morning lineup scores for April. "I'm just going to read just the top five this month. For fourth grade, fifth place goes to 4-208!"

Ms. Fiore did not move. A tall boy retrieved the certificate from the podium.

"Fourth place, 4-220!"

Kelsie, my SFA poet buddy, accepted on behalf of Ms. Mulvehill's room.

"And third place, I can't believe it, goes to 4-217!"

"YES!" I screamed, plowing forward to grab the certificate myself. I pumped one fist and gnashed my teeth insanely. "YEAH!" The kids followed my lead, going bonkers in celebration. We spilled into the aisle, cheering and stalling the announcement of the rest of the winners.

"WE DID IT!"

May

Nothing Cannes Stop You Now

Bᴇʀɴᴀʀᴅ ᴡᴀs ᴀʙsᴇɴᴛ ᴏɴ ᴅᴀʏ ᴏɴᴇ of the huge Math Test, so I filled in a special absentee Scantron grid for him. He was absent again on days two and three.

"I think Bernard moved," Eddie said.

Behaviorally, Bernard had made the most progress out of anyone in 4-217, but his foothold on the path was tenuous. In the winter, he had thrown punches as a reflex. With the March parent-teacher conference as a landmark, he was now making new and important efforts with self-control. I had helped keep his success streak going with a number of preemptive interventions when I spotted one of his personal warning signs: a certain facial expression or a specific tense movement he made with his hands.

I thought changing schools so late in the term was the worst thing that could happen to Bernard. Our fragile progress fractured, he would now have to deal with being the new kid, and he would do it with his fists. I wished his parents had mentioned something to me about the move, but I doubt I could have talked them into postponing it for seven weeks.

Bernard was the sixth student who had been with me in September who would finish the year in another class. I imagined the six — Asante, Verdad, Daniel, Deloris, Fausto, and Bernard — and felt helpless.

"Can I use Bernard's social studies book?" Cwasey asked. Several of our hardcover textbooks had taken a walk during the year, and we no longer had a complete class set, which meant reviled book-sharing during some lessons.

Cwasey walked to Bernard's old desk and pulled out the book. As he reached in, Tayshaun tossed a crumpled paper ball at his back. Cwasey turned and shoved Tayshaun's desk, knocking it over.

"Cwasey!"

"What I did?"

"You did not have to knock over Tayshaun's desk!"

"I didn't do it," Cwasey protested, his eyes pleading for me to believe him.

"I'll speak to you at lunch."

Cwasey vehemently continued to claim innocence when I pulled him aside in the cafeteria. "I saw you with my eyes, Cwasey," I said slowly, pointing at my eyeballs. "I know Tayshaun threw the paper at you, so you reacted. Just admit that you knocked over his desk."

"I didn't do it," Cwasey repeated with the same expression.

I spoke to Cwasey's mother and Mr. Schwesig about arranging some guidance sessions for him, but nothing happened. I quietly moved Cwasey into my mental category of habitual liars, right beside Marvin, Joseph, and Deloris.

Seresa came skipping over to me, a big smile on her face. "Mr. Brown! If everyone saw Cwasey do something and he still says he didn't do it, that's *ludicrous*."

The administration tapped Fran Baker to "anchor" 4-217 for the eleven days I would be in France. Ms. Rosenberg, little Ms. Strong, and big Mrs. Little (the Test tutors) cleared their schedules to cycle in so that no fewer than two teachers would be in the room at all times. I got a kick out of the fact that four full-time teachers with over seventy collective years of teaching experience were deemed necessary to assume the responsibility that I was privileged to enjoy every day alone.

In the middle of the week, Mrs. Boyd made another visit to my room with sharp criticism about my bulletin boards and threats about my future at P.S. 85. After thoroughly ripping my professionalism, she changed gears and wanted to chat about movies, offering to introduce me to the monthly book-order lady, who was the mother of an award-winning filmmaker and NYU alumnus.

To work on the classroom, I canceled the Visual Arts Club for the week, postponing our music video shoot to the end of the month. No Region One Literacy Fair showcase for us. When I stopped by Ms. Fiore's room to give the news, Ivana asked Corrina, "What are we going to do to have fun now?"

Elizabeth Camaraza stayed with me for the eleventh-hour 217 makeover. She single-handedly designed and mounted a gorgeous "*Pocahontas and the Strangers*: Responses to Literature" bulletin board, replete with green-and-gold construction-paper cornhusks. "You just needed a woman's touch," she said.

On Friday, May 7, I delivered to Mrs. Baker eleven days of lesson plans, which were politely and promptly discarded. The tutors had mountains of materials to keep the kids busy.

"You have worked like a Trojan, Mr. Brown," Mrs. Boyd said, looking at the pretty paper agriculture on my wall. "Don't miss your plane home."

The Festival de Cannes is a land of cinephile dreams. I spent my days sporting a laminated access pass as an editorial intern for the *Hollywood Reporter* and my evenings in black tie at red-carpet screenings or swank soirees, usually with Clarissa, a film student from Texas, on my arm. We drank wine and watched Truffaut's *The 400 Blows,* the movie that had blown my mind as a high school sophomore, on a giant floating movie screen at the Cinéma de la Plage by the indigo Mediterranean's edge. I saw films from fourteen countries, ranging from Bosnia to Chile. On my last day, the *Reporter* published a story I wrote called "Scarlet Fever" about the diversity of the red-carpet camp-out-spectator culture. Then I caught the first ever screening of *Kill Bill* with both volumes merged into one continuous film, introduced by Quentin Tarantino himself.

On my last night in France, the familiar, queasy dread seeped back into my stomach. Did I really have to see Mrs. Boyd or Ms. Guiterrez ever again? I preferred life in the cosmopolitan world of film. Drinking fresh grapefruit juice for breakfast in a courtyard several tables away from Pedro Almodóvar beat my bodega bagel on the D train. I was only gone eleven school days, but the idea of coming back to P.S. 85 gave me horrific goosebumps.

I left my top-floor suite to check out of the Pierre et Vacances de Verrerie at 6 a.m., and immediately noticed something strange when the elevator's lobby-floor button refused to light. I got out on the second floor and bump-dragged my massive seventy-pound suitcase down the steps, into a dark, ghost-town lobby. Where was the desk person at six on a Monday morning? Where was anybody?

I walked to the front door to find it *bolted from the outside*. All other windows and doors that led outdoors were locked too. I had never heard of a large hotel lobby being closed, let alone locked down. I *needed* an employee to call a cab for me. If I hoofed it with my giant luggage to the bus station, I'd be dangerously close to missing the only bus to Nice that would get me to the airport in time for my EasyJet flight to London. I started to sweat.

A man pushing a mop appeared. Frazzled, I pounced in his direction. "Monsieur! I need to call a taxi. Do you know the number for a taxi? A taxi!"

The shrugging man spoke zero English, and I could offer no French. He moved toward the stairwell with his bucket and mop. A flash went through me, familiar from my 4-217 crisis moments: *Assess what he can accomplish. No taxi. Get him to let you out, or find out how to let yourself out of the building. Do it calmly and cordially.*

I took a breath and followed the cleaning man, smiling and pantomiming a key turning and opening the front door. He frowned. I gave him a pleading look, fully shifted into my let's-cooperate teacher mode. He capitulated and unlocked the door.

The bus would leave for Nice in forty-one minutes, and I had clocked the beachside walk from my hotel in suburban Cannes-Bocca to the bus station in the center of Cannes to take forty-five. I steeled myself for a brutal trudge under the sweltering early morning sun.

Then something amazing happened. A taxi, the first unoccupied one I had seen in my whole stay in this neighborhood, rolled up the block with its vacancy light switched on. I wildly waved down the driver and he stopped, asking something in French and squinting in the sunglare. I nodded, and he asked again, raising his voice and miming speaking into a telephone.

He's asking if I called a cab, I deciphered.

"Yes," I lied, opening the door and hoisting my suitcase onto the seat. "Oui, oui. I called, I called." Now with both hands free, I mimicked holding two phones to my ears.

"*Get out!*"

"What?"

"Get out! I am not your taxi. Get out of here."

My stomach dropped. The French cabbies had a code of honor about stealing each other's fares. If I had in fact called, he thought one of his buddies was coming for me. I *needed* to make this man understand my side of things. "Wait! I didn't call a taxi. I *tried* to call is what I meant. I need to get to the bus station. No one else is coming for me. Please!" I could feel my insides firing up, the rising, now familiar twist of anger and frustration, of discarded hope. I dumbly dragged my luggage off the seat and it plopped to the pavement. "S'il vous plaît! Come on!"

"Get away! Fuck you, Ashton Kutcher!" the incensed cabbie barked.

"What?"

"FUCK YOU!"

His shouting set a match to my bubbling rage. *"I need to get in this cab!"* I screamed, whipping my body to bare-knuckle-punch the passenger door. I froze, suddenly aware of myself. I had snapped again.

"POLICE! POLICE!"

I grabbed my suitcase and hustled toward the beach. Forty perspiration-drenched minutes later, I staggered onto the bus, heading home and promising myself not to punch things ever again.

Four-two-seventeen cheered for fifteen seconds when I entered the cafeteria before quickly returning to normal. Several teachers asked to see pictures from the trip. Others shot me looks of thinly veiled antipathy.

"They were fine," Mrs. Baker reported. "We kept them busy with busywork. Usual problems with the usual ones. Group two [Gladys Viña, Evley, Sonandia, Gladys Ferraro, and Gloria] was a joy. They were really wonderful."

Sonandia looked worried. "Sony, what's up?" I asked.

She hesitated. "Somebody wrote something about you in the bathroom. On the third floor."

"Is that what's bothering you?" I asked. She nodded. "Don't worry about that at all. That doesn't bother me. That means nothing." Sonandia smiled because I smiled, and that was the end of it.

The moment the day ended, I jogged upstairs to the third-floor girls' bathroom to read inside the first stall door in giant magic marker letters, "MR. BROWN HAS SEX WITH MS. BAKER." I washed it off, feeling strangely legitimized to be inspiration for graffiti in the Bronx.

I returned from France to find 4-217 suffused with romantic intrigue. Rumors swirled that Eddie had the hots for Lakiya, and Evley turned beet red every time he and Julissa stood beside each other in line.

Eric Ruiz was behaving stranger than usual, grinning ceaselessly and clutching a one-dollar bill every time I looked at him. "Eric, put the dollar in your pocket or you're going to make me a hundred cents richer." He complied, but the next time I glanced his way, his grin was back, with a corner of the greenback just peeking over the edge of his desk. At the end of the day, I found a tightly crumpled sheet of loose-leaf paper on the floor near group two.

To: glyds V

Do you like me because of the $1.00
Yes or No
And what is your pone number

Sadly for Eric, the "No" was circled several times before the paper was discarded. But Gladys Viña, a quiet pal of Sonandia's, was not only receiving love letters that day. Next to Eric's rejection note, I found something else.

Dear Lito,

I love you. You like me a little bit. Answer my question and write back anything.
Pick one do you like me
A lot or a little
Write back I got another paper.

Sincerly love,

Gladys Viña

I had never seen Lito and Gladys V. even say hello to each other. Not far away from Gladys V.'s confession lay another sheet from the same miniature notepad, marked by Lito's scraggly penmanship.

Baby I LOVE YOU

The hotly anticipated book fair was a glorified toy sale. The kids loved it. Jennifer was the only student who bought a book, but ten others walked away with card games, magic sets, and stationery featuring pictures of mammals.

Eric bought the most expensive item available, a ten-dollar "Keep-Out Box" filled with activities and secrets. I had never seen perpetually blank-faced Eric in such good spirits. I could barely believe it when he raised his hand in the afternoon to ask if he could visit the library to check out a book. He returned ten minutes later, cradling a weathered hardback reference book titled *Automobiles*.

"I didn't know you were into cars," I said.

The floodgates opened. "I want to be a mechanic. My cousin works in a garage. He teaches me stuff. He's gonna teach me to build cars. He knows everything in the engines and how to take it apart and make it work again like perfect." In moments, he was explaining to me the difference between carburetors and alternators. "My dad teaches me about cars, too. But he's on vacation."

"That sounds fun."

Eric shrugged and stuck out an index finger and flexed his thumb like he was pulling a trigger. "It's not that kind of vacation."

"Oh. Well, maybe you can teach me some things about cars in writing. And I can bring in some car stuff for you. Would you like that?" Eric nodded and excitedly went back to inspecting the diagrams in *Automobiles*.

Walking down the stairs for dismissal, he mumbled something unintelligible.

"What?" I asked.

He mumbled again.

"Speak louder. I can't understand you."

"I said my Keep-Out Box was stolen!" He started sobbing, the first time I had seen him cry since Fausto strangled him back in week one.

"Stolen! When?"

"I don't know."

I halted the line. "Has anyone seen Eric's Keep-Out Box? Any information will be rewarded!" No one volunteered to speak. The line below me snaked around the lower landing, so I couldn't even see everyone. We were in the worst spot to attempt a quickie investigation. "Eric, when did you realize it was missing?"

Sensing the hopelessness, Eric bolted forward, hurtling down the steps to the exit.

The next morning, he looked miserable. He gave no answer when I asked him if he wanted to read about cars in the library with Mr. Klein. "I just want to go to Mr. Schwesig," he said. I sent him to the guidance counselor where he played Connect Four for a half hour. He put his head down on his desk.

During my prep period, I visited the book fair, now packing up on its last day. "I'm looking for something that I think is called a Keep-Out Box, or something like that. Do you have it?"

The PTA mother had not heard of it. She called in some help, and soon all four volunteers were discussing my desire for a Keep-Out Box. "I think we ran out of those," the boss lady finally determined.

I returned to 217 and summoned Eric to the hall. "What'd I do?"

"Nothing, you're not in trouble. We're going to the book fair." I told him he could pick out anything he wanted to replace the Keep-Out Box. He shrugged and selected a deck of playing cards decorated with fish.

"Are you sure that's all you want?"

He shrugged again.

At a spring PTA meeting, Jodi, Karen Adler's champion student in 4-111 and a leader in my Visual Arts Club, who was attending with her mom, posited the idea of holding a talent show as a fund-raiser for the school. The plan was set in motion for an evening talent and fashion show, with food and door prizes for the year's final PTA gathering. Maimouna and Cwasey were picked to be two of the featured dozen models and dancers, meaning they left room 217 two wonderful periods per week for rehearsal.

Seeking to put the T back in PTA at least once, Karen and I went to the culminating performance. Aside from fiancées Mulvehill and Bonn, we were the only teachers there.

"Where's Jodi?" I asked.

"She's not coming. She's punished for fighting with her sisters," Karen said.

The emcee's microphone did not work, so Ms. Llanos, the PTA president, attempted to achieve silence through raising her hand and asking for quiet. The din of chatter in the half-full auditorium did not subside. It was the *parents* making the noise. Karen and I looked at each other in horror, giving the silent signal in sync with Ms. Llanos. Mrs. Boyd finally took to the stage. "Excuse me, people, but the microphone is not working! We are going to need your cooperation to begin! *Excuse me!*" Boyd and Llanos exchanged a helpless look, somewhere between shared fury and disappointment. The crowd continued its roaring chatter, oblivious to the distressed organizers. Mrs. Boyd called again fruitlessly for quiet, then left the stage to seek a custodian.

"Thank you for coming," she said to Karen and me as she passed.

Fifty-five minutes after the scheduled start, a newly acquired microphone enabled the show to begin. It was a halfhearted performance of loosely synchronized movements punctuated by spontaneously wild poses that drew personal cheers.

"Maybe it's all right that Jodi missed this," I said.

"I got the job, muthafucka!"

"Congrizzats, bitch!"

"It's official. The hiring committee approved me. I'm in!" Karen shouted into the phone. Karen had secretly responded to a job posting she saw on a bulletin board at City College. She would teach sixth grade at a Riverdale start-up charter middle school specializing in science. Her interviewer and future supervisor, Mr. Kahn, was a funny, intelligent, laid-back character who wanted Karen to infuse her piano-playing expertise into her teaching.

"No more P.S. 85 for you."

"No more P.S. 85 ever. I am peacing out of that hellhole. Are you still thinking about leaving?"

"I think I have to," I said. "Unless a miracle happens."

After dismissal the next day, I found Karen pacing in her room with her left palm pressed to her forehead, a locomotion that usually exists only in fiction. "Are you taking the train soon?" I asked.

"I don't know. I need to talk to Boyd." Karen was flummoxed to an uncharacteristic degree.

"Are you okay?"

"Yeah, yeah, yeah. I just might be a while. I'll tell you all about it later."

I went back to my room to sort out a paperwork issue. Teachers are supposed to make two records of attendance every day: an official Scantron sheet and a backup grid. Like many swamped teachers, I had largely abandoned the backup grid in November. Now Ms. Cooper, the payroll secretary, was asking for all of the old backup grids. Our conversation that morning had gone something like this:

BROWN: I don't have the backup grids.

COOPER: I need you to give them to me.

BROWN: I physically don't have them.

COOPER: (making crazy eyebrow expressions) You have to give me the backups.

BROWN: I understand, but I don't know what to tell you. All of my originals are accurate. The backups are gone.

(Silence)

COOPER: Mr. Randazzo said you have to give me the backups or your paycheck will be withheld.

BROWN: You'll have them this afternoon.

With my pen, I invented absences and guessed tardies (Was Eric late on November 14? Sure. Was Destiny absent on November 16? Why not!) for about twenty minutes on a stack of blank grids. When I was almost done, Karen came by. "Boyd just offered PAC to Andrea Cobb and me," she gasped.

"What did you say?

"We said yes!"

"Are you serious? That's cataclysmic! What about the charter school?"

"Nothing about the charter school. I'm going to stay. My brain is mush right now!"

Shockwaves over the Performing Arts Class snub to Fiore and Solloway rocketed through the P.S. 85 halls before lineup the next morning. They ranked in seniority on their grade levels, had attended a much-discussed seminar series at Teachers College, and most of all, had acted all year as if their selection was in the bag. I thought that while Fiore and Solloway may be strong textbook teachers, their surly whininess made them poor collaborators. Picking Andrea, a young and energetic second-grade homeroom teacher, and Karen was a brilliant move by Mrs. Boyd to reinvent PAC with cooperative teachers instead of embittered ones.

Not everyone saw it that way. Fiore and Solloway claimed they were leaving P.S. 85, only to quietly retract their declarations later in the week. Ms. Boswell and Ms. Berkowitz started giving away their classroom supplies to just about everyone except Karen and Andrea. I had a good view of Fiore and Solloway's public hand-wringing on the blacktop during recess while I jumped double-dutch.

ELA Test scores came back. Except Eric and Marvin, everyone passed. *Lakiya* passed by a hair. Her docile temperament in January may have given her the edge. Lito and Christian passed, both by small margins. I called Christian's mother to give her the green light for summer camp and Disney World. No mandatory summer school. I didn't count Clara as one of my ones since she took the Test with Ms. Fiore. Besides the gifted Performing Arts Class, I had the fewest failures in the grade. Neither Ms. Guiterrez nor Mrs. Boyd ever said anything to me about it.

June

Teacher Gone Missing

THE MUCH-HYPED P.S. 85 RETIREMENT CELEBRATION at City Island was set for Wednesday evening, June 2. Mr. Randazzo, Mr. Len Daly (Randazzo's right-hand man), Ms. Corson (an expert in the outmoded Success for All program), the two PAC teachers Ms. Boswell and Ms. Berkowitz, and one other lady I had never seen before were bowing out of their Marion Avenue careers, and the $65 admission send-off party ruled the hallway talk for the preceding weeks. Women bought new dresses. Al Conway put himself on a high-impact diet.

Al's excitement about the dinner-dance was a little puzzling. I was not planning to go, expecting the affair to be a weird, expensive back-patting soiree for the school's elders, a group with which I was not pining to socialize. A few days before the party, Al cornered me in the Teacher Center. "Dan, you've got to go. This could be our only chance all year to hang out together!"

I had never figured that Al Conway earnestly wanted to hang out with me. My feelings of aversion about the party flipped into strange excitement. Barbara had told me that at one of these parties a few years ago, Ms. Guiterrez got sauced and bear-hugged Mrs. Boyd, screaming, "I love you!" Give me the spectacle, I thought.

Every other first-year Fellow except Cat Samuels had the same idea. At 6:15, I rolled into the catering hall with Allie Bowers, Trisha Pierson, and honey-haired second-grade teacher Corinne Abernathy at my side.

"Mr. Brown, you *devil!*" Ethel May Brick cooed, checking off our names.

Seeing your normally casual and haggard colleagues gussied up is a strange sensation. Tonight I was not the struggling rookie in the hell class. We were all adults at the great equalizer, an open bar.

I felt fantastic and got a drink. Len Daly made a cordial nod in my direction at the bar. "What do ya got?" he asked.

"Whiskey and ginger."

"Jack?"

"Yeah."

Daly nodded, deeming my answer satisfactory.

I broke the silence. "Hey, congratulations on everything. On all of this."

"Thanks, man," he said, crunching an ice cube from his cashed highball. "Thanks."

We stood unspeaking for another ten seconds, sharing a weird moment before he nodded and sauntered toward the crudité.

Within an hour, the room was loose. I spotted Mr. Randazzo with his arm around a paraprofessional in a maroon velour bodysuit. Janet Claxton, her boyfriend, and I shot the breeze while Camaraza sang her heart out to ELO's "Mr. Blue Sky." Tim Shea chewed the fat with Ms. Guiterrez, who rolled in wearing a spicy midriff-bearing outfit that showed off the tendrils of a sprawling, symbol-laden tattoo across her shoulder blades.

After our chicken cordon bleu, the atmosphere morphed into a bar-mitzvah-on-acid booty-dancing scene. Usher's "Yeah" came on the sound system and people went loony. Later, during a salsa number, Mr. Tejera and an ESL teacher performed an expert mambo. I got into the jam myself, twirling Trisha Pierson around the floor while a gallery of PTA volunteers cheered us on. Marge Foley's unexpectedly audacious move-busting scored her invitations to four parties. In the most surreal twist, Mrs. Boyd emerged from a back room in a sombrero and baja, doling out maracas and straw hats while "Hot! Hot! Hot!" blared in the background. I wound up between

Melissa Mulvehill and gym teacher Dick Zweben in the Public School 85 conga line.

In the valet parking queue, a vivacious Ms. Guiterrez ordered Tim Shea to pick out a downtown bar to keep the party going. Tim deferred to me, and I recommended Grass Roots on St. Mark's Place. "Let's do it!" Guiterrez roared. "Ms. Abernathy, you must drive me. Or else I will drive one hundred and fifteen miles per hour!"

I moved to another cluster on the sidewalk. "Are we going out *drinking with Guiterrez*?" Elizabeth rhetorically asked me.

I heard Guiterrez shout in the background, "One hundred and fifteen miles per hour!"

"Holy shit, have you seen Guiterrez? She's going berserk!" Karen jumped in.

"We're going to Grass Roots with her. You are absolutely coming," I said.

"Hell *yeah*!"

Just before I leaped into Trisha's Saturn and out of the giggling crowd by the main entrance, I noticed Mrs. Boyd standing about ten feet from the edge of the group, looking at her shoes, talking to no one.

The bar was a strange scene. Guiterrez seemed to have gotten drunker on the ride downtown, and unexpected designated driver Corinne Abernathy looked mortified at her boss's loss of composure. Six of us squeezed into a booth.

"Shea, get me a bay breeze. No, I meant a sea breeze! Bay breeze has pineapple and I hate that. I hate pineapple. Here!" Guiterrez gave Tim a crumpled fistful of singles. "Wait! I forget if it's sea breeze or bay breeze with pineapple!"

Tim came back a minute later. "Is it a bay breeze or sea breeze?" Guiterrez asked emphatically.

"No pineapple," Tim said.

"The Continental is right there!" Ms. Guiterrez said, pointing at the wall. "That's the only place to see good heavy metal. That's all I like. Limp Bizkit! Metal! Nothing else. I go to the Continental all the time."

I smiled wryly and looked at the table, amused with Guiterrez's horror show but possessing no desire to converse with her. The Hygienists had played the Continental in March, and everyone at the table except the assistant principal caught the show. Trisha Pierson even had a love connection.

One drink was enough. Corinne offered Ms. Guiterrez a ride. "Nah, I live right there on Bleecker," Guiterrez said, and traipsed away.

Evan Krieg had recommended *Mrs. Frisby and the Rats of NIMH* for a read-aloud. After the success of *Pocahontas and the Strangers,* I wanted to proceed with a novel only if each student could have a copy in his hands. The memory was burned in me of Destiny Rivera saying, "I can't believe I read a two-hundred-page book!" Between ransacking Krieg and Solloway's fifth-grade in-class libraries, I gathered enough copies for a class set. The reading level was a bit over their heads, but I opted to go for it anyway. We could walk through the text together at our own pace.

The book was a smash. As a prize for going the distance, I threw a movie party with popcorn and Don Bluth's animated *The Secret of NIMH,* and I was delighted when the kids unanimously voiced their preference for the book.

June is open season for lesson planning. I had never implemented my comic-book-making plan with Tayshaun, but now I introduced a class-wide project of creating comic strips. Across the board, the kids delivered the depth and creativity that I had been desperately seeking to draw out. Athena's *The Mean Friends* and Gloria's *The Romance of Chelsea and Joe* might have been their best work of the year. Seresa's *The Invisible Boy* was my favorite, a plaintive tale about a shy boy (named Evley) who, after several abortive attempts, finally asks a girl her name. I posted them in the back of the room beside the newly founded *Eddie Rollins Exhibit: Colors by Lakiya Ray.*

In a reflective end-of-the-year survey, sixteen kids wrote that they wanted to become teachers when they grew up. I felt so good that I played steady quarterback in captains Dennis and Eddie's four-on-four blacktop football game after school.

As I threw the ball around with the kids, a fateful piece of paper ran through the office copy machine. My future at P.S. 85 had been decided.

The P.S. 85 roster for 2004–2005 was distributed. Ms. Guiterrez's promotion from grades 2–3 interim assistant to grades 4–5 assistant principal became official, and four of her current third-grade teachers were moving up with her. I did not have a classroom on the list, nudged out of the fold by Guiterrez's protégés.

So much for building from the lessons of my embattled first year in the classroom. I had been demoted to a teacher-on-wheels. I looked at the classroom list with a sense of calm, even relief, that my Great Expectations School fate had finally been sealed. I sat down at the Teacher Center computer, typed a three-line letter of resignation, and signed my name.

When my letter of acceptance to the New York City Teaching Fellows had arrived fifteen months earlier, I had opened and read it with a serenity similar to what I felt now. I knew this piece of paper would change my life, but somehow its smallness, its thinness, tempered the magnitude of its contents' consequences.

After placing the letter in Mrs. Boyd's box, I headed to the months-overdue Marvin Winslow IEP (Individualized Education Plan) meeting, although I had little desire to be in a room with Marvin for extra time after his most recent "Fuck this class!" rampage. He had punched Gladys Ferraro again and I strongly suspected him of lifting Julissa's caterpillar-shaped pencil sharpener.

At a round table in the School Based Support Team office nook behind the gym, I sat across from Mrs. Winslow and Marvin, flanked by three women I had never met. Ms. Guiterrez and Dr. Kirkpatrick, who prepared the report, could not attend. Marvin's glare melted into his now familiar deer-in-headlights face, but when one of the ladies began reciting his file, Mrs. Winslow's face looked identical to her son's in her vulnerability and confusion.

The psychologist stranger began, "Marvin, your self-esteem is very, very low. You don't feel too good about yourself, do you? No, you don't. You have low skills in all subjects, but particularly in reading because you don't read so well. Your phonemic awareness needs a *lot* of work. Your teacher, Mr. . . . Brown? Yes, Mr. Brown agrees that you need a smaller class environment to succeed. So, right now you're not doing so well, but we hope that you can do better with a more intensive classroom setting."

Watching clueless Marvin and his mother listen to the woman's speech made me squirm. The next professional read from the folder: "Marvin, you have problems with speech. You run into problems forming thoughts and that affects how you talk." Her monologue turned into a terminology-laden maze that Mrs. Winslow was clearly not following.

I jumped in. "Look Marvin, this is what this is all about. Even though you had a hard time doing some of the work in 4-217, you're still a smart kid. It will be a good thing for you to have a teacher who can spend a lot of time working with just you. I couldn't do that as much as I wanted to, because I had twenty-five other kids to worry about. Your new teacher will be able to work with you all the time. Doesn't that sound good?"

Marvin nodded. I decided to go for broke. "You told me that you're not smart, but that's wrong. You are smart. You're just in a class with kids who have been doing some things for years that are brand-new to you. Let's say I went to astronaut school to learn how to be a spaceman, and they put me in a class with other astronauts who have been studying space science for three years, would I do well in that class? No, they would all know more than me. But does that mean I'm not a smart guy? No! I just need someone to take me aside and work with me, so I could catch up on the stuff that the other astronaut students have been learning for the last three years. It would be hard to learn it all, but if I worked hard and had a good teacher, I could do it. That's you! You're in a class where you need to catch up a little, and this is your chance. Do you understand what I mean?"

A long pause passed with all eyes on Marvin. He mumbled, "You want to be a spaceman?"

"I think you should go to special ed is what I'm saying."

Everyone again looked at Marvin. "I don't want to leave Mr. Brown's class!" he moaned, bursting into blubbers.

"Aww," the three special ed ladies sighed.

Mrs. Winslow cradled Marvin to her bosom while he sobbed. The ladies and I clamored to explain that this was all for *next* year, and he would be in 4-217 for the rest of this school year.

"I want to be with Mr. Brown next year! Please!"

Marvin's outpouring caught me off guard. I thought he despised me. A part of me had thought at times that I despised him. This was the second crying request by a student to stay with me.

"Everyone has a new teacher next year. No one in your class gets to stay with Mr. Brown," the third lady explained.

"Mr. Brown, will you be here for summer school?" the second lady asked.

"No." Budget cutbacks had abolished summer school at P.S. 85 anyway, allotting no teacher positions and a handful of student spots at nearby P.S. 9 for critical cases.

The first lady turned to Marvin. "But you'll be able to visit Mr. Brown all the time next year. You can talk to him all about how you're doing in your new class. I'm sure Mr. Brown would be happy to see you whenever you want. Right, Mr. Brown?"

"Right," I said, swallowing hard. My hand went to the signed letter of resignation in my pocket.

Marvin looked pacified, and Mrs. Winslow signed the requisite forms.

I had been looking forward to submitting recommendations for my students' future teachers, mentally matching up personalities for months. I wanted Lito Ruiz and Destiny Rivera with Jeanne Solloway for her maternal manner. I envisioned Eddie getting along with Evan Krieg. Evley and Gloria would mesh well with mildmannered Scott Riesling. Lakiya was prime for Marc Simmons's perennial hell room. Both Hamisi's and Gladys F.'s mouths and pens needed a dose of writing fanatic Paul Bonn. But what to do about my top three: Sonandia, Jennifer, and Seresa?

"I want them," Karen told me. "There are some open spots in PAC."

The Performing Arts Class traditionally operated on a rigid track with the same batch moving from Boswell in fourth to Berkowitz in fifth.

"It's my class now. I'll push it through," Karen said. She did.

My mom had quietly resisted visiting 4-217. I think my recountings of students' violent outbursts and disrespect made her worry that she wouldn't be able to control the kids if she came, blemishing my image of her as a master teacher.

"The kids will love it," I told her on the phone. "They've been asking over and over for Amanda, too. This will be more memorable than anything else you'd be doing on that Monday."

"You're right," she said after a pause. "I'll get some things together."

On Sunday night, June 20, my mom and sister slept in my bed and I crashed on the futon. At dawn, the three of us set out for P.S. 85.

The surprised kids were ecstatic when they entered their classroom to discover two bonus members of the Brown family. "Amanda!" Tiffany cried, running over for a hug. The two of them had quickly developed a rapport during Amanda's icy January day at P.S. 85. "And Mr. Brown's mom!"

After a special "Brown Family Math" edition of my Mental Math Mornings (teachers essentially invented their own math curriculum after the Test), my mom gathered the kids for a read-aloud

of Barbara Kerley's *The Dinosaurs of Waterhouse Hawkins*. I was mortified that Dennis, Lito, and Joseph refused to move forward to sit with
the listeners. However, within minutes of hearing Marcia Brown's
voice, they crept to the front to join their classmates. The kids were
mesmerized by Hawkins, an Englishman who constructed the first
life-sized models of dinosaurs, some of which remain buried in Central Park. Then Mom brought out the . . .

"Chocolate chip cookies!"

"Homemade?"

"Oh snap, Mrs. Brown!"

I took out my camera to capture the scene. While Mom was taking a picture of Amanda and me with group five, Marvin Winslow
tapped her shoulder.

"Mrs. Brown, can I please take a picture with the camera
please?" Marvin meekly asked.

I glared as covertly as possible, shaking my head slightly,
mouthing, "Not him. Don't do it. No." A moment later, Marvin
Winslow was handling my camera, something I had truly expected
never to happen again. Images of a spiteful camera thief spiking my
Nikon into the tile floor flashed in my head. My mom put her hand
on his shoulder as he steadied the frame. *Click.* He handed the camera back to her. He shot one of the best pictures in the roll.

During my prep, I brought Mom, Amanda, and the regular Ms.
Bowers tutors to the auditorium to watch the kindergarten graduation ceremony. Allie's beaming class performed an adorable dance
routine to "Under the Sea," choreographed and led by Trisha Pierson. When the little mermaids and mermen took their bows, my
group went bananas with applause.

After lunch, Mom overruled my advice not to read aloud to the
keyed-up afternoon crowd. "The read-alouds are the best way to
calm them down," she said, and performed Judy Sierra's *The Dancing
Pig,* a Balinese version of Hansel and Gretel. The kids were angels.

The smorgasbord of prizes thrilled even Lakiya Ray. Mom
brought goodies large (more stuffed bears from Macy's, posters, tote

bags collected from reading conventions, and enough books for each kid to pick three) and small (pencils, dinosaur figurines, notepads, candy). As each delighted student carefully picked out gifts, I stood and marveled. Our class may have had a thousand ugly moments, but this was beautiful. I couldn't believe Sonandia and Jennifer were absent, attending their older siblings' middle school graduations.

Lito looked forlorn when he inspected the table. "There are no more bookbags?" he asked.

"It doesn't look like it . . . oh, wait." Mom grabbed her personal teacher tote and emptied the contents. "This one has a little dirt on the bottom. Is that okay?"

"Yeah! Thank you!" Lito lit up with his new treasure.

Gloria Diaz hugged Love Bear to her neck. Tough Lakiya cradled Hope Bear like a delicate cub. Athena declared she was going to read her copy of *The Dinosaurs of Waterhouse Hawkins* to every member of her family. (A promise she kept several times over, according to her fifth-grader brother, Alvin.)

"You're good. I'm impressed," Mom said afterward at a diner. "Just remember not to let things lag for a second. Everything you do needs to draw them in. You started to lose them when you played with the dinosaurs too much during math."

"You're right. You were amazing."

"It's easy to give out presents and be a success for one day," she said, sipping her chamomile tea. "To be with them, pushing them, day in and day out, that's a whole different ball game."

Wilson Tejera called my extension. "Mr. Brown, sorry to bother you. I was wondering if one of your students could come over to my room to help me box up some things. Is Hamisi in the middle of anything?"

Hamisi was currently seething in the back of the room since I had just confiscated his Game Boy again. Following the Math Test, Hamisi's behavior had nosedived to intolerable, mean-spirited levels. He smirked when reprimanded and cursed a blue streak. After starting September as my line leader, his contribution to 4-217 was ultimately a disappointing one. But why did Tejera, the October face-grabber, want him?

"Hamisi, do you want to help Mr. Tejera in his room?"

"Oh yeah!" He couldn't scurry out of his seat fast enough.

Later, at lunch, Hamisi showed off the five-dollar bill that Tejera paid him for his services. Tejera said to me, "Hamisi really is a good kid. Temperamental, but a nice kid."

I arranged a 4-217 walking field trip to the New York Public Library branch on Bainbridge Avenue for June 24, the second-to-last day of school. Despite the end-of-school antsiness and June heat, the kids walked in a neat line, with our only snag coming in Clara's sudden disappearance on our way out of the building. ("I had to tell my sister something," she attempted to explain.)

The librarian, Ms. Crenshaw, drew thrilled disbelief when she explained the free Internet access and book/video checkout limit of an unfathomable *ten items*. Everyone took books home except Eric Ruiz, who, arms full of automotive-themed storybooks, was turned away for owing over ninety dollars in outstanding late fees, dating back to a similar class trip last year.

Walking back, I froze a picture in my memory of Dennis, Joseph, Lito, and Eddie swaggering down sunny Marion Avenue toward school, their arms slung around each other's shoulders. A moment later, Cwasey opined on how black and Latino kids shouldn't walk like that. I cut him off and hoped that no one else heard his ugly remark, preferring to remain in that image of four friends walking together.

Following the final full day of school, the Visual Arts Club gathered for its swan song and the world premiere of *Teacher Dance Party*. After several early-June attempts, we had finally shot the movie over two afternoons, agreeing to delete the final dancing teachers scene (for lack of participant interest) and replace it with freeze-frame reaction shots of the kids' discovery of the secret shindig. As a special finale, I cut together individual end-credit curtain calls, with each kid's name in white-on-black screen text synched with the second verse of Johnny Rivers's "Secret Agent Man." We ate snacks and, by request, watched the four-minute video nine times. I returned Lito Ruiz's phenomenal roll of pictures to him and shared his neighborhood documentary work with the group. Lito had started showing up at the Visual Arts Club after my return from France ("Don't go away again, Mr. Brown"), and I made him an official member.

On Friday, June 25, my alarm buzzed and I tumbled out of bed for the last time as the teacher of Public School 85's class 4-217. Before noon, it would all be over. I threw a bathing suit in my bag for the after-party at Elizabeth Camaraza's backyard in New Jersey.

Karen and I chattered on the D train about the summer. I had an August 18 plane ticket to London, where an open-ended European jaunt would begin. She was mulling a crossroads with her boyfriend, who was already off working at an overnight camp upstate.

At Lee's Deli, I bought a slew of Little Debbies and eight bottles of orange Vitamin Water.

Everyone was present and punctual at lineup, radiating nervous energy. Seresa gave me a "Happy Retirement" Hallmark card. Seeing this, Sonandia and Gladys Ferraro sprang on me with gifts. Sony gave me a wallet and Gladys F. had an oversized periwinkle golf shirt in a gift-wrapped box. I put the shirt on over my tie and wore it the rest of the day.

In the room, the kids finished cleaning out their desks and I emptied mine, trashing many papers I wish I had kept. I called each student to the back of the room to review the report cards' final marks and comments. By popular demand, we played "Baseball," a trivia game my high school mentor Mr. Truitt had played with us on casual days. The team's batter picks a category and requests his question's difficulty in terms of a single, double, triple, or home run. The most popular categories were "Names" and "P.S. 85," where batters needed to come up with the first names of teachers (infinitely amusing to elementary school students), name all three assistant principals in alphabetical order, or the like. Gladys Viña notched a home run when she named six first-grade teachers, earning the girls' team massive bragging rights.

During an abbreviated prep period, I delivered copies of *Teacher Dance Party* to all eleven Visual Arts Club participants and Mrs. Boyd's mailbox. While in the office, I checked my teacher rating. I was satisfactory, but placed on extra-observation probation for the next two years.

Mrs. Boyd was in the office when I swung by. "I received your letter," she said.

"Yes."

"Are you sure you want to leave?"

Minutes ticked down on 4-217. Lunch was scheduled for 10:55, with a direct dismissal from the cafeteria at 11:30. At 10:30, with Mr. Lizard tucked under my arm, I summoned the collective to the back corner for a meeting (the former site of my Reading Chair, which was literally ripped apart while I was in France), where I doled out five-ounce plastic cups. Eyes went wide when I withdrew the large Vitamin Water bottles from a grocery bag.

"I always wondered what that stuff was," Sonandia said. It was true that I taught all year with chalk in one hand and a mysterious orange health drink in the other. I poured each kid a cupful of Vitamin Water.

"Members of 4-217," I began.

"Jay-Z ain't in G-Unit!" Cwasey yelled, just forming the rebuttal for a previous dispute.

"Jay-Z ain't in G-Unit," Tayshaun mimicked in a mumble.

"Hey! Quiet!"

Cwasey frowned. I estimated twenty seconds until he pushed someone. My sensitive moment needed to happen fast. I raised my cup. Instantly every other cup went up and silence spread, in sudden reverence for this grown-up ritual.

"Boys and girls, you will have many, many years of school in your lives. And this was one of them. No matter what happens, you were all in Mr. Brown's fourth-grade class together, and I hope you remember it. Good luck!" I drank my drink and everyone followed suit.

"That tastes good!"

"I'm-a get my mom to buy that!"

"It's healthy, too," I said, and walked toward my desk to break up the meeting. Half of the class walked with me, shadowing my moves around the class for the rest of the morning.

"Last twenty-five-second challenge of the year. Let's see if we can make it!"

The kids lined up perfectly by the count of fifteen. "I knew 4-217 had the best lineruppers in the school," I said. "You just kept it a secret all year."

"Except when we won third place!"

"That's very true, Dennis."

Marvin Winslow's mother came by to pick him up early. "Marvin had a good year this year," she said.

You are nuts if you believe that, I thought. Then out loud, I replied, "Next year will be much better in Ms. Beck's class. He'll be able to start getting the help he needs."

"Oh, we're moving to Manhattan. He ain't coming to *this* school no more. Marvin, hurry up!"

"What?"

"Oh yeah. I'm getting a job. Thank you! Good-bye, Mr. Brown! Come on, Marvin, I'm in a rush!" Marvin slumped out the door and was gone.

In the cafeteria, no one wanted to eat. I sat at the lunch table, surrounded by children. "Who wants to hear a true story?" I asked. Everybody. "I don't know if you remember this, but the first week of school was very tough for me."

"We had Fausto!" Athena agreed.

"Well, there were a bunch of things. I had to yell a lot more than I ever wanted to. I hate yelling, especially yelling at kids, but I yelled all the time that first week, and there were fights and problems and I was really upset. But at dismissal on Friday of the first week, Jennifer, do you remember what you did?"

Jennifer grinned and blushed, looking at her shoes.

"It was a terrible day, and right when I let everyone go in the parking lot to go home, Jennifer said, 'Thank you, Mr. Brown,' and she gave me a hug. It meant a lot to me. All the yelling and frustration was worth it if I had at least one student who appreciated what I was trying to do. I know there was more than one, but it didn't feel like it that first week, until Jennifer gave me that hug. Then she did it every day of the year, saying thank you and giving me a hug. It didn't cost her anything, but it saved me." I looked at Sonandia. "You never know when the smallest thing that you do will change someone's life."

When Sonandia walked to the garbage can to chuck her untouched school lunch, I followed her, feeling I needed to say goodbye privately. I patted her shoulder, not knowing what to tell her. "I'm going to miss you, Sony."

She shrugged. "I'll see you again."

Soon it was time to line up and dismiss. We walked down the north stairwell, making a longer than usual walk across the width of the parking lot before reaching the awaiting parents. Seresa and Sonandia hugged me as soon as we got outside. Even *Lakiya* joined in the spirit.

"Thank you, Mr. Brown," they said.

Jennifer hung back, looking unsteady. I stepped toward her. "Thank you, Jennifer, for everything."

She hugged me and burst into tears. I felt the lump in my gullet start to expand out of control. We walked silently toward the crowd at the gate.

"Tiffany, come here. I want you to take care of him for me."

Tiffany's mouth dropped open. *"Mr. Lizard?"*

"I think he should live with you. The closet is too stuffy for him. Is that okay?" "Yes! Thank you!" Tiffany squeezed Mr. Lizard and giggled with surprise. My entourage and I continued toward the parents, my eyes getting more watery with each step.

Clara's aunt was the first to see me. "Oh boy, you're supposed to be happy!"

I replied quietly, "It's been a long year."

"Oh no, Mr. Brown! You're going to make *me* cry!"

I looked at my crew for the last time. "Have a great summer, guys."

"You too, Mr. Brown." And they dispersed.

I stood by the door, frozen. Out of the milling pack of adults and children, Sonandia came running back, throwing her arms around me. A few seconds later, she was gone, out of sight.

I leaped up the steps three at a time, knowing a second's delay could spell disaster. I reached desolate 217, shut the door, and sat in a chair against the closet wall where no one from outside could see me.

Teacher Found

On the first day of the following school term, I was in southern Croatia. Holed up in a villa outside the coastal city of Dubrovnik, overlooking the royal Adriatic Sea, I began recounting on paper my year in the Bronx. While at P.S. 85, I hadn't planned to write about my experience; I was simply focused on surviving it. Now I felt a compulsion to tell the story to *myself*, to relive the myriad failures and successes. The year had changed me. Alone in Europe, I pored over my dog-eared notebook.

After three months abroad, something else propelled me back to America: Colleen MacMillan. She was also a Fellow, a third-grade teacher at P.S. 70, a Bronx institution of 1,700 students. Our first date, dinner and drinks at downtown haunt 7A, was exactly a month before my planned departure for Europe. We laughed, told teaching stories, drank Long Island Iced Teas, and shared a quick kiss as I put her in a taxi at 3 a.m. I stood on the Houston Street sidewalk to watch the cab disappear in traffic. I *needed* to see Colleen again. The month became a whirlwind romance that put all my previous relationships in perspective. When we said goodbye at a Greyhound bus station, a shockwave of emotion overtook me. I was ridiculously in love with her.

I returned in time for Thanksgiving. I kept up with my teacher friends, as well as Sonandia, Seresa, and Jennifer via email. Sonandia thrived at the top of the PAC class and got accepted to a selective middle school academy in the Bronx. Seresa and Jennifer drifted apart, finding their niches with different groups of friends, though both had strong academic years and received solos in Karen's marvelous, reinvented

PAC show. Marvin Winslow did come back to P.S. 85 (enrolled in Ms. Beck's fourth-grade special ed class) on October 18, when his mom decided to stop keeping him at home. The family had never moved to Manhattan, but rather to a shelter in the Bronx. His mother had another baby, and Marvin missed over sixty days of school. When he came, he was relatively well behaved in his small class. Epiphany and Lakiya teamed up to raise hell in Marc Simmons's class. Eddie became an achiever in Evan Krieg's room and formed a friendship with Seresa's crowd. Destiny moved somewhere down the Grand Concourse, not to return to P.S. 85.

Eric Ruiz got moved up to fifth grade in spite of his dual Test failures and my recommendation to keep him back. This was in accordance with a much-rumored directive to promote the 2003–2004 fourth-grade failures and hold back third-graders scoring a "one" on any Test. The Department of Education's goal was to strengthen New York City's 2004–2005 fourth-grade population, whose February ELA scores would, prior to Mayor Michael Bloomberg's first reelection bid in November 2005, supply the definitive "after picture" data for measuring the effectiveness of the mayor's reforms. Needless to say, Bloomberg's political goals were met.

Dilla Zane retired, and P.S. 85 revised its stance on print-rich classroom environments. Under new leadership, the mania over bulletin boards was deemed excessive and unnecessary. Ms. Guiterrez likely would not again confront a teacher over the spelling of "announced," although she continued to strike fear into the hearts of P.S. 85 rookies.

Weekly art periods were extended to the entire school, but the Visual Arts Club was discontinued.

Barbara Chatton does not mentor anymore. Sarah Gerson, my summer training Fellow Advisor, resigned from the Department of Education.

Besides Tim Shea, who defected for a pharmaceutical sales job, and me, however, all nine of the other Cohort 6 Fellows at P.S. 85 stayed to complete their two-year commitments and Mercy College master's degrees. Each graduating Fellow received $4,750 in tuition reimbursement from Americorps. As of June 2011, five of my fellow Fellows, including Trish Pierson and Cat Samuels, are still teaching at P.S. 85.

Watchdog advocacy group Inside Schools rated P.S. 85 three stars out of five, noting the school's "indomitable spirit" and observing, "Their work, displayed with great pride and care—hallway bulletin boards are covered in protective plastic—is truly superior." Kendra Boyd also got high marks for "personifying the strong sense of continuity at the school." They noted little downside beyond "the usual strains of chronic overcapacity" and one parent's complaint that the administration may be sluggish in responding to problems.

Days before the 2006–2007 school year began, Ms. Boyd retired.

On Black Friday, an envelope arrived from the New York City Department of Education. Enclosed was a "Notice of Overpayment" invoice for $3,315. My never-received termination pay and unused vacation time were deducted from my debt, reducing the amount owed to $1,760. The stated explanation was that I had received extended-time pay when I was entitled only to the base rate. I was actually happy about the paper when I looked it over. Since I *did* work extended time at P.S. 85, clearly the DOE had made a mistake and I could receive my outstanding $1,555. A polite lady in the payroll department explained that since I had broken my contract, I was required to give back my overtime pay.

"I *worked* those hours. I taught a half-hour longer each day than base-rate schools, and I went to all that extra professional development."

"Trust me, I empathize. I wish these weren't the rules. And you're not the only one this is happening to. You're actually lucky. I know you probably don't feel lucky, but the Department is sending these notices out now to people who left two, three-and-a-half years ago. They're tracking everyone down," she said.

"This is insane. No one ever mentioned anything about giving back money for time that you were physically there. I've never heard of anything like this."

"It's the rule. Three-year contract to keep your extended-time earnings."

"You mean two years," I said. "The Teaching Fellows contract is for two years."

"I don't know anything about that, but it's three years for an extended-time school, Teaching Fellow or not. If you leave before that, you owe a year's worth of the overtime. Or else it will be a serious problem for your W–2."

My mentor, Barbara Chatton, an email enthusiast, did not respond when I wrote to her. I learned that Article 12.II.C of the United Federation of Teachers' contract (lapsed on May 31, 2003) outlined this three-year requirement for Schools Under Registration Review (SURR) and ex-SURR school overtime pay. P.S. 85 had used extended-time salary as a carrot for prospective teachers, banking that no one would comb the thirty-two-article contract for loopholes in which the DOE could take back paychecks. There had been no fine print on the Teaching Fellows commitment form. I buried my anger and sent my pay back to the Department of Education.

A year after I left the Bronx, the United Federation of Teachers agreed to a new contract with the city, raising teachers' salaries and increasing hours, effectively switching every school to an extended-hours schedule.

I knew my future was in the classroom. After leaving P.S. 85 I felt a continual itch: a longing for some kind of a second chance with a kid like Lakiya Ray. Her hug on the last day of school had stuck with me. I couldn't—didn't—want to shake a nascent, giddy epiphany that I *really mattered* when I taught.

But my New York City Department of Education file was unsavory. A return to the classroom had to happen outside the public schools, the place where I most wanted to work.

For several months after my return from Europe, I delivered flowers until, with the help of a Teacher Dance Party screening, I was asked to teach Digital Filmmaking at a summer arts camp in Brooklyn. Several weeks later, the Collegiate School, an all-boys Upper West Side independent school that serves the polar opposite of P.S. 85's socioeconomic community, hired me as a fourth-grade co-teacher. According to the school's website, yearly tuition for a K–12 Collegiate student in 2011–2012 was $37,500. Elizabeth Camaraza wrote my letter of reference.

Life at Collegiate was different and delightful, yet not without a culture shock. On my first day a fourth-grader, writing about his summer, asked me, "Mr. Brown, how do you spell *Tuscany*?" Soon after, the boys enjoyed the buffet-style school lunch of tilapia, corn chowder soup, organic Greek salad, and strawberry shortcake.

I got the green light to lead a daily read-aloud and selected Neil Gaiman's *Coraline*. I wrote on the board the book's epigraph by G. K. Chesterton:

Fairy tales are more than true: not because they tell us that dragons exist, but because they tell us that dragons can be beaten.

The students were rapt, and vigorously offered predictions and analysis. This was how I should have started my year in the Bronx, I thought. But then I checked myself—for this type of classroom discussion to work, the students had to balance enthusiasm with self-control, a skill that seemed to be well practiced on the Upper West Side. In class 4-217, the same lesson would likely have stirred up bedlam.

Our opening discussion on *Coraline* was the tip of the iceberg. The students had great stamina for read-aloud time and independent work, so we covered material more quickly, avoiding stagnation or boredom. Teachers collaborated constructively, with minimal rivalry—not at all the case with the faction-splintered staff back in the Bronx. We took an overnight trip to Boston and walked the Freedom Trail.

Each year, the Lower School staff voted to select a topic of study to build a special school-wide unit from scratch. We picked "Structures" and I signed on as the resident expert on canals. This assignment sent me off on my own inquiry process since I knew virtually nothing about canals. I built from scratch lessons on the science and engineering of canals, world geography, canal math on locks and water levels, and the in-class building of our own canals. We sang "Fifteen Miles on the Erie Canal" and examined how building the Erie Canal changed New

York City forever. It was beautiful. I improved as a team member and as a teacher.

The boys received both physical education and recess four times a week, with two sessions of art, computers, library, and science lab. Reading, writing, and math coaches join the two classroom teachers for most core subject lessons, putting three teachers with twenty-two students, or sometimes eleven, if a half-group is away at art or science. Every child experiences many opportunities for public speaking and one-on-one support. Weekly assemblies and intergrade "buddy" systems foster school unity. There are no standardized tests, or even grades until middle school.

Of course, a well-endowed independent institution is bound to differ from a massive public system. Strikingly though, many sources of Collegiate's success derive from efforts with no line items in the school budget. For example, administrators in the Collegiate Lower School know every child. Their priorities are clear, because they meet with each set of classroom teachers once a week and often drop in for lessons. This community spirit emanating from the top runs deep. Parents understand and appreciate the administrators' commitment to their children and thus view them as allies, not adversaries.

The students are invested in their academic future, so disruptive behavior is rare. Simply, the kids recognize that school is important. They are surrounded by role models who value scholastic achievement, and their calm, professional school environment implicitly does not tolerate anti-school rebelliousness. Standardized tests are not necessary to ensure diligence from teachers and achievement from students. Rather, comprehensive portfolios of student work, evaluated by teachers, administrators, and parents, demonstrate a more rounded picture of a student's readiness to move forward. The absence of testing pressure affords flexibility in scheduling too. Unlike the public system, Collegiate does not mandate five blocks of in-class reading per week. Instead, they fit in three reading periods to make room for creative, exploratory "specials" like art, science, music, and computers.

Teacher collaboration is built into the schedule. During weekly faculty meetings and students' daily gym periods, lesson planning becomes a cooperative process, rather than a solitary one. In delivering lessons and handling classroom business, two or more teachers are in the room at a time. The dividends of this investment in personalizing education are manifold.

Midway through my first year at Collegiate, I was no longer a shell-shocked rookie and the mistakes I did make did not incite an instant fracas as they had in P.S. 85. Still, I saw every day that the most successful teachers wisely leveraged their experience and relationships to coax the best out of their students. As a new guy, I had a ceiling on how much I could accomplish.

This was never clearer to me than the day I happened to look at a first-grade bulletin board. Each kid had written one sentence about the book *Old Henry* and had drawn a corresponding picture. One of these caught my eye every time I passed by. The picture was chicken scratch and the words read: "HE WAS DFAT AND THAT WAS OK."

There was something charming to me about how this six-year-old had mangled whatever adjective this was supposed to be. I brought over another young colleague and showed it to her, and she couldn't make sense of it either. It became a running joke where one of us might say during a prep period "I'm feeling dfat," and the other would immediately assure that it was okay. It's okay to be dfat.

A week later, I mentioned to the veteran first-grade teacher how much that one phrase tickled me. Without a moment's hesitation, she said: "Oh yeah. He was different and that was okay."

The translation made perfect sense. The teacher, in her eighth year working with first-graders, understood the child's intent immediately. She spoke the language of first-graders.

This exchange stuck with me. I think it crystallized the challenge of being a rookie. I thought of myself as dedicated, enthusiastic, and relatively intelligent, but so many times, I just didn't speak the language. I imagined if I had been assigned to teach that first-grade class, there's no way I would be able to bring those students nearly as far in their learning as their veteran teacher would. I couldn't even decipher what they were communicating.

Interestingly, when Mayor Bloomberg's appointment of magazine publisher Cathie Black to be New York City public schools chancellor ended calamitously in early 2011, less than four months after she took the job, Black told *Fortune Magazine*: "It was like having to learn Russian in a weekend—and then give speeches in Russian and speak Russian in budget committee and City Council meetings." Experience and institutional knowledge count in education. Black was too dfat to be OK.

As the year at Collegiate drew towards a close, I knew I had to make a move. I was twenty-five and engaged to Colleen. I enjoyed so much about Collegiate, but after two laps of teaching fourth grade, I didn't see myself surrounded by elementary school kids when I gazed five or ten years down the line.

Literature was what I really loved. Well-told stories had drawn me to film school. I wanted to explore creative and reflective writing with young people who needed outlets for their tangled, evolving worldviews.

I wanted to become a high school English teacher: an ink-stained sharer of the best ideas ever conceived, an agent for sparking adolescents' power of expression. My students would read widely, debate vigorously, write passionately, and in the end, depart my class with the unmatchable, lasting confidence of someone who can genuinely express himself with the written and spoken word. Grandiose visions swam through my head: I'd be a man of letters, Teddy Roosevelt's "man in the arena."

"It is not the critic who counts; not the man who points out how the strong man stumbles, or where the doer of deeds could have done them better. The credit belongs to the man who is actually in the arena, whose face is marred by dust and sweat and blood; who strives valiantly; who errs, who comes short again and again, because there is no effort without error and shortcoming; but who does actually strive to do the deeds;

who knows great enthusiasms, the great devotions; who spends himself in a worthy cause; who at the best knows in the end the triumph of high achievement, and who at the worst, if he fails, at least fails while daring greatly, so that his place shall never be with those cold and timid souls who neither know victory nor defeat."

As a naïve college grad enrolling in an alternative certification program, I had drunk the Kool-Aid that intelligence, grit, and a prestigious degree predestined me for success in the classroom; that had been a folly. Now, with better reference points for navigating classrooms and a focus on high school English, I felt ready to go through a legitimate teacher education program and come out the other side, in the parlance of federal legislation, "highly qualified."

Half of all new teachers leave the profession within five years. I had already contributed to that statistic once; I was determined to arm myself with the skills to stay and thrive. In May 2007, I started a graduate degree program for Teaching of English (Grades 7–12) at Teachers College, Columbia University (TC).

Preparing myself to be a good teacher, and not cannon fodder, was expensive. In the 2010–2011 academic year, TC tuition cost $1,178 per credit, plus books and fees. My program required thirty-eight credits.

Fortunately my parents covered my costs in graduate school. My socioeconomic advantages were reflected in the homogeneity of much of my TC cohort: mid-twenties, upper-middle-class, and white. It's extremely problematic that most top-tier programs preparing people for public service are cost-prohibitive to a majority of would-be applicants.

The dividends for those who attended were many. Teachers College blended well the elements of theory and practice. I took hardcore pedagogy courses in English Methods, Teaching of Reading, Teaching of Writing, and Teaching Shakespeare, as well as a mixed salad of "foundations" courses like The History of Student Activism, and Diversity in the Secondary Classroom. Classes were in the evenings to accommodate teachers' schedules, so most nights I came home around ten o'clock to my wife. Colleen and I got married the summer I started at TC.

It was time to get back in the New York City public school fracas. My fall student teaching assignment led me to East Harlem's Francis Bacon Middle School, under the wing of mentor-teacher Denise Silva, a hyperkinetic Theatre Arts teacher who loved kids but went berserk when they didn't do what she wanted. When no one volunteered to play her warm-up improv games, she lashed out with harangues of disappointment. When the class was chatty upon entering the room, she screamed her frustration. She called it "tough love."

I felt awkward playing second fiddle to Denise. On the fourth day of class, a boy called her "sexist" and, neck veins bulging, she got into it with him right there. "*Do you have any idea . . .* " was an opening she recycled liberally. Later in the hallway, another student, Hector, quietly assured me, "Don't worry, we know *you* not sexist." I said thanks, but pointed out that neither was Ms. Silva. I knew it was my professional responsibility to back her up—even though she did, in my perception, display a marked preference for her female students.

Even when the kids were hooked on a class activity, forces at Francis Bacon seemed to conspire to prevent coherent lessons. The school stood adjacent to a massive construction site, and the grating industrial groans of heavy machinery never took a coffee break. During one fifty-eight-minute lesson I led on extracting key information from monologues, the construction equipment went mercifully quiet, but we were interrupted by a lengthy public address announcement about something called a "penny harvest," three loud-ringing phone calls notifying individual students about their guidance counselor appointments, NYU undergraduates entering the room to observe, a woman from the Settlement House somehow affiliated with the guidance department showing up to give out literature about her organization, and a tutor arriving to spirit away five students. The lesson required sustained concentration; achieving it from the whole group was impossible.

Still, there was much to learn by parachuting into a school for fourteen weeks to survey the lay of the land. For example, Francis Bacon held a Fall Field Day, which was a real success as a community building exercise. I thought it was a great idea to have Field Day at the beginning of the year, instead of the very end. I placed second in the faculty egg-and-spoon race.

Also, Denise had a great system called "Notes of Praise" that set clear criteria for students to earn a positive note home. The kids bought into this; those fourteen-year-olds *really* wanted their families to be proud of them. Unfortunately, Denise got overwhelmed within a month and the Notes of Praise fell by the wayside. The kids were resentful when they finally caught on that their earned Notes of Praise were long overdue. I saw firsthand that even when you're overburdened, consistency is crucial.

I was also reminded of the power of out-of-classroom interactions with kids. One morning I was spacing out while riding the First Avenue bus to school when Denise climbed on. She sat next to me and we chatted about class. A stop later, Henry, one of our volatile seventh-graders, boarded the bus. Just the day before, Denise had nailed him with lunch detention and a searing lecture about self-sabotaging his future prospects in life.

I quietly cringed, since Henry was about to see Denise and me riding the bus to school together and would certainly assume we were an item, information that would spread like wildfire among our students. I was stunned when Henry calmly leaned in for a quick, one-arm hug from Denise and said with a smile and a charming mock bow "Good morning, my teachers!" Then he shuffled to the back of the bus.

Later in the day, Henry came into our empty classroom during lunchtime. Denise was out of the room, so I was the only one there. Henry was on some kind of gum-scraping detail. I said hello to him, and he came over to me.

"I saw you on the bus today," Henry said.

"Yes. I was there with Ms. S.," I replied, not sure where to take the conversation.

"I get on at 96th Street. Two stops on the limited and bam, I'm at school." The floodgates were open. "I know I need school to get a good education and a good job. You and Ms. S. are my nicest teachers."

Here was a boy who just wanted to talk. We made a standing lunchtime date.

One day, I shadowed eighth-grader Hector Gago and his peers in class 822. I picked Hector and his class because they already knew me well as their Theatre Arts student teacher, and it would be easy for me to be invisible among them. Since I'd spent so much time with these kids, I was interested to see what their day was like outside of my class.

Hector seemed able to strike an impressive tightrope balance between achieving academically and being a male who fit in with his pals in El Barrio. Navigating the two worlds of "cool" and "smart" was challenging, if not impossible for many kids, but Hector seemed to pull it off. He was the class treasurer, a consistent participant in class discussions, and an animated presence in the hallways between classes. On Back to School Night, his extended family beamed when I told them how well Hector was doing in our class. I wanted to see the trajectory of his day.

I was profoundly let down.

The day began with a ninety-minute humanities class, devoted entirely to test prep. Ms. Jones, the student teacher running the class, actually opened by saying, "Okay guys, today we're doing more test prep. I know it's boring, but the Test is in January, so we gotta get through it." The kids, some of whom can frequently act rambunctious and oppositional, seemed terrified of the Test and did exactly as they were told for the full hour and a half.

Each kid got a copy of last year's English Language Arts (ELA) test. It seemed that the school photocopier was in need of new toner, as I had to strain to read the light grey print on the pages. I sat in the back of the room with Hector and some other children and could not read a single word of the transparency Ms. Jones was annotating on the overhead projector. There was no room for student participation; Ms.

Jones told the students—in a genial tone, at least—which sentences were important and should be underlined. Then she looked at the questions, gave the kids a minute to come up with their answers, and told them which answers were correct. On two of the questions, they were allowed to conference in pairs.

"Now you guys do the rest," she said, prompting fifty minutes of quiet while the kids worked over the problems.

I did the test too, and after an interminable silence, Ms. Jones asked for the students' answers. Other students cheered when they agreed with an answer announced to be correct.

The hallway transition from the test prep period to Spanish was predictably raucous. For my part, I felt like freaking out too, after the boring, pressure-laden ninety minutes we had all just tolerated.

Spanish class didn't provide much of a reprieve. The kids started with fifteen minutes of copying words and definitions. The teacher announced he had a personal situation going on, and took a cell phone call in the hall. When the actual lesson started, the kids participated eagerly and the teacher praised them for their answers.

After Spanish, the students returned to their homeroom for a one-hour formal "diagnostic" standardized math test. The hour was silent and awful. I was so bored that I left. What I missed was an afternoon math class where the teacher reviewed the answers to the standardized diagnostic test.

I came away feeling sorry for the kids. They were silent, bored, and scared. Also, they didn't get to walk away as I did, since they had been trained not to question what was demanded of them involving the scary Test. Their trusted principal and teachers—with varying amounts of zeal—shoved it down their throats. I'd like to see advocates of high-stakes testing actually try to sit through a day in the life of this assessment regime.

I'd planned to observe Hector specifically, but his experience was no different than the other kids'. At least I had a little more context for why they blew up in Theatre Arts class.

When my time was about to expire at Francis Bacon, I asked the students the fill out a "Report Card for Mr. Brown." The sheet prompted: How much do you feel you learned in Mr. Brown's class? What did Mr. Brown do well as a teacher? What do you think Mr. Brown could do better? Please explain your answers. Almost all of the seventh- and eighth-graders appeared to take time and give thought to their responses. Here's a representative sample:

He could do better I think if he could controle his temper.

You didn't yell that's why everyone liked so he really didn't have a reason. He doesn't need teachers like ms. s to help him because all she does is scream.

Mr. Brown explained a lot and he also gave chances. I think Mr. Brown should not yell a lot.

Mr. Brown can do better when the class is misbehaving yell as much as I know he Dont like yelling.

I learned a lot because he didn't screamed a us and he took it step by step.

Sometimes it boarding and sometimes it fun. Have patantion with kids. Don't tell alot. unless they are bad. Give exaple more often. I like you teaching.

Mr. Brown could screm or be louder to the class when they don't pay attention because he has to wait for the class and we miss some of the lesson. His a fun teacher to learn from and gives us an apportunity to say what we have to say on question he asks on the lesson he teach even though we're wrong.

—⁓—

He screamed and made kids raise there hands and made the lessons fun.

The kids were fixated on yelling and not yelling. My first year in the Bronx was fraught with shouting and in the time since, I'd cultivated a teaching persona that—I thought—never yelled out in anger or frustration.

Yelling in the classroom under any circumstances is counterproductive and emotionally exhausting from a teacher's perspective, and evidenced by the report card comments, for the kids it's downright scarring. Even so, a number of my Francis Bacon students still perceived me as a yeller. In a classroom full of human beings, you never know what comes across.

My second student-teaching placement lasted from January to June as the main teacher of two eleventh-grade Honors English classes at DeWitt Clinton High School in the Bronx. I'd long awaited this return to the borough that had knocked me out. Four and a half years had passed since my first day as a teacher, and here was my opportunity to get it right.

Since classes at Clinton are semester-based, I got to be the lead teacher from the first day of the course. My juniors didn't know I was a student-teacher and I never told them. My mentor, Jim Garrity, sat in the back and offered incisive lesson dissections and planning ideas.

Working with Jim at DeWitt Clinton was a desirable placement that I had angled for. The school, one of the last large comprehensive high schools in New York, served close to 5,000 students and boasted an august hit parade of alumni including legendary writers James Baldwin and Countee Cullen, composers Richard Rodgers and Bernard

Hermann, the creators of Batman (Bob Kane) *and* Spider-Man (Stan Lee) . . . Within the building, "small learning communities" (SLC) operated on their own schedules. My classes were part of the "Macy Honors" SLC, a prestigious college-prep program that was the pride of the principal. Landing in the Macy program was a relief because—indicated by an unsettling dropout rate and the main entrance metal detectors—not all of Clinton's classrooms were conducive to focused, high-level inquiry.

My first day ever as a teacher, back in the P.S. 85 days, had devolved into a fracas partly because of my transparently benign, help-me-help-you stance. One would think that now, over four years later, when I stepped in at Clinton to face my Bronx teenagers, I'd take a harder edge.

However, by this time, I'd learned that you do not need to fashion yourself into some kind of drill sergeant to teach in a tough neighborhood. By presenting yourself as organized and interesting, you can actually win over the students who might disrupt; they'll *want* to be part of the community if you make it enticing enough. A majority of behavior management issues can be defused by a teacher's organization and students' engagement. Juggling that solid teacher persona and student buy-in with substantive academic activities is the great challenge. Being new—lacking experience and institutional knowledge—compounds this challenge and can tip the scales towards chaos.

Yelling and scaring students have ephemeral benefits—you'll achieve quiet for a moment—but negative long-term returns. I hadn't grasped that as a rookie. With a renewed opportunity at DeWitt Clinton, I wanted these students to *want* to impress me. I also knew that, at five-foot-eight, I had no shot of intimidating them.

I also weighed the advantages I had going in; these kids had applied for the Macy Honors program, so their grades mattered to them. When kids bring intrinsic motivation for academics, they are far less likely to antagonize the teacher. While my ultimate goal was to engender a love of reading and learning and all that good stuff, it was comforting to know that I could, if absolutely necessary, dangle grades over them to further my ends.

My opening gambit was a syllabus review complete with an anti-plagiarism speech modeled after a TC professor's style. The students actually seemed to perk up during my amateur psychoanalytic probe into why people plagiarize. (They've procrastinated and they're freaked out.) I think some bells were ringing. I liked feeling the focused attention of the group, and the speech had the added benefit of making it sound like I had experience teaching high school students.

Next I handed out a personal letter; their first assignment was to respond in kind.

Dear Students,

Hello, I'm Mr. Brown, your English 6 teacher. Although we will get to know each other pretty well in person in our five periods per week together, I wanted to introduce myself to you in black and white as well.

I was born in Philadelphia, Pennsylvania in 1981, which makes me a lifetime Philly sports fan. Every year, the Eagles break my heart. (I'm pulling for the Giants over the Patriots in the Super Bowl, though.)

I attended public school in Cherry Hill, New Jersey. As a high school student, I became obsessed with movies. There was an elective course in the school called "Film Appreciation," where Mr. Truitt, a teacher who had been there for thirty years, showed all kinds of movies on an old-school 16 mm projector. I had never seen a foreign movie, or a silent film, or really very much besides Hollywood stuff like *Indiana Jones* movies. Mr. Truitt showed films from all over the world, and we had amazing—and often heated—discussions picking them apart. He introduced me to artists that I came to love and never would have found on my own.

One film that Mr. Truitt showed that stands out in my mind is *The 400 Blows*, a French movie from 1959. It's a low-budget, semi-autobiographical work by Francois Truffaut, about himself as a fourteen-year-old in a working-class Paris neighborhood. I was used to movies where the main character is heroic, but Antoine, the main character of *The 400 Blows*, is not heroic in any normal way. He lies, steals, and ultimately gets disowned by his parents and sent to a reform school. There's no happy ending.

At the end of *The 400 Blows*, I didn't quite know what to think about it. Everyone in the class had different opinions. Some dismissed Antoine as a worthless troublemaker; others thought he was a Jesus-like martyr. My classmates' opinions were all over the place, and Mr. Truitt forced each student to back up his argument. We never came to a consensus about one correct way to interpret *The 400 Blows*, and we eventually realized that wasn't the point. The valuable part was the exploration. This was a revelation to me.

After graduating from high school, I moved to New York to attend New York University. In 2003, I became a teacher. I am excited about the journey we will take together this semester. We will explore a wide range of material, and I look forward to picking it apart with you. My goal is for you to feel that when you walk into English class, you are walking into a place where ideas matter and everybody has a voice.

Sincerely,
Mr. Brown

This worked well. The next day I received thoughtful replies filled with admirable goals—ones that I could leverage in one-on-ones if their behavior or work ever strayed. I was happy. So I drowned them in homework.

I didn't mean to. Our first unit was on the Harlem Renaissance, so I'd decided to set it up with some essays by Booker T. Washington and W.E.B. DuBois to provide some historical context. Our second class together, my students followed me into—and then took over— a nuanced analysis of Washington's "cast down your bucket" brand of self-help as public policy. We were on fire!

From the back of the room, Jim signaled discreetly that we had two minutes left before the bell. Snapped out of my reverie, I responded by sweeping up several manila folders I'd laid out containing future assignments and, in an irrational rush, handed out the next three nights' work. I dumped on them the challenging *The Souls of Black Folk* excerpt with an accompanying written response, a T-chart comparing/contrasting Washington and DuBois's ideas, and then a prompt to write a newspaper election editorial endorsing one of the candidates, Washington or DuBois over the other, for the mantle of Chief African American Spokesman. For models on editorial writing, I threw them the *New York Post* presidential primary endorsement of Barack Obama and the *New York Times* piece supporting Hillary Clinton. In the final minute of class, each of the thirty-three students received five different sheets of instructions. Of course, the bell sounded in the midst of my frantic paper-passing, and immediately around me a huddle of kids materialized. They were eager to get all the papers and get jogging to their next honors class across the massive building. A physics teacher waited for me to get out so he could use the classroom.

I regretted overloading the kids, and I gave lighter assignments over the next few days, including a generous extra credit opportunity for memorizing twelve more lines of Langston Hughes's poetry. But I never indicated to the students that I thought I had screwed up. Almost all handed in the work, and the quality was surprisingly good.

I worked on memorizing my sixty-six kids' names quickly; this went a long way. A week into the semester, when during a discussion I aimed my gaze at a reticent student and said, "What do you think, Sierra Divina Shaneequa Lee?" Sierra looked a little startled and then responded thoughtfully. She participated regularly for the rest of semester, and later told me that my remembering her name surprised her in a really positive way. I was glad for this; in my previous classes, I had felt the invisible cost of students' alienation. For Sierra, a small gesture was enough to activate her participation and engagement; for others, I couldn't crack the code.

During my first year at P.S. 85, I had a small clutch of students led by my star, Sonandia, whom I could usually count on to participate, and responded by relying heavily on them to keep lessons alive. I later decided that those kids were likely to speak up and share with or without Mr. Brown at the front of the room. It was the less inclined students that I needed to coax out of their shells if I was going to be a truly successful teacher.

I sought to account for the quieter contingent by assigning a handful of presentations and group projects throughout the semester with checks to make sure each student participated. Under Jim's guidance, I fashioned a literary criticism project that involved groups of students becoming experts on a critical lens and then applying it to *The Great Gatsby*. Groups re-imagined *Gatsby* as a Hollywood film that emphasized their critical lens. The groups wrote a movie pitch and designed a poster to show their new vision, then presented to their peers, who had a hand in grading them. One group using the Freudian psychoanalytic lens transformed all of the characters into animals. Tom Buchanan was a grizzly bear; Meyer Wolfsheim's lupine likeness was self-evident.

Most days, the forty-five minute lesson whizzed by. The kids were reading closely and chomping on ideas in the texts. Our Langston Hughes poetry celebration featuring students' original, Hughes-inspired works alongside the classics got ink in the school newspaper. Our culminating project involving in-character monologues based on *To Kill a Mockingbird*—inspired by a TC professor—was a hit. The assistant principal for the English department, Maggie O'Dowd, observed me twice and offered encouragement.

Jim helped me immeasurably through our daily conferences. During classes, he sat in the back of the room, let me run the show entirely, and composed longhand letters on a yellow notepad. His notes helped me focus on the nuts and bolts of good teaching. The gathered wisdom in his words leapt off the page. Some excerpts:

On your "Elements and Expectations of This Course" handout, I am especially impressed by your presentation of "original work" by trying first to understand the motivation for plagiarism. Yes, students get overwhelmed and some feel inadequate and yearn for the kind of recognition that becomes available through handing in "good writing" that they may be incapable of achieving on their own. Perhaps you could invite them to share their stress or anxiety with you in constructive ways—that's vital to establishing a sense of trust that I think will go a long way.

—

You gave out the Zora Neale Hurston reading and asked for a notebook response for HW. One of the systems I've developed is to set up a kind of form for students to label each entry in a unit as, for instance with the Harlem Renaissance, HH #1, HR #2, etc. (with dates). It's helped students to organize and it's helped me when evaluating notebooks. Consider adopting the system—it's up to you.

—

Good choice to have today available for students to express some of their anxiety about Locke's difficult text—it worked to just have students express their understanding and for others to hear these interpretations. It was almost therapeutic in a psychoanalytic sense for students to voice their anxiety as a way to dispel it.

—

I think your approach and the tone you've maintained about plagiarism are constant and fair. You seem honestly irritated by the circumstances of the four cases and baffled by the phenomenon, meanwhile making it clear and certain that you will not tolerate the act. It still might be interesting to explore the psychological aspect as further reinforcement.

Not plagiarizing isn't just a rule (like so many in school), but a moral issue.

—⁂—

What made the activity for me was the reflection afterward—interesting insight into characters shared. Perhaps a follow-up activity might be for students to compose and construct monologues—not necessarily finding them—but composing them from what characters are reported saying or what thinking may be implied. This would also allow students (like Britney) to get deeper into the assignment and highlight their acting/speaking abilities.

—⁂—

Yes, it was teacher-led and traditional, but it was a very interesting "word talk." Did you enjoy it? Because you seemed to be enjoying it and what I think the real value here (and what you convey) is the love of words. The only thing I would have done differently was being sure that everyone had a partner or made eye contact with a partner before letting them go. At least nine students seemed to be inactive or sat alone without sharing.

I felt like a success; in the final week of the school year, I had no idea that my biggest test at DeWitt Clinton still awaited me.

On June 12, my classes and I celebrated our last week together by watching the movie adaptation of *To Kill a Mockingbird*. It was over ninety degrees for the third straight day and our classroom had no air conditioning, but the students were engrossed with Jem and Scout, characters to whom they'd become so close. I was proud that despite the conditions, we were still viewing this film and talking substantively about literature.

Meanwhile, the rest of DeWitt Clinton High School was in lackluster shape. A water fight on a stairwell led to a teacher slipping and falling. Fights were breaking out. Security guards indulged in stunningly unrestrained cursing sprees. A stroll down the hallway glancing into classrooms revealed bored kids spacing out, pacing around while teachers sat behind their desks, reading or fidgeting with a Blackberry. The school calendar had four days left before Regents exams, but really, the year was over. People were cashed out.

On the screen in my room, Miss Maudie was telling Jem, "There are some men in this world who were born to do our unpleasant jobs for us. Your father's one of them." I tore my gaze from the screen to look at the students, who were totally hooked in. Then there was a sudden pounding at the classroom door—BAM! BAM BAM!—and before I could reach the handle, a uniformed female security guard strode into our room. This had never happened before—an officer in the class. I decided to handle it, rather than invite Jim from the back of the room.

"Alright, we're taking the water. You, you, and you," she yell-talked, pointing to Britney, Marielmer, and Yessica, three students who had bottles of water on their desks. "Give me the water." Two older students I didn't know, holding large plastic lawn bags, had followed the officer into the room. It seemed that there was a small collection of plastic water bottles rolling around the bottoms of those giant bags. The two minions roved around the dark room, scooping up the girls' water.

I was bewildered, and suddenly, sharply angry. We were sitting in stultifying heat—and this *stranger* (my protective switch flipped) wanted to *take away* the water? It made no sense. The kids were nonplussed, jarred out of the movie.

"Wait, wait, wait. What's going on?" I said.

But she and her flunkies just headed for the door. I followed them into the hall, closing the door behind me. By the time we reached the corridor I was furious, and ready to channel my inner Atticus Finch.

"Excuse me, but this doesn't seem right," I said, my pulse skyrocketing.

"Water fight. Downstairs. A teacher slipped. We're confiscatin' the waters. A direct order," the officer mumbled.

One of the older students opened the lawn bag, and Officer Gant—I read her nametag—tossed one of the bottles toward it. My Jedi reflex kicked in; I speared out my arm and caught it. Now that she held two bottles and I had one, the power struggle took on a new shape.

"Look, sir. I got a direct order. If you have a problem, you can tell the principal."

No! I wasn't going to have these thirsty students' water trashed, only to take it up with the bureaucracy later. Screw the direct order. This needed to be handled now. "I need to talk to your supervisor," I said.

Gant didn't seem inclined to get into it with me. I was clearly steamed and she probably wasn't invested enough in her direct order to take on my livid protest. She clicked on her radio and called for Mr. Alvarez, the assistant principal whose sole charge was to run security. I heard staticky yelling on his end.

"He's coming up," Gant said.

While we waited for Alvarez to arrive, something fortunate happened. Gant absently passed the two bottles in her hands to me. Maybe she was tired of holding them. Maybe now she counted herself out of the negotiation. Either way, the three bottles were now in my possession and Alvarez would have to physically wrest them from my death grip.

I was amped up. I again thought of Attitcus, advising his daughter: "I wanted you to see what real courage is, instead of getting the idea that courage is a man with a gun in his hand. It's when you know you're licked before you begin, but you begin anyway and you see it through no matter what. You rarely win, but sometimes you do . . . "

"Hey! What's going on? What's the problem here?! I gave a direct order!" Alvarez appeared at the far end of the hallway, hollering as he speed-walked towards us. "*A direct order!*" He reached us and scowled. "Who are you?"

"I'm Mr. Brown."

"I don't know you."

"I've been teaching this English 6 class all semester. I don't want these water bottles taken away. It's hot and the kids need them."

"There was a water fight. An adult slipped and got hurt. A *pregnant* teacher. I put out an order all over the school. It's not just this class. It's a school-wide policy."

"Okay, but these are honors students. They're not involved in any trouble. And we're like the only class on the hall still doing something."

This was true. In the final week of classes, the un-air-conditioned rooms were stifling and in every window I passed, I glimpsed tableaux of glazed-out teachers and students resembling coach class passengers on a red-eye flight.

"Mr. Brown, I can't operate like this. The kids can't hold the bottles. If they need a drink, they can go out to the water fountain."

"But that means they're missing class. Plus those water fountains are disgusting."

He paused. Was I wearing him down? I know he couldn't disagree with me about the rust-encrusted fountains; they belonged in a dungeon. But then he took a deep breath and leaned in, inches from my sweaty face.

"I don't have time for this, Mr. Brown," Alvarez said with renewed frustration. "I'm *taking* these water bottles. If you have a problem, you can talk to the principal after class."

"No." My cheeks were on fire. "Here's what's going to happen: I'm going back to my class *with* the waters, and if *you* have a problem with it, you can tell the principal. But this is over. Goodbye."

I stormed back into the classroom and slammed the door behind me with unexpected violence. The sound was sudden and intense. All eyes fixed on me. A few kids applauded. The movie continued to play. Atticus was in the courtroom—in the arena.

Adrenaline rocketing through me, I delivered the three water bottles to their owners, then sat in the back next to Jim. He looked at me with a "What was that?" expression.

A few minutes later, there was a knock at the door. I went to it to find the school secretary.

"Are you Mr. Brown?" she asked.

"Yes."

She paused, perplexed. "This is your class? We . . . don't have any record of you in the office."

"I'm a student teacher," I said under my breath. I hadn't disclosed this openly to my students, although the dots were available in plain sight for connecting. Down the hall to my right I heard a burst of exasperated laughter. It was Alvarez, listening in from a distance. He threw up his hands in mock amusement and walked off.

"Okay," the secretary said. "I think the principal's going to want to speak to you."

"Now?"

"No. We'll find you." She walked away.

I watched the end of *To Kill a Mockingbird* with my students. When the bell rang, the students whose water I rescued thanked me, and everybody left.

My buzz from the confrontation subsided. I felt sure that I had done the right thing in protecting the kids from their drinking water being chucked, but I knew I was about to be dealt a consequence for my ethical stand.

Assistant Principal Maggie O'Dowd, who had supported me throughout the semester, met me in the hallway with a grave expression. "Dan, what happened? They want you out of the building now."

Jim and I related what had occurred. I admitted it was wrong to have slammed the door and I agreed that I should have involved Jim from the start. Maggie seemed pessimistic. "I hear what you're saying, but I don't know if I can protect you on this. Alvarez wants you out of the building today. Let me talk to Terry [Theresa Harmon, the principal and see where things stand."

While I waited for Ms. O'Dowd's return, I queried other English teachers if they'd been visited by security for bottled water disposal during the previous period. Only a couple, the ones who shared my hallway, had. I walked to another wing of the school and innocently asked a security guard if they were still confiscating bottled water.

"Nah," he said, waving it off as if it were unimportant. I returned to the English department office.

Twenty minutes later, Ms. O'Dowd was back. "The only way for you to stay is to apologize to Alvarez and admit what you did was wrong. That's what we agreed on. If you do that, we can probably work something out. I set up a meeting at twelve with all of us, Mr. Alvarez, and Ms. Harmon in Gerry's office. I hope we can get this resolved then and there and that'll be it."

The meeting was one hour away. I asked Jim what to do. He said he thought I had done the right thing, the Atticus thing, but he couldn't tell me what to do from here on. We had one week left of class and I *really* wanted to be there for that week. After the rapport I had built with my students, I couldn't imagine abruptly disappearing forever without warning. I had written my students a letter, not yet distributed, to bookend the semester and planned to ask them to reply for the final assignment of the year.

My courage in confronting Alvarez was partly artificial too. I was only a student teacher, unpaid and preparing to leave not just DeWitt Clinton, but all of New York City in just a few weeks. I knew what it was like to be a full-fledged teacher, on the payroll, relying on your salary, taking the long view with relationships with colleagues. My imminent departure emboldened me to burn my bridges in the name of taking a stand.

If I stood by my principles and went down in a blaze of self-sacrificial civil disobedience, maybe my students would be somehow inspired. Probably not. I'd be another teacher who vanished into the vacuum of the Bronx public school universe.

I really wanted to stay and finish what I'd started that semester. Still, the idea of abjectly apologizing to Alvarez felt so dirty and wrong.

I considered my position darkly. Was this dilemma a harbinger for the rest of my professional adult life? I had plenty of experience with compromise, but now I was essentially being forced to renounce what I wholly believed to be right. The institution held the power; I didn't. I had to conform to what it wanted—even if that entailed arbitrary,

Gestapo-like confiscations—for the privilege of working with students and earning my daily bread. Well, maybe my daily bread wasn't a factor on this gig, but it certainly would be in all the ones to follow. Maybe this was why teachers aren't taking to the streets and screaming their heads off about how insane our schools' mechanized high-stakes testing culture has become; they need the jobs and they strategize on the promise of sticking around to fight another day.

Submission and conformity are necessary on many levels—where would we be if everyone treated traffic lights as optional?—but everyone has a breaking point. What is asking too much? Was it really too much for me to jot off a note to Mr. Alvarez, a letter that would instantly disappear into a bureaucratic void, addressed to a person I'd probably never see again?

I walked with Jim to Principal Harmon's office a few minutes before noon still unsure of what to do. Anticipating the worst, I'd left a note in the faculty lounge spelling out what had happened; writing it gave me a melodramatic by-the-time-you-read-this-I-will-be-gone feeling.

The principal's office had a large conference table, and when Jim and I were shown in, Ms. Harmon, Ms. O'Dowd, and another assistant principal, Mr. Jenkins, were there. The three administrators all looked to be in their fifties. Career educators. Alvarez wasn't in sight. We sat down.

When prompted, I recited what happened, and this time I opened with an apology for slamming the door. That prompted a round of nods from the tribunal. "I know that slamming the door was unprofessional. It was wrong. I am very sorry that I did that. But I do very much want to stay and finish out the year with my students. We've had a great semester. The water being taken away was disconcerting, especially the way it was done, without an announcement or clear rationale. I'd encouraged my students to bring water bottles to class so they could stay hydrated without leaving the lesson. I've very publicly brought a water bottle every day. I know that Mr. Alvarez has a tough job to do, securing the whole school, but this felt . . . off." I felt like they were really hearing me, and I went for broke "And you know, we were finishing our study of *To Kill a Mockingbird*. I guess I was feeling all excited about Atticus . . . "

They were laughing. Then they abruptly stopped. The three administrators seemed to exchange meaningful glances. Mr. Jenkins put his fingertips together in a pyramid. "Look, Dan. Mr. Alvarez asked for you to be removed from the school community. We talked about it and we agreed that an apology could . . . ease the upset. Mr. Alvarez has another commitment right now so he can't be here. We heard your apology for slamming the door and you're right—that's completely out of bounds. Everyone seems to say you have a bright future in this profession, but doing something like that is exactly the way it could get messed up. I've seen good teachers' tempers really bring them down. What do you say?"

My temper in the classroom had nearly destroyed me before. Back at P.S. 85, at the lowest low moment in a day of disappointments and frustrations, I had snapped, screamed, and pummeled my fist through the chalkboard—all in front of my traumatized students. The incident was literally papered over—I put a poster in front of the cracked surface for the balance of the school year—but I'll never know the damage my fourth-grade students absorbed by seeing their teacher go berserk. This was something I needed to fix.

"I'm really sorry that I slammed the door. I appreciate the importance of security being able to do its job. I really don't see how taking away my few students' water bottles made sense though. I'm sorry it escalated into this heated power struggle, but that sort of thing—someone entering the class unannounced—hadn't happened before and was truly alarming. That said, my actions were born out of a real closeness and I guess a sort of protectiveness I feel for the students—our students. I'd really like to finish out the year with them. If you need to eject me or fire me, I understand, but I'd *really* like and I'm sure my students would really like to conclude our time together on a positive, continuous note. I appreciate the opportunity to say my piece."

Jenkins broke the silence with an expulsion of air that sounded like a half-laugh. He leaned back. "Look Dan, I hear what you're saying. And I've heard what Jim and Maggie [O'Dowd] have offered on your behalf. You've clearly got a real passion for teaching and you're very energetic. Honestly, your . . . spiritedness reminds me a little of myself when I was just starting out—"

I was saved! Each administrator took a turn to reiterate that slamming doors was bad and to recount wistfully their own brashness as a young teacher, many moons ago.

It emerged that Alvarez's direct order was hastily made and sloppily enforced, and no one in the room felt comfortable owning or defending the decision. I left duly chastened for my door-slamming, and discreetly encouraged to avoid Mr. Alvarez. That was easily done since it was the last week of school and I'd never seen him before that day.

I walked away awash with relief and new appreciation for the administrators; they had looked past the cut-and-dry breach of protocol in my rejection of the direct order. In my brief career in public schools I'd already crossed paths with bureaucrats from whom I would not have expected understanding and good faith.

My final days at Clinton were extra-sweet, since I knew how close they had come to being yanked away. After receiving my pardon from the bosses, I revised my farewell letter to the kids and poured in a little extra.

June 11, 2008
Dear Students,

I don't know how much of a secret it was, but you were part of the first high school class that I have ever taught. Each period we spent together was for me a new, uncharted adventure. Now that our time as teacher and student is ending, I want to express to you my true gratitude for your sharing of your personality and working each day as you did, educating me, little by little, how to be a more effective teacher.

One thing I have learned is that when there are thirty or more people in the room, one book or conversation or activity can be experienced so many different ways. I got feedback that the Langston Hughes poetry celebration felt to some like a special class. Others were bored. Many of you acknowledged that reading Hughes led you to interact with poetry in different ways than you had before. When we read *Bodega Dreams*, many members of the class responded enthusiastically to the gritty, streetwise tone of the book. A few students told me it is now among their all-time favorite books. Some, however, quietly expressed disappointment with the story for a variety of reasons.

Abraham Lincoln famously said, "You can't please all the people all the time." He may be right; I know I haven't pleased all of you all of the time. However, my great hope has been to challenge all of you all the time. I have sought to test your limits, to push you into unfamiliar intellectual places, and you have always risen to the task. I hope that this semester has broadened your understanding and skills in seeing the world. In my opening letter to you, I wrote that I wanted our classroom to be a place where ideas matter and everyone has a voice. I hope that the reality matched the aspiration.

I became an English teacher because I believe that words are power. The greater your ability to use words and respond to others' words, the greater your power will be to kick open doors of opportunity. I have the highest confidence in you as you move forward. Still, if you would like to keep in touch, I would be very happy about it. Email me anytime to talk about school, books, college, or anything. I will still be available to write college recommendation letters in the fall if you would like one. Just send me a line and we'll make it happen.

Each of you will leave your unique mark on the world. I can assure you that during and after this semester, you have left your mark permanently in my memory and my heart.

Keep reading, writing, asking tough questions, making connections, advocating for yourself, and always aiming high. To offer a little bonus life advice from Gandhi, "Be the change you want to see in the world."

Thank you for a wonderful semester.

Best wishes,
Dan Brown

On the 4 train home, when I read their responses after our final day, I knew I'd be a teacher for a long time.

I liked the fact that on ALL work that we were given you took time to comment on everything I mean everything. In my notebook you paid mind to the time [on the clock] which I wrote down [next to my entries]. I was shocked when you said: "This was great (my poem) and you wrote this at one in the morning." This made me more determined to work hard knowing that you see I put pride into my work.

Usually in English classes, you have to read books that are only about racism or are "classics." And for once I read a book in class where it had to do with Hispanics and wasn't necessarily considered "classic literature." And that was different because a lot of teachers would find *Bodega Dreams* unacceptable literature.

If you were ever to give or suggest having vocabulary words as summer homework, I would certainly acquiesce to that offer. But as for now, I wish you the best of luck or blessings for your future. Continue to be a laudable teacher who will always be known to vigor a sullen class, and empower or inspire young minds to aim high, never stop reading or writing, and realize that English doesn't always have to be formidable. You are greatly appreciated.

⸺⁓⸺

I know I haven't participated much in class discussions, but I don't like to speak much in a room full of people. However, I am increasing my speaking ability. The two presentations that we've had in class helped me and I hope you continue to have more presentations like that in your future class. It's a great way to help students overcome their obstacles of speaking to a large group.

⸺⁓⸺

I have always been a person who loves to think about why life is the way it is, why there is so much hate and pain, why there is so much anguish in the world . . . etc. I keep to myself and love to think while I am alone. And it felt great to write those thoughts out and have someone else read them, it meant the world to me, to have someone else "listen."

⸺⁓⸺

The last note hit the hardest. I read it twice and promised myself to earn more of these.

Dear Mr. Brown,

. . . I never really took to poetry and avoided it at all costs, but I guess that was just because I was never introduced to Langston Hughes' poetry. Now I even write my own poems sometimes. I thought it was strange that I went through many years of American history class and I was deprived of knowledge about these great Americans. Take no offense, but I found it ironic that my English class was more like a combination of history (Black) and literature and that it was being taught by a young Caucasian male.

Literature hasn't always been an interest of mine and I only read literary novels when I was required to. From freshman year until now, I managed to avoid *The Great Gatsby* or *To Kill a Mockingbird.* I thought I'd be lucky if I made it through high school without having to read the aforesaid novels because I thought that they would be boring and old-fashioned. I was wrong. *The Great Gatsby* and *To Kill a Mockingbird* challenged me to think differently and to scrutinize works of literature. I also think that *To Kill a Mockingbird* is now one of my favorite books; it is a moral story that I learned along with Jem and Scout. I also learned about new critical lenses. The psychoanalytic lens stood out to me the most. Even though I was supposed to use the lens to interpret novels, the psychoanalytic lens gave me insights on my life. It educated me on the reasons why I behave and think the way I do and it helped me cope with personal problems that I have.

There are many other positive things about our experiences together, but if I was to tell you everything, I wouldn't close this letter. Dr. Seuss said, "don't cry because it's over, smile because it happened." I will miss having you as a teacher and I hate saying goodbye but as I sat here and wrote this letter, it dawned on me that this isn't goodbye but a new beginning to new experiences. I wish you the best of luck with your relocation and I hope your students in Washington are as enthusiastic as our English class. I'm glad to be a part of your teaching experiences and I hope that I have left a positive mark in your memory. I will read the novels you purchased for me and again, thank you.

★   ★   ★

The 2011-2012 school year will be my fourth as an eleventh- and twelfth-grade English teacher at the SEED Public Charter School of Washington, D. C. I'm not a super-teacher, like anything you've seen in Hollywood, but I know how to run a rigorous, engaging classroom. Each year I get better at refining my curriculum, anticipating students' needs, collaborating with parents, and participating in the school community. I inaugurated a tradition of publishing a senior class literary anthology, and I co-direct students in a Shakespeare play each spring. I'm even a founding member of the school's New Teacher Induction team, designed to help rookies through their treacherous first year.

These successes are possible because SEED is a functional learning community. My classes range from ten to seventeen students, so I'm able to give individualized feedback to each student on each assignment. Teachers at DeWitt Clinton carried workloads of five classes with thirty-four students apiece; it's staggering to consider the time involved in grading 170 essays.

My school leaders are supportive former teachers who know all of the students and their extended families. They clearly care about test scores, but they don't force disproportionate test prep on teachers and students. The principal encourages her teachers to seek out opportunities for professional growth and she footed much of the bill for two other colleagues and me to pursue National Board Certification. This rigorous year-long process—assembling a four-piece, sixty-plus page portfolio and taking six essay tests—constituted the most rewarding professional development experience of my career. I had never even heard of National Board Certification at P.S. 85, where a choking anxiety seized me every time I saw an administrator headed my way.

At SEED, I'm able to shape my curriculum. My classes belong to me to invent and re-invent. When I wanted to order class sets of Sherman Alexie's *The Absolutely True Diary of a Part-Time Indian*, I got the green light. When an English department colleague and I sought a partnership with the PEN/Faulkner Foundation to bring authors into our classrooms, my principal gave us a thumbs-up and now we each host three writers a year.

Being a confident teacher is fun. At P.S. 85, I looked to Sonandia as my beacon in a tempest. Now, there's no storm; I have primary control of the atmosphere in my classroom, putting me in a much stronger position to elicit real growth from my students. I teach my students to lead structured literary discussions and by the time we're wrapping up books like *The Great Gatsby* or *Their Eyes Were Watching God*, there is no doubt that they are becoming stronger analysts and deeper thinkers.

It's not always sunny. Plenty of days, I still come home feeling like a failure; working with teenagers can be heartbreaking. But my lows aren't as low anymore—I've learned to avoid or defuse no-win power struggles with defiant students. My expectations for myself and my charges are higher.

People rise to the occasion when they feel ownership. My children at P.S. 85 had their finest hours—Dr. Seuss day and the *Pocahontas and the Strangers* unit, to name two—when both the children and I felt this sense of ownership over our work. As a clueless rookie operating in a hostile environment, I couldn't sustain, let alone build on that sense of ownership. Now I can, and the palpable progress propels me like rocket fuel.

Epilogue

My daughter Sadie was born during D.C.'s "Snowpocalypse" of December 2009. Now she's toddling around, hoisting herself up wherever possible, and pressing her favorite board books into Colleen's and my hands. At the time of publication, *Hippos Go Berserk* is a top pick.

I obsess over Sadie's education. Colleen and I are both products of suburban public schools and we want to educate Sadie the same way.

Sending my daughter to public school fills me with hope and fear. In my hopes, I see a kindergarten class with fifteen kids with a well-prepared teacher who loves children and sees them as individuals. I envision time to play and figure things out. I imagine that if Sadie is learning something quickly—say, her numbers from one to ten—then the teacher will notice and help her learn about numbers up to 100 and beyond. If she's having difficulty with a concept—like patterns—the teacher will notice and give her some different strategies and extra attention to help her get it. I want her teacher to model curiosity, kindness, and passion for learning. Basically, when I think about Sadie's education, I think about her classroom: who's in it and what's going on.

But then the fears creep in. If she were assigned to a class like 4-217 with a twenty-two-year-old version of me as the teacher, I'd have a heart attack, break out of my hospital room, and camp out in the principal's office until new arrangements were made.

Every successful adult I know can name at least one teacher who made a significant, even life-changing impact. Of my great teachers, *none* were rookies. My mentor, Mr. Truitt, had taught for three decades when I took his film appreciation class for five straight semesters.

I want Sadie to learn from passionate, experienced teachers—professionals who know their craft and speak the language of young people. My fear is that so many would-be-great teachers aren't choosing the profession because of the mediocre pay, low respect, and increasingly mechanistic conditions. Perhaps even more would-be-great teachers try teaching but leave after a few years, creating a perpetual staffing crisis.

Attracting top college grads to teaching is essential; retaining them for the long haul is what matters most. Compensation is *the* prohibitive factor. No one wants to move down the socioeconomic ladder. I'm an example: I grew up with my own bedroom, occasional vacations, and a college savings fund. It's very important for me to try to provide these things for Sadie. On a teacher's salary, I really can't. Candidly, I could not commit to teaching if my wife didn't have a lucrative job. (Colleen left teaching in 2008 after five years.)

The altruism that recruiting organizations like Teach For America harnesses lasts for a while, but not the long run. Affluent new grads may leap at the opportunity to earn $40,000 a year for doing public service, but it's much less attractive when they're nearing thirty, wanting a house and family, and seeing their peers earn much more.

On top of that, teaching is increasingly becoming a profession of suspicion, disrespect, and warped priorities. Teachers are constantly wondering if they will be marked as deadbeats, with Michelle Rhee holding a broom and glaring out from the cover of *Time* magazine, ready to sweep you away like trash.

Some Republican governors have mined political gold portraying teachers as welfare queens with easy jobs and cushy benefits. This has opened the door to shredding collective bargaining rights and ushering in reform policies abhorrent to teachers. "Accountability," a universally accepted term above reproach, has been co-opted to provide cover for ramping up testing to extraordinary levels. Preemptively dismissed as corrupt defenders of a despicable status quo, teachers' voices are drowned out. Of course, teachers are the ones who actually have to implement these policies that overemphasize testing, depersonalize education, and strip ownership from the classroom.

Democrat leaders, apparently unable to come up with any better ideas, have ceded to No Child Left Behind's oppressive assessment regime.

Expanded high-stakes testing— more often and for younger children— appears imminent.

Meanwhile, on the ground, would-be-great teachers are straitjacketed by out-of-touch bureaucratic mandates and then running for the hills before they can master their craft and make a real difference.

How can Sadie's public school classroom be a haven for learning and discovery amid all this? I fill with dread when I think of Sadie being taught by someone terrified of losing her job over a teacher evaluation based on high-stakes test scores.

And yet when I think about the people doing the hard work in classrooms, my spirits lift. In my journey across the education landscape since the crazy NYC Teaching Fellows placement fair in 2003, I've taught alongside educators in elementary, middle, and high schools, in public, private, and charter schools, in New York City and Washington, D. C. Overwhelmingly, they are talented and caring individuals. Since my P.S. 85 initiation, I've worked with excellent school leaders who toil relentlessly, often thanklessly, to develop their staff and to educate their students. Kind, smart administrators can pump vitality through a school community like a beating heart. Parents I've met want fiercely for their children to succeed. And most of all, students— young, curious, vulnerable, hilarious, heartbreaking, sensitive, posturing, growing people— provide the fire that fuels all of the work.

I want Sadie to be in the classroom with them.

Many people who choose inner-city teaching burn out and leave. Others burn out and stay. But some teachers, like Trish Pierson and Carol Slocumb and Marnie Beck, are warrior-poets for their students. Surrounded by disharmony and heartbreak, they do not slow down, quietly blooming into supernovas behind classroom doors.

"It's never as good as you think it is, and it's never as bad as you think it is." I think Barbara's words are right, but not how she intended them, as a mind-easing crutch about how all experiences gravitate to the middle. If you teach, especially in the hostile, neglected inner city, you hold children's hopes and empowerment in your hands. It's true that it's never as good or as bad as you think it is; it's much better or much worse.

On my last day at P.S. 85, as I was boxing up my teacher's desk, I found a jagged paper scrap, ripped from a worksheet about Finding the Main Idea, containing a message I had written to myself at some dark moment that winter:

> #1: I care.
> #2: Because of #1, I am not a failure.

> Footnote: Caring is more than hoping; it is acting and being a constant, relentless agent for Good Things.

I think about these things often, and about how to mitigate the personal toll of inner-city teaching and create a healthier academic and social experience for students. I remember little moments, like when Seresa used the word *ludicrous*. And big moments, like when Sonandia fought to stay in my class.

And I think about disappearing before I could correct my mistakes.

I left P.S. 85 and moved on to another community where I've found my footing as an educator. As ever-prophetic aphorism fan Barbara Chatton once reminded me, one door closes and another opens. I have enough open doors to be alright. For the out-of-sight, out-of-mind children of the Bronx, there are still many doors to wrench open, many doors to build.

Acknowledgments

I am indebted to each of my colleagues and students at P.S. 85 for playing a role in a life-changing experience.

During the process of writing this book, I was sustained and encouraged by many extraordinarily generous people, particularly my parents, my sister Amanda, Colleen, Mr. Joe Truitt, and my friends who read early drafts and offered constructive criticism.

I am also indebted to my tireless and resourceful agent, Linda Langton at Langtons International Agency, as well as my dedicated, insightful editors, Cal Barksdale and Tessa Aye at Arcade Publishing. Many thanks are also owed to Dick Seaver and Jeannette Seaver for believing in this story and helping it to find a place in the world.